Sarah Siddons

To Stuart Rock, without whom this would not have been possible, with my eternal thanks and love.

Sarah Siddons

The First Celebrity Actress

Jo Willett

First published in Great Britain in 2024 by
Pen & Sword History
An imprint of Pen & Sword Books Limited
Yorkshire – Philadelphia

Copyright © Jo Willett 2024

ISBN 978 1 39901 862 3

The right of Jo Willett to be identified as
Author of this Work has been asserted by her in accordance
with the Copyright, Designs and Patents Act 1988.

A CIP catalogue record for this book is
available from the British Library

All rights reserved. No part of this book may be reproduced or
transmitted in any form or by any means, electronic or mechanical
including photocopying, recording or by any information storage and
retrieval system, without permission from the Publisher in writing.

Typeset by Mac Style
Printed in the UK by CPI Group (UK) Ltd, Croydon, CR0 4YY.

Pen & Sword Books Limited incorporates the imprints of After
the Battle, Atlas, Archaeology, Aviation, Discovery, Family History,
Fiction, History, Maritime, Military, Military Classics, Politics,
Select, Transport, True Crime, Air World, Frontline Publishing, Leo
Cooper, Remember When, Seaforth Publishing, The Praetorian Press,
Wharncliffe Local History, Wharncliffe Transport, Wharncliffe True
Crime and White Owl.

For a complete list of Pen & Sword titles please contact

PEN & SWORD BOOKS LIMITED
47 Church Street, Barnsley, South Yorkshire, S70 2AS, England
E-mail: enquiries@pen-and-sword.co.uk
Website: www.pen-and-sword.co.uk
or
PEN AND SWORD BOOKS
1950 Lawrence Rd, Havertown, PA 19083, USA
E-mail: uspen-and-sword@casematepublishers.com
Website: www.penandswordbooks.com

She raised Tragedy to the skies, or brought it down from thence. It was something above nature ... She was not less than a goddess, or than a prophetess inspired by the gods. Power was seated on her brow, passion emanated from her breast as from a shrine. She was Tragedy personified. She was the stateliest ornament of the public mind.
          William Hazlitt, 'Mrs Siddons' in *The Examiner*, 15 June 1816

Contents

Introduction		viii
Chapter 1	Childhood	1
Chapter 2	Mister Siddons	10
Chapter 3	Starting Out	20
Chapter 4	Bath	30
Chapter 5	Triumph	38
Chapter 6	Lady Macbeth	47
Chapter 7	Ireland	55
Chapter 8	Behind the Scenes	67
Chapter 9	Celebrity	77
Chapter 10	Royalty	88
Chapter 11	Revolution and Society	97
Chapter 12	The Kembles	104
Chapter 13	Working Life in the Theatre	116
Chapter 14	Maria	129
Chapter 15	Sally	140
Chapter 16	The Galindo Affair	148
Chapter 17	Marriage's End	159
Chapter 18	Retirement	167
Epilogue		177
Appendix I: Characters		185
Appendix II: Sarah's Main Stage Roles		193
Bibliography		200
Notes		206
Index		217

Introduction

'A worthless candidate for fame and fortune'[1]

On the night of Friday 29 December 1775, a 20-year-old actress steps onto the stage of the Drury Lane Theatre. It is her London debut. Drury Lane is one of only two theatres in the city to have a prestigious royal patent. It is packed nightly with the fashionable, political and literary elite who come here to watch the finest performances of the most popular plays. Its celebrated actor/manager, David Garrick, will retire once this season is finished, so anyone who is anyone wants to come and see his work. Over many years, the talented and energetic Garrick has built up the reputation of Drury Lane. The opportunity for the young actress to join his company and perform here is truly a golden one.

The new actress is playing the part of Portia in *The Merchant of Venice*. She is billed simply as 'a Young Lady (being her first appearance)'.[2] She is Sarah Siddons, a married mother of two, who has been acting all her life. Her parents own a travelling company of players, and she has performed in the various plays they have put on for as long as she can remember. But appearing here at this famous venue, in the holiday season between Christmas and New Year, in front of the great and the good, the 'splendid and numerous' feels a totally different experience for her.[3] Sarah has never been to London before, and the capital city is far larger than any other in Britain.

Just eight weeks before this evening, Sarah gave birth to her second child, a daughter, named Sarah after her mother, but always called Sally. Sarah's pregnancy has delayed her arrival at Drury Lane. The season started in September, but she has only been able to join now, in December. Her labour started in Gloucester, while she was midway through a performance there. She has brought the new baby with her to London, along with her 14-month-old toddler son, Henry, and her husband of two years, William, whom she affectionately calls 'Sid'. Nobody involved seems to have considered the toll this hurried birth will have taken on her, both emotionally and physically. Sarah's 'Sid' is an actor too, but it is already evident that he does not have the skill to make his living as a leading professional actor. The couple have both been hired on the same terms – £5 per week (£678.60 today) – but it is understood that 'Sid' will be playing smaller roles. The Siddons have known of the famous Garrick throughout their working lives, but they have almost certainly never met him. Garrick sent a scout to appraise Sarah's acting talents rather than seeing her for himself. He carried out the negotiation to contract both Sarah and William to join the Drury Lane company entirely through correspondence.

Sarah is so nervous that even her first entrance as Portia onto the Drury Lane stage appears tentative. Rather than striding confidently on, she totters, a delicate and fragile-looking figure, seemingly totally overcome by the vast audience in front of her. Many years later, she will write about the experience, admitting that:

> The awful consciousness that one is the sole object of attention to that immense space, lined as it were with human intellect from top to bottom, and on all sides round, may perhaps be imagined but cannot be described, and never never to be forgotten.[4]

Her nerves overpower her.

She is not helped by her costume. Sarah is tall, dark and striking but what she is wearing – faded and salmon-coloured with an untailored back that hangs down like a sack – does nothing to accentuate her good features. There has been little time for her to sort out a costume. Often actors provide their own, but Sarah has been loaned hers by the Drury Lane wardrobe. To make things worse, it seems to the audience as if their Portia is not entirely sure either where to fix her eyes or where to plant her feet. And worst of all, no sooner does she start saying her lines than her voice dries up almost completely. As one audience member later puts it: 'She spoke in broken, tremulous tones, and at the close of each sentence her voice sank into a horrid whisper that was almost inaudible.'[5]

The London audience packed into Drury Lane are all too aware that the press will pass their verdict the following day. The young actress before them seems overwhelmed by this. The exposure on this huge London stage is clearly too much for her. Nevertheless, she does manage to rally slightly in the final act, adequately delivering 'The quality of mercy' speech in the famous trial scene towards the end of the play. But she talks far too faintly, not projecting her voice to reach those seated in the back rows. Besides, the audience have already made up their minds: 'After her first exit, the judgement of the pit was unanimous as to her beauty but declared her awkward and provincial,' writes one.[6] As a debut, it could hardly be worse.

The next day the newspapers' verdict is, as expected, one of almost universal condemnation. *The Morning Chronicle* advises Sarah to 'throw more fire and spirit into her performance.'[7] *The Middlesex Journal* pronounces her face and figure agreeable but judges her acting ability to be nothing particularly special: 'There is not room to expect anything beyond mediocrity.'[8] To be mediocre is worse than anything. She is a creature of the provinces and must be sent back there to appear in mediocre theatres, acting in mediocre plays, with mediocre colleagues, far from the bright lights of the prestigious London stage. The newspapers single out her voice as a particular weakness and pick up on 'a vulgarity in her tones'.[9] It is a fundamental requirement for a London actress, as the darling of the great and good, to appear classless, refined, and not to reveal any traces of early vulgarity, regardless of her origins. The reviewers are clear: Sarah is 'ill-calculated to sustain that line in a theatre she had at first been held forth in.'[10] Not only does she lack the required refinement, but she has also been over-promoted. They simply do not see the promise which Garrick thinks he has spotted in her.

Only *The Morning Herald* is more forgiving, and that is only because the owner of the paper, the Reverend Henry Bate, has been partly responsible for recruiting Sarah. He had been sent by Garrick as a scout to see Sarah perform in the provinces. It was Bate who negotiated for Sarah to appear at Drury Lane – at what Sarah would later describe as 'very low terms'.[11] So he does not want to lose face. Surely his critic can find something positive to write about her? She has a fine figure, with expressive features, enthuses the journalist in *The Morning Herald*, but 'Her fears last night so prevented her doing justice to her powers.'[12] The problem, it is clear, is stage fright. If it were not for that, she may well have what it takes. But the 20-year-old is so scared by the prospect of all these people staring at her that she loses the ability to perform in front of them. She might be a powerful actress, but she is so hobbled by such crippling anxiety that all her talent goes for nothing. These reviews will rankle with Sarah for ever after.

After the main play has been performed of an evening, it is the custom to present what is called an 'afterpiece', using the cast in different guises from the roles they have been given earlier. The afterpiece this first night is a pageant called *The Jubilee* which Garrick conceived in honour of William Shakespeare. Garrick's regular cast are not much enamoured of it as part of the repertoire, mainly because they are compelled to represent silent Shakespearean characters, and often not those characters for which they have made their names. His three other leading ladies this season – 47-year-old Mary Ann Yates, who is the most celebrated tragedienne of the time; 35-year-old Elizabeth Younge, a previous protégée of Garrick's, who is famed for her portrayal of Shakespearean heroines; and 38-year-old Frances Abington, who specialises in comedy – do not welcome their new rival. Their instinct is that Garrick's casting Sarah as Venus indicates favouritism. They conspire to ensure that they block Sarah's eyeline, so she cannot be seen by the audience. Garrick, old hand that he is, immediately notices what is going on. Gallantly, he leads Sarah as Venus downstage, right past all her scheming rivals, so the audience can still see her. But he later admits to Sarah that he dares not cast her in any better roles in case the other actresses poison her.

Five nights later, on Wednesday 3 January 1776, Sarah reprises the role of Portia in *The Merchant of Venice*. This time she seems to fare slightly better. At least the audience can now hear her reciting Shakespeare's blank verse. The first night might linger as a shameful, miserable memory, but she has no choice but to keep on trying. Next Garrick casts her as the title role in a new abridgement of a play by Ben Jonson called *Epicoene, or The Silent Woman*. The title role implies that Sarah has a large part to play. In fact, the comedy revolves around a set-up where the lead character looks as if he is marrying someone silent, who is to be played by Sarah. Yet, right up to the first night, Garrick cannot make up his mind as to whether the part should be played by a woman or a man. Throughout the action Epicoene appears to be a woman, but at the end she reveals herself to be a boy. As soon as the play opens, the critics complain that this vital moment in the play simply does not work. After only three performances, Garrick replaces Sarah – with a male actor.

The next play in which Garrick casts Sarah is a new piece by none other than the Reverend Henry Bate, the newspaper owner who went to scout Sarah and was responsible for her coming to London. Perhaps Bate envisaged her playing a part in his new work when he recommended her to Garrick. The play is called *The Blackamoor Wash'd White* and is based on one of Aesop's fables. It never makes it into print but is probably about the contentious slave trade. Regardless of how it deals with its subject matter, Bate's play only runs for three nights. Then the audience can bear it no more. Mayhem ensues. Fighting breaks out in the stalls, some members of the audience attacking Bate's writing and some defending him. When Garrick comes forward to try to restore some sort of order, he is pelted by an orange. The play is never performed again.

Sarah might have hoped that the reaction to the play itself would draw the attention of the critics away from her. But she does not get away so lightly. *The Morning Chronicle* is positive about how the cast overall manage this piece of tosh, but they are excoriating about poor Sarah's performance:

> All played well except Mrs Siddons, who, having no comedy in her nature, rendered *that ridiculous which the author evidently intended to be pleasant*.[13]

They have spotted yet another weakness. Sarah is not particularly strong when it comes to comedy, despite having suggested to Garrick during their written negotiations that comedy is one of her strengths. *The Morning Chronicle* describes her as being ridiculous in the role. It is a further opportunity for backbiting from her fellow actresses. And another reason for Garrick to wonder whether he has done the right thing in recruiting her.

Later the same month Garrick gives Sarah the part of Emily in Hannah Cowley's *The Runaway*, another comedy, this time revolving around marriage and how women strive to overcome the injustices imposed by family life. Elizabeth Younge has been cast as Bella, the better of the female roles. The play will run for seventeen nights, but Garrick recasts Sarah after only five.

Two more comedies follow. In April Sarah plays the part of Maria in a new farce, Thomas Vaughan's *Love's Metamorphoses*, in which her performance is judged as substandard by one spectator – her future unofficial biographer James Boaden. Then, in May, she gets her first professional billing at Drury Lane. Appearing in the programme for the first time as Mrs Siddons, Sarah takes the role of Mrs Strickland in Benjamin Hoadley's *The Suspicious Husband*. But the critics hardly mention her.

Sarah's fellow actresses gossip among themselves that Garrick has hired Sarah to keep them subdued. He has a history of playing his actresses off against each other. And Sarah too believes that this is his motivation. Garrick asks Sarah to sit in his personal box and watch him on stage whenever she is not in the cast. She might have preferred to spend time with her two young children, but instead she dutifully sits watching him perform. She brands his gesture as 'cruel, cruel treatment' and fears it will only increase the already spiteful jealousy.[14] At other times Garrick leads Sarah out from the green room, where all the actors relax when not performing, and sits her down at his side, in another act of seeming favouritism. There are rumours that Garrick may have hired Sarah to show himself off to the audience to his best advantage. If she fumbles her way through a part, it makes him look all the better. Perhaps. But Garrick has no need to use such tactics at this point in his career.

As Garrick is due to retire at the end of the season, he wants to show off his skills as a leading actor for the final time. He decides to put on Shakespeare's *Richard III*. His performance in the title role has always been a particular highlight of his repertoire. To the consternation of the other actresses in the company, he casts Sarah as Richard III's wife, Lady Anne. Sarah cannot help but be delighted at this news. It feels like a break. Perhaps he rates her, after all? But her nerves are already shredded. She cannot relax. In rehearsal Garrick picks her up on a habit noticed by one of the critics, that her arms just hang stiffly by her sides on stage. Can she ensure she moves them with greater fluidity, he asks her? At this piece of direction, she defiantly flings her arms preposterously wide. Garrick again asks her to make the move more naturally. She tries once more. Garrick begins to grumble to himself. If she goes on like this, she will be in danger of knocking off his wig, he murmurs. Quick as a flash, Sarah replies that the great Garrick must be nervous she is going to overshadow his nose. In other words, she makes a poorly judged joke that he must be worrying that she will upstage him. Garrick merely bursts into laughter at Sarah's obstructive attitude. She clearly cannot take direction from him. But at least she is showing some spirit.

Garrick knows that the audience will be coming to the play primarily to see him in this famous role, not the rest of the cast. He choreographs the blocking so that Sarah, as Lady Anne, has her back to the audience and delivers one of her lines to him upstage, so he is looking straight out towards the auditorium, and everyone can see his face clearly. On the first night, Sarah is so overcome with nerves that she completely forgets where she has been directed to stand. In saying her line, she obscures Garrick from the audience. At this, Garrick glares at her. So ferocious is his scowl that Sarah will never forget it. She includes the incident in the notes she makes for her official biographer, Thomas Campbell, fifty years later, so he can put the record straight. The memory still leaves its scars. For their part, the critics simply condemn Sarah as 'lamentable' in the role of Lady Anne.[15] Garrick's final Drury Lane season comes to an end in June 1776 with a production of Susanna Centilivre's *The Wonder*. He does not cast Sarah.

For the past six months Sarah has been short of sleep, feeding her youngest child and caring for a demanding toddler. She is in a city that she does not know, in lodgings with little space for a young family. She married William for love, but he is not the most sympathetic of husbands. While he is also a member of Garrick's company, they both know that he will never shine as an actor. Sarah may be failing in her lead roles, but William will never even get the chance to play a substantial part here in London. He has his own demons.

Sarah does have real strengths as an actress. She is beautiful. She has an arresting stage presence. She knows her stagecraft – how to interact with other actors, how to handle props – but she has not yet worked out where her strengths and weaknesses lie as a performer. True, she has been acting all her life, but never at this level. It must feel very different when the famous David Garrick gives her direction from the times her father tells her to move downstage at a certain point in the action. Sarah knows her parents will be disappointed in her. They never rated William as an actor, and now their fears about how the young family will make their living are turning out to be well founded. It would be difficult to go back them, their tails between their legs.

The two royal patent London theatres, Drury Lane and its rival Covent Garden, operate a seasonal system where they put on plays from autumn through to late spring. Outside those times, the convention is that actors are free to find work in the regional theatres, or to take a rest. There is no question of Sarah stopping work. She has four mouths to feed. The young family head to the New Street Theatre, Birmingham, for the summer. Here they await their fate. The Siddons' contract is up, after all, and they are wholly reliant on Garrick putting in a good word for them with the incoming management who are taking over at Drury Lane. The new management consists of a triumvirate: the promising young playwright, Richard Brinsley Sheridan; his father-in-law, Thomas Linley; and a successful, wealthy physician, James Ford. These three have surely read Sarah's disastrous reviews. They may have seen both Sarah and William perform. Do they discern any talent in either which will induce them to invite the pair back for the following season?

Back in February, William has already written to Garrick, tentatively suggesting a new contract of £3 per week for Sarah and £2 for himself – a halving of their combined earnings from the first season. It is an admission of their lack of bargaining power. This would be the first time that Sarah earned more than her husband, but William is simply accepting the fact that, although his wife may have struggled at Drury Lane, he is even less attractive than her to the management. Garrick does not respond. Instead, a letter for Sarah now arrives at the New Street Theatre, Birmingham. It is written by William Hopkins, the prompt at Drury Lane. It has been decided, writes Hopkins, that the services of Mr and Mrs Siddons are no longer required. Their contracts have not been renewed. Sarah and William are of so little significance that even the task of writing to them has been delegated to the prompt. Later, the couple learn that Frances Abington, one of Sarah's rival actresses in the Drury Lane company, has told Richard Brinsley Sheridan that he is making a mistake in letting the young Sarah go. But Sheridan ignores her.

Sarah feels utterly betrayed by the departing Garrick. He has clearly not stood up for them. He has 'rather depreciated my talents.'[16] She believes that he made a promise to put in a good word for them. But instead, he has let them down 'in the most humiliating manner'.[17] She is proud. She knows the season has gone disastrously badly. But she nevertheless loathes being shamed and humiliated. Now she is finished, a washed-up young mother of two with a potentially unemployable husband, her own reputation shattered. To make matters worse, the verdict is a very public one. The reviews are there for all to read. She knows the word of mouth on her is poor, as audience members relate to their friends and relatives what they think of the new actress at Drury Lane. The critics in Birmingham agree with the verdict of their London colleagues: 'She motions nicely, but she can't shout out loud.'[18] Her voice is just not up to it. Sarah is devastated and sinks into deep despair.

For the next year and a half, the accumulated stress leads Sarah into some kind of mental breakdown, probably a clinical depression. By her own admission she seems to be hastening to her decline. As she wrote in her notes for her biographer, over fifty years later, with the memory still raw for her:

> Who can conceive the size of this cruel disappointment, this dreadful reverse of all my ambitious hopes in which too was involved the subsistence of two helpless infants![19]

This is not simply about her professional reputation as an actress. The fate of her children is also at stake. She has been 'banished from Drury Lane as a worthless candidate for fame and fortune.'[20] Acting is all she knows and yet even that is now being called into question. There is no welfare state to support them. The workhouse may very well beckon. And who there will give a moment's thought to a striking young mother telling everyone she meets all about how it looked for a brief interval as if she might have made it as an actress at the famous Drury Lane?

Six and a half years later, the night of Thursday 10 October 1782 turns out to be one of the most remarkable ever to take place in the history of British theatre. Drury Lane presents a production of Thomas Southerne's *Isabella or The Fatal Marriage*. The tragedy is so affecting that almost the entire audience find themselves moved to tears, while several members have hysterics at the power displayed by the actress who has been cast in the lead role of Isabella. The reviews are ecstatic. Never has a performer played the part of a tragic heroine with such intensity. She makes the story come to vivid life in a way no-one else has ever done before.

The young woman, still only 27, is described as having founded a new religion. She instantly becomes a celebrity, more immediately famous than any of her predecessors. From now on, a life beckons for her where she will never be out of the spotlight. She will be mobbed by her fans, wherever she goes. The newspapers will feature gossipy details about her private life. Aristocratic society will fall over itself to make her acquaintance. She will become the darling of the royal family. As for money, she will go on to earn more even than her predecessor, David Garrick. She will learn how to play the all-important fame game. She will ensure that she is painted by the greatest portrait artists of the day, and that engraved copies of these painted images are widely sold so that her face becomes familiar even to those who never see her perform. She will travel the length and breadth of the British Isles to appear before her adoring fans at theatres packed to the rafters. She will seek to control what the newspapers write about her, and even come on stage to argue her case to her audience direct, when her behaviour is occasionally called into question. For the whole of the rest of her life, she will be a superstar – the first celebrity actress.

The name of that triumphant young performer treading the boards of Drury Lane as Isabella that evening in 1782? Sarah Siddons.

Chapter 1

Childhood

'Common Players of Interludes'[1]

Sarah Kemble was born in a rented upstairs room at The Shoulder of Mutton Inn in Brecon on 5 July 1755. Her parents, Roger and Sarah (or Sally) Kemble, were actors in The Warwickshire Company of Comedians, a troupe of itinerant players putting on shows as they travelled from town to town. Always on the move and without a permanent home, the company of actors had come to Brecon for the May Fair and to use the town as a base for touring Wales for the following couple of months. Along with the other actors in the company, the Kembles needed somewhere to lodge and The Shoulder of Mutton took them in. The pub was frequented by farmers on market day. It was known for good ale and for its legs of mutton, roasted on a kitchen fire. Sally Kemble was left behind here in a rented room to give birth all alone, the rest of the company having travelled on to Llandrindod Wells to perform without her. Her husband Roger was presumably needed on stage. She gave her first child her own name. Sarah's very arrival in the world felt hurried and inconvenient.

Sarah's mother had been born Sarah, or Sally, Ward in Clonmel in Ireland. Her grandfather, John Ward, was originally from Ireland and had settled in England. John Ward was a Methodist, and also a travelling player, who had established The Warwickshire Company of Comedians in 1740, touring the West Midlands and parts of Wales, including Staffordshire, Gloucestershire and Warwickshire. He and his wife Sarah married in Leominster. She was the daughter of yet another set of theatrical players, the Butchers. So, on her mother's side Sarah Siddons came from three generations of actors and grew up to be part of a fourth. Strikingly, both her parents and her grandparents, once they were married, took on the management of their theatrical companies.

Both Sarah's maternal grandmother and her mother acted in The Warwickshire Company of Comedians. They played in Stratford – indeed, John Ward's was the first recorded company to perform a Shakespeare play there. John Ward wrote the two earliest surviving prompt books for Shakespeare's *Hamlet*, and in later life he organised a benefit to restore Shakespeare's statue in Stratford. John and Sarah Ward retired to Leominster, where they died in the 1770s when our Sarah was in her early twenties.

The Wards were not best pleased when their daughter Sally fell in love with a travelling actor in their company, Roger Kemble. Born a Roman Catholic in Hereford on 1 March 1721, and fourteen years older than Sally, Kemble had started his working life as a barber, but had soon begun to earn his living as an actor. His private life had been turbulent; in 1745, when he was in his early twenties, a defamation lawsuit had been taken out against him in Gloucestershire by a widow named Sarah Hawkins, presumably the result of a falling out over their relationship. Seven years later, in 1752, Roger had become romantically involved with an actress called Fanny Furnival, who was separated from her husband. Although Fanny and Roger never married, she appeared on stage as 'Mrs Kemble'. After some kind of argument with their previous company of actors, Roger Kemble and Fanny Furnival answered an advertisement to join John Ward's Warwickshire Company of Comedians instead. There, Roger Kemble's relationship with Fanny Furnival came to an end and he met his future wife – the owner's young daughter, Sally Ward. So, by the time Sarah's parents became a couple, Roger Kemble's name had been controversially linked to two other women, one of whom he left to become involved with the much younger Sally.

Kemble is a Herefordshire and Wiltshire surname and earlier generations of the family seem to have lost land by staying loyal to the king in the Civil War. Sarah Siddons and her siblings made much of how the family were descended from a Captain Kemble – who displayed such bravery after the Battle of Worcester that Charles II gifted him a war horse – and a Father John Kemble – who was involved in the Titus Oates plot and then sentenced to death, aged 80. Sarah even visited Father Kemble's grave in Welsh Newton in the Wye Valley when she was an established middle-aged actress and arranged to pay a monthly stipend for its upkeep. This focus on past heroes provided a useful means of detracting from any whiff of scandal around her father's early life.

When Roger did declare his intentions to his future in-laws, John Ward was reported to have quipped that he had not wanted his daughter to marry an actor, but since Roger Kemble could not act then his daughter had not disobeyed him. In fact, the Wards, the Kembles and the Butchers before them were unusual in that they chose to marry, rather than to live together unmarried. This yearning for respectability ran through all three generations, and into Sarah Siddons' own as well.

Life for the touring or 'strolling' companies was not easy. While such troupes had existed since the Middle Ages, they had been under constant pressure since the restoration of the monarchy in 1660. They were compelled by law to carry Letters Patent from the king or a licence from the lord chamberlain. In the hundred years or so before Sarah's birth, throughout the late seventeenth and early eighteenth centuries, the status of these troupes was continually under attack. In 1713, a law was passed that classed 'common players of interludes' in the same category as mountebanks (in other words, charlatans or tricksters) and performing animals.[2] Religious elements within the local communities saw the travelling troupes of actors as dangerously subversive and, in 1737, eight years before Sarah was born, a yet more stringent Licensing Act was made law, whereby the travelling players were prevented from acting 'for hire, gain or reward' in any place where they did not live.[3] Additionally, no new play could be performed unless its contents had previously been approved by the lord chamberlain.

So, by the time Sarah's parents were making their living as travelling players, the law prevented them from charging audiences any money to see them perform and censored the content of whatever play they decided to put on. They had to pretend to be doing something else other than acting. Often, they would claim to be holding a concert, for which they would charge an entry fee and then during the interval perform the play which was the real reason their audience had come to see them. Another device commonly used was to sell something such as tooth powder and then give the purchasers free tickets to the play as part of the sale. The strolling players travelled from venue to venue, often simply using agricultural barns or local halls in which to perform, finding lodgings where they could. Gradually different companies adopted different circuits and each one developed their own touring system. They would deliberately arrive in towns when the life there was at its fullest and busiest, such as during race weeks or when assizes were being held. Hence John Ward's company was in Brecon for the May Fair at the time of Sarah's birth.

Roger and Sally Kemble married in June 1753 in Cirencester and, for thirteen years, they remained as part of John Ward's company. They were still only actors within the company, rather than actor/proprietors, when their eldest daughter, Sarah, was born, two years after they were married. Since Roger was a Roman Catholic the couple agreed – in a compromise many mixed marriages such as theirs adopted at the time – that their sons should be brought up Catholic and their daughters as Anglicans. The baby Sarah was christened on 14 July, when she was only nine days old, at the Church of St Mary in Brecon. The curate who conducted the ceremony got Roger's name wrong on the paperwork and called him George. Perhaps Roger and the company were still away, and Sally organised this christening by herself. Clearly the error of the father's Christian name did not matter to her.

Roger and Sally Kemble had twelve children in all, of whom eight made it to adulthood. John Philip was born in Prescott, Lancashire, seventeen months after Sarah's birth. A second brother, Stephen, was born one year later in Kington in Herefordshire. Sarah's two brothers were closely followed by four sisters, Fanny,

Anne, Elizabeth and Jane. Three other children, Mary, Henry and Lucy died in infancy and a fourth, Catherine, as a teenager. The couple's final child, Charles, was born in 1775, when his oldest sister Sarah was already 20 years old, and herself a mother of two.

Looking at Sally Kemble's life from today's perspective, the physical strength required to give birth to this number of children, while touring the country, putting on plays, and sleeping wherever a bed could be found, is striking. She performed on stage throughout her pregnancies, as her daughter Sarah Siddons would go on to do. She was playing Anne Boleyn the night her third child, Stephen, was born and reputedly only just had time to finish the performance before the baby arrived. She would have breastfed the babies herself – no wet nurse for her – and the new arrivals would immediately have been thrown into theatrical life with the rest of the family, travelling around the circuit. Her seventh child, Anne, was disabled from birth, but she too joined the family troupe and travelled from place to place like everyone else.

Sarah Siddons' biographers have often romanticised this life. She has been described walking into a town on the circuit either with a drum or a crown on her head, dressed in white satin and spangles, her train held up by her brother John Philip, himself dressed in black velvet. This has been characterised as pre-figuring her later success as the queen of her theatrical generation. In truth it was a crude way of drumming up support. First, Roger Kemble would go into the town to ask permission for his actors to perform and only then would the company of actors be allowed to make their entrance. The satin and velvet costumes of Roger Kemble's children would doubtless have been dirty and bedraggled. The travelling players processed through the town, giving out handbills to advertise their coming performances. They needed to make enough money to pay for their board and lodging, feed themselves, buy or mend any costumes and props, and cover their travel to the next venue.

The proprietors in a strolling troupe would usually travel by cart from place to place, carrying the simple costumes and props with them, but the actors themselves were expected to walk between the various towns where they performed. As soon as they were strong enough, Sarah and her siblings would have joined them on foot. There was a carefully agreed system within the companies of strolling players for the splitting of profits, whereby the proprietor/manager collected any money they made. Expenses were then deducted and the profits were divided into shares, one for each member of the troupe and four 'dead shares' for the manager. So, the more family members working in the company, the more money Roger and Sally Kemble collected for them. Finances were inevitably often tight. The life was hand to mouth. Sarah's younger brother, Stephen, used to recount how he lay in bed hungry for two long days until eventually he resorted to digging up a raw turnip from a distant field so he had something to eat. It is easy to see how, once she became a successful actress, Sarah's determination to earn as much as she possibly could to support her own family derived from these early experiences.

The uncertain, transient life as a strolling player inevitably resulted in a whole array of disputes between individual members of the company, sometimes erupting into physical violence. Alcoholism was rife. Roger Kemble was not unusual in leaving one troupe, probably under a cloud, and joining another to try his luck there. Since travelling players were classed as vagabonds, it was hard for them not to see themselves as such. Petty thievery abounded. A whole company would often slip away at night, leaving their unpaid debts behind them. If the manager built up a good reputation somewhere, and if a member of the gentry in the area where they were performing then forged a friendship with him, then the manager would often rely on this patronage to protect his company when they returned. The local squire might help procure a good venue for them, for instance. In the hand-to-mouth life that actor/managers led, they needed all the support they could get. The workhouse was only a week's earnings away. Inevitably, just as most actors' economic lives were unstable, so were their relationships. Extramarital affairs were common, as was illegitimacy. To be married was unusual. Very few actors among Sarah's contemporaries had been born in wedlock.

The experiences of her early life informed Sarah's way of looking at the world. She was remarkably physically strong but pushed herself to the limit throughout her life, just like the adults among whom she grew up. Inevitably her health suffered as a result. She proved resourceful and adaptable as an adult professional, skills she learned as a child. Hardly surprisingly, she longed for a permanent home and put down deep roots as soon as this was achievable. We know from her letters that, even once she was hugely successful. she dreamed of a comfortable, secure escape from the world, an idyllic country cottage. She was often troubled by competitive relationships with other actors, or more often actresses, as if she were subconsciously reproducing her early experiences with her siblings. She was often accused – with good reason – of nepotism. The Kemble children as adults proved to be remarkably strongly bonded.

In 1766, when Sarah was aged 11, her grandparents retired and Roger Kemble took over the ownership and management of the troupe, which was renamed Mr Kemble's Company of Comedians. One of the actors in the company, Thomas Holcroft, wrote that it was:

> more respectable than many other companies of strolling players; but it was not in so flourishing a condition as to place the manager beyond the reach of immediate smiles or frowns of fortune.[4]

The Kembles did well touring the circuit and their finances improved sufficiently for them to contemplate sending their eldest son, John Philip, away to a Catholic seminary at Sedgley Park, Wolverhampton. He studied there for four years and then, in 1771, he was sent to Douai, in Northern France, to an English college to continue his studies. An income account book shows Roger Kemble to be earning £350 a year at the time (£51,780 today). The Kembles now travelled between towns in their own coach, squashing the whole family in. Behind them came two lumbering wagons, piled with props and costumes, while the rest of the company no longer walked but were transported by stagecoach. Their lives were constantly changing as they travelled from place to place, and yet the rhythms were always the same. They arrived, they advertised the fact they were in town, they performed, and they left again. There was little or no chance to make bonds with anyone outside the company. For the Kemble children, their only contemporaries were their immediate family.

All the accounts from the time agree that Sally Kemble, Sarah's mother, was the life force who kept the family together. She had an iron will and a strong sense of purpose. The marriage to Sally had been the making of Roger Kemble. Their eldest son, John Philip, compared his mother to Volumnia in *Coriolanus* – a part which Sarah Siddons would go on to make her own. The artist Thomas Lawrence, who knew the family well, described her affectionately as 'the old lioness'.[5] Sally was totally devoted to Roger, who his children claimed to have been an excellent actor. He played the title role in Robert Dodsley's *The Miller of Mansfield* at Drury Lane in later life, aged 67, thanks to his children securing him the role. Sarah wrote that she 'always loved my father and respected his sound understanding.'[6] She was said to look like her father and sound like her mother. Sarah remained emotionally close to both her parents throughout adulthood.

The strength of their parents' marriage and the security of the family life they created must surely go some way to explaining the later success of the Kemble children. It is striking that Roger and Sally Kemble's ambition for all their offspring was that they should leave acting and find other occupations for themselves. The couple tried hard to place their children elsewhere, but these plans came to nothing. All the Kembles' many children worked in the theatre in some form, and all, apart from one, married performers. As the Kemble children grew up there were more chances to establish themselves as adult, professional actors than there had been for their parents. Gradually a series of permanent theatres, with royal patents, were being established in many of the large towns and cities, such as Bath in 1768, Liverpool in 1772, Bristol in 1778 and Birmingham in 1807. These did not have the same prestige as the two London theatres, but they did provide more permanent, lucrative employment for actors than the strolling circuit. The Kembles would take advantage of this. And they were all good at their craft. Their childhoods had given them a fantastic training, so they all went on to have better lives economically, with more stability, than their parents ever enjoyed.

Sarah could never remember her first performance on stage. She may well have been carried on as a baby. Several of her early biographers tell the story of how, as a very small child, she had been billed as some kind of infant phenomenon, but when it came to the moment for her to perform, she was overcome with stage fright. So her mother took her by the hand and led her down to the footlights. There she was made to recite Aesop's fable, *The Boy and the Frogs* and gained the applause, which was to hold such power for her, all her life.

Her first documented stage appearance acting a role as one of the cast was in Coventry on 22 December 1766, aged 11, the same year that her parents had taken over the management. She played Ariel in *The Tempest*. She admitted to Thomas Campbell, her official biographer, that she did not remember it. After all, being around the theatre and appearing, either in speaking or non-speaking roles, was just something she had always done. A Victorian biographer quoted from an unspecified local paper that:

> she seemed to be so entirely a creature born of the loves of a breeze and a sunbeam, that the whole audience broke into frantic applause at the end of the play, and her proud happy father began dimly to foresee his daughter's future.[7]

She played the part of Rosetta in *Love in a Village* in Worcester and acted with some soldiers in Arthur Murphy's new play *The Grecian Daughter* at Stourbridge in Worcestershire, where her amateur fellow actors were dismayed when she burst into laughter at a particularly tragic moment. She would make this role one of her most celebrated in later life once she had controlled the urge to laugh (see Appendix 2 for more details of Sarah's lead roles).

Leading this itinerant life, educating their children must have been difficult for Roger and Sally Kemble. When Sarah was just 10 years old, she professed a great love of *Paradise Lost*. Her fondness for John Milton's poetry persisted throughout her life. Perhaps she connected to the combination of Milton's simple, strong faith and his commanding language. Sarah's mother taught her elocution, as well as how to sing and play the harpsichord. Whenever the

Kembles stayed somewhere for a longer period, they would enrol their children in local day schools. The family stopped in Worcester for an extended period in 1767, and Sarah was sent to Thorneloe School in Barbourne. The headmistress, Mrs Harries, apparently offered to teach Sarah for nothing. One of the pupils at the school wrote to her mother that Sarah was initially unpopular, with her simple clothing, long nose and reserved manner. This pupil was shocked when she asked Sarah about her father's profession, only to be told that he was the manager of a troupe of strolling players. However, Sarah won round her snobbish fellow pupils when they put on an amateur play and she showed them how to make a sack-backed costume (perhaps like the one she wore for Portia at Drury Lane a few years later) using thick, brown, sugar paper which they purchased from the local grocer. All her life, Sarah was a people-pleaser.

Sarah was always very much the eldest daughter, a willing disciple, learning at her mother's feet. She doubtless felt maternal and protective towards her many younger siblings, and this then translated itself into powerful feelings for her own children. Being a mother was fundamental to her sense of self. Her brothers and sisters must have needed help walking those roads between venues, and Sarah would have made sure they all got their fair share of whatever food was available. But they were also her fellow workers. All the children became part of the company from the earliest age. Long before the term 'child protection' was even invented, Sarah would have made sure her siblings were protected from other members of the company or from the many strangers they continually encountered, any of whom might have had designs on them. She took her role as the oldest child extremely seriously. Unsurprisingly, these bonds were exceptionally strong.

Sarah also grew up accustomed to a fully functioning matriarchy, where her mother was the person to whom everyone deferred. Like her daughter, Sally had been the daughter of actors. She had fallen in love with someone whose past had several skeletons not so very hidden from view, but her love and their subsequent marriage had been the making of him. Despite Sally's father not rating him, Sally's husband had turned out to be a good manager of the family business and an excellent father. Her daughter Sarah would try to replicate this in her own life, albeit largely unconsciously. A future husband was someone to be brought into the fold and tamed. Then all would come good.

Sarah also learned at her parents' feet that respectability was hugely important, in the largely unrespectable world in which she grew up. Since the law classed the Kembles as being no more than 'sturdy beggars and vagrants', it would have been easy to accept that label and live as such.[8] Yet the Kembles defined themselves as something very different. They were owners and managers of a small, successful business. Importantly, their children had all been born in wedlock and none of their daughters would go on to have illegitimate children. In an age where there was little social mobility, as a family of actors they did not fit easily into any defined social class. As such, they were able to move seamlessly between different strata of society. So Sarah could be enrolled in a private school for young ladies – albeit for free – but she would soon be on the road again, sleeping wherever the troupe could find lodgings and foraging turnips when they went hungry.

Doubtless the Kemble parents' wishes that their children leave acting and find employment elsewhere were largely motivated by their desire that the next generation better themselves, both socially and economically. Sarah would go on to be employed as a servant in an aristocratic household, but she later dined with duchesses. She certainly fulfilled her parents' ambitions in that respect. Her parents set her oldest brother, John Philip, on the path to becoming a Catholic priest, a role with ambiguous social status, but one with more stability than that of an actor. John Philip gave the priesthood up in favour of a life in theatre, and, like his sister, he also achieved great success, both professionally and socially. Again, his parents must have been delighted.

The Kemble children all had theatre in their bones. Before their earliest memories they were surrounded by the trappings of the family business. They knew from very early on that they must be quiet while others performed. Soon they were given small parts in the productions and learned sufficient discipline to memorise their lines and deliver them as required. They were taught the importance of respecting other actors in the company, of making the right exits and entrances, of ensuring that the blocking they had been taught was carried out correctly, and that the props they took on stage were the right ones, to be used as required. Within that framework they could bring their own imaginations to bear on the roles they played. If someone in the family had been cast in a part in the previous production, then someone else could try making their mark by playing it rather differently in the next. Creativity was encouraged and it flourished, but this creativity was to do with adaptation and interpretation rather than with making something from nothing. Certainly, the life they led was tough, but it was also the stuff of romantic dreams. They were artists; they were storytellers. They were the people who arrived in a dull, everyday, unexceptional place and made magic before the eyes of those who came to see them.

Chapter 2

Mister Siddons

'A damned rascally player, but a civil fellow'[1]

On 12 February 1767 Mr Kemble's Company of Comedians were performing in the city of Worcester. A playbill announced that there would be a concert of music in which the 11-year-old Sarah Kemble and another member of the troupe, a Mrs Fowler, would sing, and that in the interval there would be presented, 'gratis', as the law required, the Worcester premiere of William Havard's *Charles the First*. The characters would be wearing costumes 'according to the fashions of those times'.[2] Clearly the Kembles were doing well enough to be able to afford historical costumes for their players, something unusual for touring companies such as theirs.

The family appeared in force. Roger Kemble played General Fairfax, and Sally, his wife, who was five months pregnant, played Lady Fairfax. Sarah took the part of The Young Princess Elizabeth, while John Philip, who had not yet been sent to his Catholic seminary, played James, Duke of York. Their younger sister Fanny, aged 7, played his brother, the Duke of Gloucester. Transgender casting was not a problem when parts needed to be shared out amongst the available children. No mention was made of 5-year-old Elizabeth Kemble, nor her disabled 3-year-old sister Anne, nor 18-month-old Catherine. Presumably they knew to keep quiet backstage or had non-speaking parts. The other roles were divided between eleven other adult members of the company, including two married couples, the Vaughans and the Fowlers. The part of the Duke of Richmond, the second most important role, was to be played by a newcomer to the company – a Mr Siddons.

William Siddons had been born in September 1744 in Walsall, Staffordshire, the son of a publican. His father, Joseph Siddons, kept The London Apprentice public house, in Rushall Street, but died in a wrestling match when William was only 6. There is no record of his mother, Mary, remarrying, so life would have been tough for the widow and her son. James Boaden, Sarah's first biographer, described William as being 'brought up to business' so perhaps Mary kept the pub going.[3] William soon left his hometown and began life as an actor. He performed as an amateur, aged 22, in a play in a malthouse in Walsall. The experience must have been a good one, since he then left to seek his fortune as a professional actor and appeared in *Charles the First* as part of Roger Kemble's company a few months later, in February 1767. Here he first met 11-year-old Sarah. James Boaden, who wrote an unauthorised biography of Sarah during her lifetime, knew William Siddons well. William was, he wrote, extremely handsome, fair in colouring, with a graceful, sedate manner, able to play both harlequin and Hamlet, and excellent at learning lines – a 'quick study', as this was termed. He must have made a strong impression on the adolescent Sarah. They acted opposite each other later that season in a romantic comic opera, *Love in a Village*.

It is impossible to know when the couple began to have strong feelings for each other. Most biographers tactfully talk about love developing some three years later in 1770, when Sarah was a more respectable 14 or 15, and William, 25 or 26. Even then, it feels very young to us for a teenage girl to be committing herself romantically. But these were different times and different circumstances. There was little opportunity for privacy in the itinerant life they were both leading. They lived and worked alongside each other, intimately involved physically, even before they revealed their feelings for each other. They soon started referring to themselves by the nicknames they would use all their married lives: 'Sal' and 'Sid'.

Sarah was already acknowledged as a phenomenon – strikingly beautiful, with a remarkable voice, entirely at ease both performing the various plays in the repertoire and singing as well. For the couple being cast in the roles of romantic leads opposite each other must surely have encouraged the relationship to develop. Offstage they spent their days rehearsing lines together, buttoning each other into costumes as they hurriedly changed in a barn, or handing over a vital prop as they waited to make their entrances. At night the members of the company slept wherever a room could be procured for them. Any time for the two of them to be alone together must have been more difficult to engineer. For the next three years Sal and Sid toured Kemble's circuit together – Droitwich, Bromsgrove, Bath, Worcester, Wolverhampton, Warwick and Coventry.

After some time, the couple announced that they were engaged. It immediately became clear that both Roger and Sally Kemble were wary of the romance. Since Sarah was so young, Sal and Sid would have needed her parents' formal consent to marry. Roger and Sally were experienced professionals in the world of touring theatre. They could see that William Siddons had little talent as an actor and that William and Sarah's financial prospects would be poor. They must have dreaded the thought that their talented daughter and her uninspiring future fiancé, however handsome and steady, would simply remain as jobbing actors within the company, continuing to take their share of the meagre profits.

Roger and Sally Kemble's hopes for social advancement for their eldest daughter looked unlikely. They had wished for more for her.

History seemed to be repeating itself, as Sarah must have been all too aware. Roger was fourteen years older than Sally. The age gap between William and Sarah was eleven years. Perhaps it did not matter. Sally had only been 18 when she and Roger had married, so William and Sarah might hope to marry young too. Sally had been the making of Roger. Sarah doubtless saw herself as rescuing William. Just as Sally's parents had made the point that the man on whom she had set her heart was no good at acting, so Sarah's parents clearly felt the same about their daughter's prospective husband.

Here, Sarah's official biographer, Thomas Campbell, takes up the story. James Boaden had avoided writing about Sarah's youth. We have Sarah's written notes to Thomas Campbell, but these only concern her professional life, not this early period. She must have been nervous that the facts around her decision to marry William be presented in the best possible light. I suspect Campbell's account is not entirely factually accurate. The story of Sarah's life over the next few years was reworked, to present both husband and wife in a positive and flattering light.

As told by Campbell, Roger Kemble's company moved to Brecon in the autumn of 1770, where Sarah reputedly sang a song entitled *Robin, sweet Robin* on stage. On hearing her rendition, an eligible squire fell madly in love with her. His name is given as Mr Evans of Pennant, and his income is faithfully recorded as £300 a year (£44,240 today). It immediately became clear that Roger and Sally both felt strongly that Mr Evans would make a far better match for their young daughter, bringing with him the respectability and stability they longed for. They told her so, and promptly withdrew the parental consent they had given for her marriage to William Siddons. For his part, William was thrown into paroxysms of jealousy and suggested to Sarah that they should elope. Sensibly, she refused.

Even by the time Thomas Campbell published his biography, Mr Evans seems to have disappeared. It is impossible to trace the conveniently commonly named Mr Evans. Campbell noted Evans' annual income but recorded that 'he lived to consume it and died a bachelor.'[4] In other words, he drank himself to death, having never found anyone to replace Sarah in his affections. Better for the biography if Mr Evans' love continued, unrequited. He feels like a convenient cypher.

Campbell then says that Roger Kemble promptly sacked William Siddons but, out of the kindness of his heart, he agreed that the young actor should be allowed a benefit night before departing – a popular convention whereby all the takings from that evening's performance would go to William, rather than being shared among the company. Instead of accepting this gracefully and taking his leave with dignity, William composed a subversive song entitled *The Discarded Lover*, which he performed at the end of his benefit, to the delight of the Brecon audience but doubtless to the horror of Roger and Sally Kemble. The tone of the piece is clear from the very first verse:

> Ye ladies of Brecon, whose hearts ever feel
> For wrongs like to this I'm about to reveal;
> Excuse the first product, nor pass unregarded
> The complaints of poor Colin, a lover *discarded*.[5]

William portrayed himself as Colin, who had been rejected by his lover, Phyllis, despite adoring her. The doggerel continues in eleven whole verses. A wealthy young squire, William explained, had heard her sing *Robin, sweet robin* and this had thrilled his heart. Her mother then took it upon herself to drive Colin away. Phyllis was swayed by the £300 a year, which 'Made her find out a thousand she n'er saw before.'[6] She had broken her vows to him. William ended by appealing to the audience for their support, since 'a jilt is the devil'.[7] The audience lapped this up. Their hearts were touched by his plight at losing the love of his inconstant Sarah. And they took against her parents for getting involved. William's benefit was a huge success. But as he came off stage, Sarah's mother, Sally Kemble, boxed his ears.

All this may well have taken place. But it may also be a fabrication by Thomas Campbell and by the then elderly Sarah Siddons to disguise what really happened. Campbell, or even Sarah herself, might have written *The Discarded Lover* to be included in her authorised biography. All her life, Sarah wrote clichéd rhyming verses very like this. There are no records in Brecon of William Siddons' popular benefit night. He himself was long dead by the time Campbell wrote his tale of what happened.

To continue with Thomas Campbell's account – one which his biographers have always accepted as a reputable source – Roger and Sally decided to send Sarah away from the company for a time immediately after William had left. After all, their aspirations for her were that she should have a respectable life, not one on the stage. They arranged for Sarah to go into domestic service, working for a Lady Mary Greatheed in the grand house of Guy's Cliffe in Warwickshire. Here she stayed for three whole years from 1770 to 1773. The exact dates are unclear, some biographers saying she was only there for two years.

Sarah certainly did work for the Greatheeds for some time. And William Siddons did stop acting with Mr Kemble's Company of Comedians for a few years. Yet there are several unlikely elements in this story. The Kembles were doubtless dismayed at their daughter's romantic attachment and may well have sacked William Siddons from the company, particularly if he had suggested eloping with their underage daughter. But in that case, would they really have allowed a benefit for this relatively untalented jobbing actor, who had behaved so unacceptably? It is also unlikely that the Kembles would have chosen this moment to send their daughter – then a valuable member of the company and an extremely promising performer – into domestic service. Surely, they would have wanted to keep her close while she recovered after the turbulent end of her relationship with William? She was only 15, after all.

The church of St Bartholomew, Wednesbury, in Staffordshire, is not far from William Siddons' birthplace of Walsall. And in this very summer, on 27 July 1770, is recorded the baptism of a baby boy named William Siddons. Siddons was an extremely unusual surname and there are no records of anyone else by the name of Siddons in the area. The baby's father's name is given as Joseph Siddons, the name of our William Siddons' deceased father. The mother's surname is not recorded, and her Christian name is simply given as Jane. Sarah's younger sister, Jane, had not yet been born, so the name would have had no emotional associations for her at this point. Ideal for an alias. As we know from Sarah's own baptism, names were often confused. Since the baby was illegitimate, his surname should have been recorded as Kemble, not Siddons, but perhaps the couple, who could not marry without her parents' consent, nevertheless wanted their child to be given his father's surname. They presumably still intended to marry once she was old enough.

There are no more records to indicate that this baby, William Siddons, or William Siddowns as he also appears further down the register, lived for very long. It is impossible to prove, but it seems highly likely that this was the illegitimate child of William Siddons and the young Sarah Kemble. Their daughter's pregnancy out of wedlock, when she was only 15, would have given Roger and Sally Kemble a far more powerful reason for sacking the young, untalented actor. We know the company were in Coventry in February before the crisis in Brecon, but the whereabouts of the troupe in the spring and summer are unclear.

My contention is that, once the truth was revealed that Sarah was pregnant, some kind of rupture took place between the young lovers and her parents. Then William and Sarah left Coventry and went to find William's mother, who was living in Staffordshire – perhaps still in Walsall or perhaps in nearby Wednesbury – to see if she would help them. Where else would they have gone at such a time? There, the underage Sarah gave birth, and the baby was baptised but then died. The couple may well have decided to call their first child William. Notably, they never gave any of their subsequent sons the name William, even though they did name their eldest daughter Sarah, after her mother. Perhaps the name William for a boy child had bad memories for them.

Several times in her life Sarah suffered from severe clinical depression. She acknowledged this when things went wrong after her first, disastrous London acting season in 1776. The significant trauma at this time, when she was aged just 15, may well have resulted in some kind of post-natal mental collapse. In that state, it would probably have been impossible for her to appear on stage and perform. Perhaps the couple did part at this time. The two of them could not marry without the consent of her parents, and their prospects were poor. Having a child out of wedlock was not seen as particularly shameful among strolling players, but being married was an article of faith for Sarah's parents. They would have wanted the same respectability for her, so the events would have been all the more traumatic for everyone involved. If Sarah returned to the family in Brecon that autumn, her parents must have despaired as to what to do with her. Perhaps this was the trigger for them to see if they could find work for Sarah as a domestic servant.

As a successful professional actress Sarah would go on to excel playing tragedy. The roles which she made particularly her own concentrated on the tragic heroine as mother. In *The Fatal Marriage*, for instance, she played a woman who stalwartly refused to give up her beloved only son to her powerful father-in-law. This was the quintessentially Siddonian role. Was Sarah mining these early experiences, while keeping as a closely guarded secret what had really happened? In her own personal life, too, she was particularly exercised by always wanting to keep her children safe. She was passionately conflicted whenever she worked away from them. As we shall see, she was the archetypal guilty working mother. Again, the ghostly imprint of her early experiences looks to have played out in the way she behaved towards her subsequent children.

What is beyond dispute is that Sarah went to work as a maid at Guy's Cliffe at some point in the early 1770s. Guy's Cliffe House was the ancestral home of the Greatheed family. Samuel Greatheed had been the local member of parliament, but had died around five years earlier, leaving his aristocratic wife, Lady Mary, and their two sons living there. Lady Mary had been born Lady Mary Bertie, the daughter of the Duke of Ancaster. Guy's Cliffe, of which only the ruins remain today, was close to Coventry where the company performed in February 1770. It was a particularly beautiful Gothic manor house with romantic, mullioned windows, set in the Warwickshire countryside. The River Avon flowed through the grounds. There was a nearby cave, which still exists today, and a noted collection of cedar trees.

It may well have been that Roger and his wife came to the attention of the Greatheed family that spring, while they were performing nearby. Perhaps the widowed Lady Mary Greatheed took her sons – Peregrine and Bertie – to see one of the productions. Bertie was only a boy at the time, but he loved theatre all his life. So, when Roger and Sally Kemble needed somewhere for their daughter to stay and gather her strength, the opportunity for working for one of their patrons presented itself. Thomas Campbell was writing his biography when Sarah was an old woman, by which time her talent had taken her to the other end of the social scale. Her aristocratic connections were very important to her by then. That she worked for the Greatheeds was not in doubt, but her work in the household had to be presented to Campbell's readers, over fifty years later, as something refined and respectable, in keeping with her later eminence. She had not been employed as a simple kitchen maid, scrubbing potatoes. Campbell carefully referred to her being 'placed under the protection' of Lady Mary, as if trying to skate over the real nature of the relationship there.[8]

Lady Mary Greatheed was in her early forties when Sarah came to work for her, several years older than Sarah's mother. Sarah must have contrasted the women's two lives. Lady Mary and her older son Peregrine were to die soon after Sarah's time at Guy's Cliffe finished, but the second son, Bertie, was to remain a friend of Sarah's for the rest of her life. As we shall see, he had ambitions as a playwright. He was only four years younger than Sarah herself and would have been 11 or 12 years old when she started working for the family. She soon proved herself very good at reading aloud. As an adult he would recall her bringing *Macbeth* to life for his enjoyment.

Sarah had never experienced the life of a stately home before. In fact, she had rarely lived for any length of time in any permanent house at all. She was profoundly affected by everything at Guy's Cliffe. She loved the comfort, the tasteful furnishings, the security that life here provided. She must have vowed to see if she could create something of this kind of home for herself as an adult. Providing a wonderful domestic life for her children – and for her husband – was something she strived to do as soon as she had any measure of success. And whenever she visited other grand homes, she nearly always commented on the life there. Good table linen, shining cutlery, soft beds and her own carriage were luxuries she would always work to ensure she could afford.

But the Greatheeds' wealth, like that of many landowners in England at the time, was based on slavery. They owned a sugar plantation on the island of St Kitts in the Caribbean. In the early 1780s, some years after Sarah had left, the Greatheeds were recorded as paying tax on as many as 230 enslaved people. We do not know if Sarah was aware of this, or even whether she stopped to think how the life she was now leading was being paid for. As an adult, Bertie supported the abolition of slavery, which was passed into law in Britain a couple of years after Sarah's death. He renounced his plantation as something odious, but nevertheless continued to own enslaved people for the rest of his life. There is no recorded comment from Sarah about slavery.

Sarah's role was as a lady's maid and companion to Lady Mary. She was paid £10 a year (£1,475 today). She could not have supported herself on this money. It feels like a token sum, as if she were on some kind of eighteenth-century gap year. Talented, striking and eloquent, she soon made her mark. She quickly acquired a special status at Guy's Cliffe and grew to be a valued member of staff. For her part, too, she enjoyed the experience of living and working at such a grand house. She has been described as spending any free time she was given by beginning to learn how to sculpt (a later hobby) and by reciting passages from Milton and Shakespeare to whoever cared to listen to her. Lady Mary's brother supposedly heard her declaiming Shakespeare to the other servants and saw she had potential. Soon she was reading to her employers. She went with Lady Mary to visit the Duchess of Ancaster, Lady Mary's sister-in-law, at the family seat in Lincolnshire, and the duchess later told the Reverend John Genest that the young girl 'was fond of spouting in the servants' hall.'[9]

Thomas Campbell wrote in his biography that he had seen the copy of Milton's works which the Greatheeds gave to Sarah, perhaps as a parting gift. Lady Mary was said to have confessed to 'Conservation' Sharp – a banker and poet – that whenever the young Sarah entered the room while in her service, Lady Mary herself felt an irresistible urge to rise from her chair, so queenly was the young girl. This feels like another apocryphal story, since 'Conversation' Sharp was only in his teens when Lady Mary died.

One story which is also surely fictional is that Sarah performed for David Garrick for the first time when he came to visit the Greatheeds at Guy's Cliffe during the time she was working there. Garrick was by now the famous owner and manager of Drury Lane Theatre. He had been born in Lichfield, roughly in the same area of the country as Guy's Cliffe, and he may well have visited at some point, particularly as he was involved in planning a jubilee in Shakespeare's birthplace, nearby Stratford-upon-Avon. Like Sarah after him, Garrick's success meant that he made friendships with many of the aristocracy. The story goes that Lady Mary was so impressed by her maid's acting skills that she encouraged Sarah to recite a speech from Nicholas Rowe's play *Jane Shore* in front of the famous visitor. Another version tells how the teenage Sarah went to London during this period to perform the same piece for the famous actor/manager. If either of these meetings took place, it begs the question why neither Sarah nor Garrick raised the fact they had met before when Garrick began his efforts to recruit Sarah to act for him at Drury Lane, only a couple of years later. Again, it feels as if Sarah's early biographers were happy to embroider the truth, to enhance her reputation.

Throughout her time at Guy's Cliffe, Sarah remained steadfast in her loyalty to William, just like the tragic heroines she would go on to play to such enormous success. Steadfastness was one of her signatures. Whatever had been the circumstances of William's leaving Roger Kemble's troupe and Sarah's coming to work there, the two young lovers were now reconciled. William visited Sarah at Guy's Cliffe. They resolved to wait until she was at least 18 and try to marry then. She wrote to him:

> Say not, Strephon, I'm untrue,
> When I only think of you;
> If you do but think of me
> As I of you, then shall you be
> Without a rival in my heart,
> Which ne'er can play a traitor's part.[10]

These lines feel derivative, the equivalent of a poem in a greeting card today. Sarah never did claim to be a great writer. One of her main tasks at Guy's Cliffe was to read aloud to Lady Mary, and she was perhaps inspired by verse written a hundred or so years earlier in this approximate style, which she had read to her employer. But the few lines do convey Sarah's nervousness that William might not forgive her for whatever had gone on between them, while at the same time the meter and the rhymes make light of that request for forgiveness. The overall effect feels trite, clichéd and arch. Sarah's poetry never did convey her true feelings.

William and Sarah probably strolled in the gardens together whenever he visited. His mother died during this period. We do not know whether he continued as a professional actor while Sarah was at Guy's Cliffe, and, if so, which rival company he joined. But he made sure to visit Sarah. The two discussed how much they meant to each other and planned their joint future.

They remained steadfast. Despite everything they had been through, they were still determined to be married. In 1773 Sarah reached the age of 18. Her Sid was 29. Although they still needed consent from her parents to become husband and wife and would continue to need it for a further three years, they presumably obtained a reluctant agreement to their plan. Roger and Sally bowed to the inevitable. Sarah could not continue as a lady's maid in a grand house such as this once she was married. Any hopes that she might forge a life for herself away from acting had come to nothing. Early biographers claimed that Sarah's sister Fanny was apprenticed to a milliner in Worcester and her sister Elizabeth to a dressmaker in Leominster while Sarah was at Guy's Cliffe, but they would have been very young to be sent away to work like this – 11 and 9 respectively. Perhaps their parents did try them with these two professions over the next few years, but both would, like their older sister, return to theatrical life in due course. Or perhaps, again, this is a convenient fiction.

William and Sarah were married on 26 November 1773 at Holy Trinity Church, Coventry, not far from Guy's Cliffe. What should have felt like a day of joy instead seemed like the end to a long struggle. Sarah had a handsome groom, who was even-tempered but not overly intelligent. As the Reverend Henry Bate later described William, he was 'A damn rascally player, but a civil fellow'.[11] Yet this civil fellow was the man Sarah wanted to marry. For his part he was marrying someone spirited, beautiful, eloquent and talented. The bride's father gave her away. Sally Kemble, Sarah's mother, was pregnant yet again. The baby, Henry, would be born a month later, but would not survive. There is no record of Sally making it to the service, but she would surely have wanted to be there. Roger Kemble stood witness, as did a Mary Godfrey, and the assistant curate, who conducted the service. Mary Godfrey may well have been another maid at Guy's Cliffe.

In comedies, marriage is often the end of the story. And this might indeed have been an end point for the young married couple. They would perhaps have expected to make some kind of living on the travelling circuit, bringing up their family in much the same way Sarah had herself spent her childhood. Perhaps, like Sarah's parents before them, they could have taken over the management of the Kemble troupe and improved their financial circumstances to a modest extent. But their future together would prove to be a very different one. Their first few years of married life turned out to be far more turbulent than they might have predicted. There would be emotional highs but also painful lows for them both. It was not, after all, in performing comedies that Sarah excelled.

Chapter 3

Starting Out

'I should be glad to know her cast of parts.'[1]

Sal and Sid embarked on their married life as two young actors, keen to earn their living the only way they knew how, as members of a company of travelling players. The couple's immediate prospects did not look particularly good. It probably seemed inevitable that they would start their married life together working for Sarah's parents. After all, Roger and Sally Kemble had worked for Sarah's grandparents in the same way. Yet, far too soon as it turned out, they would be recruited by David Garrick to join his Drury Lane company. And when that went disastrously wrong, they would have to work out for themselves how to pick up the pieces.

A month after their wedding, Sarah and William returned to Mr Kemble's Company of Comedians. How else were they to earn a living? Sarah was billed for the first time as Mrs Siddons when she appeared in Worcester on 13 December 1773. She played the role of Charlotte Rusport in Richard Cumberland's comedy, *The West Indian* and as Leonora in Isaac Bickerstaff's two-act opera, *The Padlock*. The former, which had proved a success when it was first put on at Drury Lane a couple of years earlier, told the story of a young West Indian plantation owner who returns to London, rum- and sugar-soaked, to marry his sweetheart. The cast includes his black servant from the West Indies. Someone in the cast, perhaps William, would have blacked up to play the part of the servant. Did Sarah ponder the connection with her old employers? The same month there had been some controversy over the company appearing in Wolverhampton, where they were originally banned from putting on shows during the Christmas season, but eventually they were reluctantly allowed to enter the town to perform there. The Kembles' battle for respectability seemed as distant as ever.

Sarah was soon pregnant with their first child. But within a few months the Siddons had left Sarah's parents to join a rival company, Chamberlain and Crump's Barnstormers. Sarah's early biographers gloss over this move and whether there was any fallout with Sarah's parents. It indicates that the couple felt they could do better for themselves. They may well have earned more money with the Barnstormers and Sarah was probably offered better roles. They started performing with the new troupe in Cheltenham that summer. In October, a respectable eleven months after their wedding, their son Henry Siddons was born in Wolverhampton.

While she was still pregnant with Henry, that first summer working for Chamberlain and Crump, 19-year-old Sarah had a stroke of luck. This was the very first thing she recounted in the notes she wrote many years later for Thomas Campbell, her official biographer. She was playing the lead female role of Belvidera in Thomas Otway's *Venice Preserved*. The play had been written about a hundred years earlier but was extremely popular with audiences. It tells the story of a group of conspirators who plot to overthrow the regime in Venice, where the play is set. Sarah's character, Belvidera, is married to one of the main conspirators, Jaffier, despite her father having opposed the match. Sarah would not have had to dig deep within herself to know how to play those scenes. Belvidera remains steadfastly loyal to Jaffier as the conspiracy to overthrow the Venetian government goes from bad to worse. Jaffier turns traitor, and is put to death, while the steadfast Belvidera is driven mad by this news and dies of grief (see Appendix 2).

One night a party of aristocrats was in the audience, which included the wealthy, influential Lord Bruce, and his stepdaughter, Henrietta Boyle. Sarah could hear the fashionable group making noises during the performance, and she took these to be suppressed snorts of laughter. Understandably her self-esteem was not particularly high at this point. She had only very recently started working as an actress for anyone outside her own family. The next day, though, William happened to be in the town when he came across Lord Bruce, who presumably recognised Sarah's husband as one of the cast. To his surprise and delight, William learned that, far from laughing at Sarah's acting, the party had been trying to suppress their sobs, so moved had they been at the fate of Belvidera.

The Siddons were soon invited to meet Sarah's new fans, and Sarah and Henrietta immediately became fast friends. The 16-year-old Henrietta was three years younger than Sarah. The two forged a bond which had all the intensity of a teenage female friendship. Henrietta was the daughter of an Anglo-Irish aristocrat and would marry and settle in County Antrim at Shanes Castle, where Sarah visited her. For now, though, Henrietta took a keen interest in Sarah's costumes. She would advise on what Sarah should wear, sometimes lending Sarah clothing and, as Sarah wrote in her notes for Thomas Campbell, 'even condescended to make part of my Dresses with her own dear hand.'[2] Since it fell to Sarah to provide her own costumes for her acting work, this was also a very practical offer of help.

It was Lord Bruce, once he returned to London, who suggested to David Garrick that the famous actor/manager might like to send a scout to appraise

Sarah's acting talent and consider recruiting her for his company in Drury Lane. Garrick soon sent his deputy, Tom King, to take a look. King was impressed by what he saw. Garrick then sent a second scout, the Reverend Henry Bate, together with Bate's wife, to Cheltenham and Gloucester to see for himself what he thought of the provincial young actress. There they saw Sarah perform the role of Rosalind in Shakespeare's *As You Like It*.

Henry Bate was a characteristically eighteenth-century clergyman, in that he inherited his father's ministry in Essex, but, since he was of aristocratic birth and would later be made a baronet, he never worked as a clergyman. Instead, he owned and ran a daily national newspaper, *The Morning Herald*, and he also fancied himself as a playwright, primarily writing the scripts for comic operas. Bate and Garrick were firm friends. In July 1775 Garrick wrote to Bate that he had heard Sarah 'has a desire I hear to try her Fortune with us.'[3] Garrick always enjoyed the sport of spotting talent and recruiting the best actors to join the Drury Lane company. There was inevitably keen rivalry with Covent Garden, the other London theatre which held a royal patent, as to who could find the brightest and best young actors and sign them up the fastest. But Sarah was not entirely a passive figure in this. Such a move would be highly advantageous to her. She had clearly indicated to Tom King that she would potentially be interested.

Henry Bate was impressed by what he saw. He and his wife had a difficult journey to Cheltenham to see Sarah's Rosalind, and then they were forced to watch her from the wings of what Bate described as a small barn. Clearly the Cheltenham theatre was not up to much. To make the assessment even more challenging, Sarah was pregnant again. Henry Bate found it hard to get a sense of what she might look like without her big belly. And yet he had no hesitation in recommending her to his influential friend. Sarah's face he described as 'one of the most strikingly beautiful for stage effect that ever I beheld.'[4] As for her performance style, it was 'remarkably pleasing and characteristic'.[5] Already, Sarah's genius for inhabiting the characters she played and enabling her audience to connect to them had been noted. Bate reported that Sarah brought great variety to her lines of dialogue, which she spoke beautifully, and she did more with one particular scene – a two-hander between Sarah's character Rosalind and the male lead Orlando – than he had even seen the famed earlier actress Elizabeth Barry achieving.

But he did have some reservations. He found Sarah's voice rather dissonant when he first heard it. He was concerned that it might come across as grating when she was playing less passionate scenes. Nevertheless, as the evening went on, he found this aspect less troubling. He advised Garrick that the way Sarah pronounced her lines might just be an affectation, which the great man could simply correct.

In his conversation with Sarah after the show, Henry Bate must have asked which roles she already had in her repertoire. He was favourably impressed by the large number of parts she knew and reported this to his friend. He admitted he himself had only at this point seen Sarah in *As You Like It*, but it was useful intelligence, nevertheless. Others he spoke to that evening assured him that she was particularly good in what was known as 'breeches roles', where actresses played men, either cross-dressing in comedies like *As You Like It*, or in playing parts which were originally written for men, not women. Sarah made an excellent Hamlet, he was told. Garrick should take care, he joked. The Worcestershire critics had particularly liked her in that role, which was one for which Garrick was particularly famed.

David Garrick and Henry Bate saw themselves as engaged in what was a military campaign to attract the best talent to Drury Lane. Bate reported that some 'Covent Garden Mohawks were entrenched near the place,' which is why he decided to meet Sarah and William immediately after the performance and drop heavy hints about the reason for his visit.[6] The rival bidders from Covent Garden, he wrote, 'intended carrying her by surprise', as if she were some medieval castle they were storming.[7] Any negotiations would be with William, as the husband, rather than with his wife Sarah. What they would do with William, and whether he could also be given a role in the Drury Lane company, was not discussed.

Once the performance of *As You Like It* finished, the Siddons were already waiting for Bate when he came to talk to them. Sarah told him that she was naturally delighted at the prospect. It represented a dream come true. The Siddons would not make a financial proposal for their services, Sarah explained, but would wait to hear what Garrick might think appropriate.

Garrick wrote back immediately, confirming that he would indeed like Bate to secure the young actress. Bate should indicate to William that he must be happy with the fact his wife was so talented and not expect much for himself. The fact Sarah was pregnant did concern Garrick, he admitted to his friend. Could Bate let him know how soon the baby was to be born, and how quickly after that Sarah would be able to appear on stage again? It is easy to see from this exchange how the Siddons must have felt pressured to get Sarah to London and on stage at Drury Lane as soon as they could after their baby's birth – with disastrous consequences.

Garrick had laughed at his friend's description of Sarah's recruitment in terms of a military campaign. Bate should tell her that if she were good at the job and was prepared to be 'wholly governed by me, I will make her theatrical fortune.'[8] She must be prepared to do exactly what he asked of her. Again, Garrick was already outlining a problem area. Once she joined his London company, Sarah would not find it easy to take direction from him. Using the same military terms in his letter to his friend, Garrick confessed that if any of his other London actresses began to be difficult in the coming season then 'I will immediately play off my masked battery of Siddons.'[9] Sarah is now described as a military weapon, not a living, breathing person, and a weapon Garrick can use to his own advantage at Drury Lane.

Bate replied on the same day. He had revised his opinion of William, he admitted to his friend. All William required was to be employed in Garrick's London company, however the great man saw fit to use him. Bate had been to see William perform and had now concluded that 'he is much more tolerable than I thought him at first.'[10] Meanwhile, the management of Chamberlain and Crump had heard word that the Siddons might be contemplating leaving them and had refused to cast Sarah in any substantial part which would allow Bate to get more of a sense of her range as an actress. The scouts from Covent Garden were also sniffing around. But Henry Bate remained confident, he wrote to Garrick, continuing their joking military metaphor, that, without Sarah's skill to raise their game, Chamberlain and Crump's 'garrison must fall by famine.'[11]

Bate then lists twenty-three different roles which Sarah has told him she would be able to perform. She was, he boasted, 'an extraordinary quick study' when it came to learning new roles.[12] Looking at them with the benefit of hindsight, it is striking to see that the majority of these were comic roles, and how most of the tragic heroines for which Sarah would later make her name were absent from her list. Six of these roles were underlined as her favourites, and the only tragic role to be highlighted was Belvidera, which had so moved Sarah's new friend, Henrietta Boyle. Sarah had not yet honed her skills and worked out her strengths as a performer. Garrick had sent his scouts far too early. If he had waited a couple of years, once Sarah had gained more experience working for Chamberlain and Crump, Sarah's first London season might have been very different. But at the slightest hint that there might be a talented actress in the provinces whom they could sign up, the two big London theatres had started circling. Inevitably, the Siddons took the bait.

A letter from William Siddons to Henry Bate revealed the couple's nervousness about the deal. They had precipitously resigned from Chamberlain and Crump's company before they had heard back officially from Garrick. Would their finances be secure? William admitted to being very relieved when Garrick confirmed his offer. It was decided that Sarah should give birth in Gloucester and that the Siddons would then travel to London as quickly as possible. The London theatre season always started in early autumn, so Sarah's pregnancy was acknowledged by all involved to be highly inconvenient, although Garrick was at pains to respect the situation. He considered delaying Sarah's arrival until the following season, but this idea was quickly dismissed by the over-eager William.

Garrick also asked that the Siddons suggest which role Sarah would like to play for her debut. He wrote that he would not object to Rosalind in *As You Like It*, except that he had hired another actress, Mary King, who had already made her first appearance the same season playing that part. Garrick was known for playing one actress off against another. This was yet another element of the deal which he struck with the Siddons that would contribute to Sarah's downfall. The Siddons were both engaged as actors, at the rate of £5 each (a joint weekly income of £1,357 today). They would need to be careful with their rent, living expenses and childcare costs. But this still represented a good offer.

Sarah's labour started midway through a performance at Barton Street Theatre in Gloucester on 4 November. She gave birth the next day to her first daughter, Sarah 'Sally' Martha Siddons. A month later the family set out for London, having baptised the baby at St Michael's Church, Gloucester. Meanwhile, on 13 December William received an angry note from John de la Bere, of Covent Garden, who was furious to have heard the news that the Siddons were starting work at Drury Lane. He was under the impression he had already agreed terms with William. In his view William was infringing an existing contract. Once William was able to give up acting, he would become Sarah's manager, but his skills were already proving suspect.

The Siddons' first London season was a disaster. Sarah's nerves would cause her voice to fail. The reviews she received those next few months would rankle with her for ever after. She was condemned as provincial, as not having the skill required to play comedy, and as being at best a mediocre talent – not worthy of appearing in Garrick's final season. Her relationship with Garrick himself was a troubled one, while her fellow actresses seemed to Sarah to be conspiring against her. And at the end of the season, she would suffer the indignity of hearing not from the new management but instead from the prompt that the Siddons' contracts would not be renewed.

At this, Sarah fell into a deep depression. Aged only 21, she must have felt that her chances of any kind of meaningful career were over. It was already acknowledged that she had a husband who was far less talented an actor than her. Yet neither of them knew any way of making their living except on the stage. They had two small children to look after while they fretted about their future. To go back to work for her parents would feel like a surrender. They had to go on. There was no question of Sarah pausing and taking stock.

A few of the less prestigious provincial theatres showed themselves prepared to hire Sarah, despite her reputation and the deadening effect of the depression which hung over her. She must have wished she could crawl quietly away from the spotlight. But instead, every evening she had to go out and perform. The Siddons were in Birmingham when they heard the news that they would not be returning to Drury Lane. In October they went from Birmingham to Liverpool to take up work there. Next, Sarah appeared in Manchester and then again in Birmingham. And gradually she began to find herself. She refined her style. She puzzled out for herself the roles which worked for her. She might have thought comedies were her strength, but from this vantage point she began to see that her emotional power was far better suited to tragedy. Most of the tragedies so loved by Sarah's audiences are very rarely, if ever, performed today, and if they were we would probably class them as melodramas rather than classic tragedies. But they spoke to the theatregoers of the time and Sarah, always playing the tragic heroine, would affect those who went to see her like no-one else before or since.

A Siddons heroine is principled. She is noble. She is brave. Romantic involvement always leads to unhappiness for her. Affairs of the heart are almost inevitably doomed. The heroine can never be anything but completely faithful to the man she loves. One of the male characters often forces her into another sexual relationship, but this is always against her will. If the play includes the character of a father figure for the Sarah Siddons role – and they often do – then she will invariably show him heroic filial loyalty, going far further than simple duty requires. The plots of Sarah's tragedies are littered with disastrous misunderstandings, extraordinary twists of fate and catastrophic calamities. In the final act, she often commits suicide on stage, to the dismay of those watching her. As she suffers in front of them, they suffer along with her. When she hopes for redemption, they too dare to dream. When she cries, they weep buckets in sympathy. (See Appendix 2 for short synopses of Sarah's most famous roles.)

For the next eighteen months Sarah felt she did not perform at her best. But gradually she rallied. Her life was given meaning again by her two children. By March 1777 she was playing the title role of Hamlet in Birmingham, himself a character not so very far from a classic Siddons heroine. Henry Bate had written to Garrick about how the Worcester critics had admired her in the role and now she felt able to play it again. She would take the breeches part of Hamlet on several occasions as a young actress, while she was honing her style, but once she returned to London for a second season, she would then not play the part of Hamlet again for another twenty or more years.

Even though Sarah did not return to her parents' company of travelling players, she always remained very close to her parents and siblings. The Siddons were joined in Manchester for their next winter season by Sarah's eldest brother, John Philip Kemble. For six years John Philip had trained as a priest in Douai, in France, but despite the long time away he found he could not give up his desire to succeed as an actor. There were rumours that Roger Kemble was angry with his oldest son for leaving the priesthood. John Philip had first appeared as a professional on the English stage in Wolverhampton during Sarah's disastrous Garrick season in London. Perhaps Sarah lobbied for him to join the company in Manchester. One early biographer makes an unsubstantiated claim that Sarah had rescued John Philip from a debtors' prison. Destitution was never far away for either brother or sister in these early years.

John Philip had been well educated at Douai and could read and write Latin and Greek. He wore his learning with pride and his approach to acting was more scholarly than that of his sister. His career from now on would be intertwined with hers. Yet, while she was content only ever to act, he would go on to manage theatres as well as appearing as the lead actor, and he would even write a play of his own. Like his sister, he was a 'quick study'. He was always fascinated by oratory and would give lectures on the theme in later life. He had a particularly characterful voice, like his sister, which was an important element in his stage presence. Unlike Sarah, he retained a Welsh accent, so the way he pronounced certain words felt particularly unusual and distinctive for his audiences.

There was a very particular Kemble 'look' shared by both brother and sister. They were tall and dark, with piercing eyes. John Philip had a largish Roman nose, which made him appear extremely distinguished. Sarah's nose was distinctive, but it was not beaked like John Philip's. When Thomas Gainsborough painted her portrait, he complained that there was no end to Sarah Siddons' nose. Besides their physical similarities, the two siblings had an easy emotional shorthand. They had acted alongside each other all their lives. Having John Philip on stage opposite her must have helped Sarah to scale the emotional heights a part required of her, knowing that she could trust her brother to respond to what she was giving him.

Sarah and John Philip were both in Liverpool in early 1777, acting for Joseph Younger's company there, when they met the actress, Elizabeth Inchbald. Elizabeth had been born the daughter of a Suffolk farmer, and raised as a Roman Catholic, like John Philip. The stage always held a magnetic attraction for her, just as it had for the Kemble siblings. Despite her family's disapproval, Elizabeth began earning her living on stage as an actress. But she suffered all her life from a bad stammer, which inevitably made a life on the stage even more challenging. She had come to London, but, young and vulnerable, had suffered sexual harassment from male company members. So she had agreed to marry her fellow actor, Joseph Inchbald, largely as a pragmatic move. He was also a Roman Catholic, but he was twice her age and already had two illegitimate children. The marriage was never easy, and the couple did not go on to have any children of their own. For a time, they tried to work in France, but financial difficulties brought them back to England, where they joined Joseph Younger's company in Liverpool. Elizabeth would remain a friend of Sarah's and of John Philip's for the rest of their lives.

In April 1777 Sarah made her debut for the well-respected Tate Wilkinson's company at Blake Street in York. Wilkinson had seen Sarah's performance as Hamlet in Birmingham and had made her an offer to come to York. He realised Sarah was still not fully recovered from the depressive illness from which she had been suffering since her failure in London. Nevertheless, he took the inspired step of casting her as the lead in one of the tragedies for which she would make her name, Euphrasia in Arthur Murphy's *The Grecian Daughter*. The play had been written in 1772, for another actress, Ann Crawford, but Sarah would go on to make it her own. Wilkinson was nervous about casting the young Sarah, admitting:

> I actually trembled from her apparent weakness, fearing she would never be able to sustain that fatiguing character with proper energy and spirit.[13]

The play is set in Sicily, where the Greek princess, Euphrasia, has been taken captive by the Roman army. Meanwhile, her dying father, Evander, is being held in a cave nearby. Euphrasia visits him, where she is tremendously loving and dutiful, as befits a Siddons heroine (see Appendix 2 for more detail about the play). Tate Wilkinson himself took the part of Evander. He need not have fretted that Sarah would not be strong enough to sustain the character. The production was a triumph.

The audiences and critics in York adored Sarah from this moment on. Tate Wilkinson's management style was caring and paternal, and Sarah found he created an environment in which she felt both supported and trusted. She could continue to raise her game. Wilkinson began to cast her as a whole range of characters, and even found acting work for William. The Wilkinsons and the Siddons soon became close. Tate Wilkinson later wrote in his memoirs that Sarah was almost constantly at his house at that time, to the great satisfaction of his wife, and that Tate himself often took snuff with Sarah. Here was an older couple, with a good reputation in regional theatre, who went out of their way to take the Siddons under their wing.

The memory of the shame and misery Sarah had suffered in London remained very vivid for her. She admitted to Wilkinson and his wife that she thought the way she had been treated was so cruel and unjust that she had no desire to return there. The Wilkinsons' friend, theatre critic William Woodfall, gave her some career advice. She should keep away from London theatres, he told her. Her style was better suited to the smaller, regional establishments where audiences could hear her properly.

As Sarah's confidence grew and her reputation was gradually repairing itself, so the Siddons' finances improved. Wilkinson arranged a benefit in Sarah's honour in York. The following spring, Sarah was playing Hamlet again in Liverpool and wrote to Elizabeth Inchbald, who was herself performing in York, to tell her that the family finances now seemed to be on a far better footing. Perhaps as a result, the Siddons family decided to take a holiday in Yorkshire along with John Philip and the Inchbalds. This was a first for Sarah, and probably for the others in the party as well. Sarah would look back on it as an exceptionally happy time. In the mornings she assuaged her maternal guilt – something she felt even more keenly as her career took off – by doing the washing and ironing for the party, singing as she worked. Then, in the afternoons the party would all venture onto the moors together to play games. In the evenings the grown-ups played cards, while Sarah sometimes sang duets with her brother.

Although she wrote about the holiday as an idyllic interlude, it is noticeable that Sarah does not mention William. Perhaps, by now, they were rubbing along as husband and wife and the parents of two children, but without the romantic feelings they had felt for each other when they were first married. The emotional journey Sarah had been through, as she processed the London failure and then began to rebuild her career and to hone her real strengths as an actress, was one that she had made alone. William had played only a small part in it. The more intense emotions on their holiday, though, were the preserve of their friends. It was evident to everyone staying in the house on the Yorkshire moors that John Philip and Elizabeth Inchbald were falling in love. Elizabeth's older husband, Joseph, seemed to have daily explosive rows with her before taking himself off alone to paint.

During these two and a half years working in the regions, refining her acting style, Sarah often played opposite an actor named John Henderson. He could see how she was refining her technique and wrote to John Palmer, a contact of his, who ran the Old Orchard Street Theatre in Bath, recommending that Palmer take Sarah on. Henderson's early death meant that he did not get the reputation as one of the finest actors of the time which he perhaps deserves. He was a tireless advocate for Sarah. Tate Wilkinson tried to secure a permanent place for her within his York company with the offer of fine clothing if she stayed, but she refused. Her old ambition was still there. Bath was more established and crucially had secured for itself a prestigious royal patent ten years earlier, in 1768. And so, in autumn 1778, Sarah accepted John Palmer's offer to join his company, where, it was agreed, she would play leading roles. The Siddons set out for Bath.

Chapter 4

Bath

'My industry and perseverance were indefatigable.'[1]

Bath proved a haven for the Siddons. For the first time the couple and their young family had a permanent home. They settled in the city with its fashionable spa for four years. Now that Sarah had the security of more permanent employment, she was able to hone her acting skills. She gained valuable further experience in Bath, playing over 100 roles during her time here. Some were not as successful as others, but as a valued member of a reputable company she could afford to experiment and work out her own strengths and weaknesses as a performer. Failure no longer haunted her. It quickly became evident that she might think she was suited to comedy, but it was as a tragic actress that she excelled. And her increasing success brought her social advantage as well. The city of Bath attracted most of fashionable society, and Sarah found herself with well-connected fans. Here she began to make friendships which would last her a lifetime.

John Henderson, who had recommended Sarah to John Palmer, the manager of the Old Orchard Street Theatre, played opposite her in Bath as Hamlet to her Gertrude, Shylock to her Portia, and Benedick to her Beatrice. Once it was evident that Palmer had secured the services of someone very special, Henderson wrote to Richard Brinsley Sheridan at Drury Lane, praising Sarah. But for the moment his recommendation was ignored. Sarah needed to build her reputation in Bath before Sheridan would consider her for his Drury Lane company.

It had been the custom in Bath that every Thursday a social event called the Cotillion Balls, a costumed evening of dancing, attracted the whole of fashionable society. As a result, attendance at the Old Orchard Street Theatre was much lower on a Thursday than on other nights. John Palmer had the bright idea of casting Sarah in a series of tragedies which played each Thursday. Soon the Cotillion Balls were deserted in favour of the beautiful new tragic actress. Sarah's weekly tragic performances became the talk of the town. As her reputation grew, Sarah declared that she had no desire ever to leave her sympathetic Bath audiences. Performing for them felt totally different from the cold indifference she had experienced at Drury Lane.

John Palmer's father had founded the theatre in Bath some thirty years before Sarah first started acting there. Palmer himself spent £1,000 (approximately £140,000 today) enlarging and redecorating the building in the popular classical style, soon before he recruited Sarah. Most importantly, he successfully petitioned parliament to grant him a patent so that his theatre could be put on the same footing as the two main London theatres of the time, Drury Lane and Covent Garden. It had thereby gained the prestigious classification of Theatre Royal in 1768, ten years before the Siddons' arrival – the first playhouse outside London to earn this accolade.

Not that life in John Palmer's company was an easy one. He also owned a sister theatre at Bristol, and his actors, along with his stagehands, props, costumes and scenery, all trundled the twelve miles between the two theatres in specially designed coaches to give performances on alternate evenings. This meant that Sarah had to be away from her young family every other night.

At first, Sarah was simply one of John Palmer's company. She was engaged for the sum of £3 a week (£406.80 today), hardly enough to keep her small family, particularly as she needed to employ someone to look after her children; William's duties did not extend that far. She was not always given the leading role. As she herself wrote many years later about her time in Bath: 'I had the mortification of being obliged to personate many subordinate characters in comedy.'[2] If she refused, she would be compelled to forfeit part of her salary. She learned a huge number of new roles over the four years she was living in Bath. William set himself up as her line coach and there were reports that he was quick to show anger if she got her words wrong. As usual, she was expected to provide her own costume whenever she appeared in a new role. She frequently mislaid items of clothing as she travelled between the two theatres in Bristol and Bath.

As Sarah's reputation grew, so did the salary she could command. Soon she was earning £6 or £7 a week (£798.50 or £915.50 today). This was then greatly augmented by the system of 'benefits' which existed in all professional theatres at the time, and which Sarah would go on to use to increase her earnings for the rest of her professional life. In every season special 'benefit nights' would be held, whereby the entire takings from a single performance would be given to one of the actors in the company, or to another good cause associated with them. In Sarah's successful 1781–82 season in Bath, for instance, her takings from the three benefits held in her honour amounted in total to £398 11s 0d (£52,120 today).

Sarah might have learned many new roles, but she began to develop her own repertoire of the specific tragic parts in which she excelled, and to repeat those performances frequently, thereby consolidating her strengths as an actress. Her

Bath audiences enjoyed watching her take the lead in plays which are rarely, if ever, performed today. (Appendix 2 contains simple synopses of Sarah's most popular tragedies.) She would have been aware of these plays before she came to Bath and already played the lead roles in some of them, but it was here that she made them her own. The emotional highs and lows which a Siddons heroine experienced in the course of the play feel contrived to us, but they affected Sarah's audiences deeply. William Shakespeare's tragedies were performed as well, but often in bowdlerised versions. A version of *King Lear* existed, with a happy ending for Cordelia. Shakespeare's *King John* and *Henry VIII* were popular with Sarah's audiences but are rarely staged today. Sarah would go on to make her mark as Lady Macbeth – her most famous role – and as Desdemona in *Othello*. For John Palmer she was still playing the title role in *Hamlet*, which she would drop once she went to London, and she also played Juliet in *Romeo and Juliet*.

Sarah and William Siddons had perhaps the happiest four years of their marriage during their time in Bath. The greater financial security they experienced meant that William could give up permanently the notion of making a living as an actor. From now on he became officially Sarah Siddons' manager and line coach. The Siddons first moved into Southgate Street in Bath and then to a more permanent home at Axford's Buildings in the centre of the city. Their two children, Henry and Sally, were by now 4 and 3 years old respectively. Sarah gave birth to their third child, Maria, in July 1779, during the first summer recess from John Palmer's company. There would have been no objection to her continuing to act while visibly pregnant, even when this made a mockery of the plot of the plays in which she starred. Two years later, in April 1781, Sarah gave birth to a third daughter, Frances Emilia Siddons, and had her christened in Bath Abbey, but this time the baby died after only three months.

While her financial hardships lessened, Sarah's life was still not easy. She always prided herself on being a supportive spouse, a devoted mother and an exemplary housewife, cooking, cleaning and ironing whenever she had a moment. Her notebook from the time is packed full of recipes. She had to supervise the childcare and run the home, and then prepare herself to appear on stage several nights a week. Her performance schedule was far harder than anything a theatre company would attempt today. Looking back on this time in Bath, when she was writing her notes for her authorised biographer, Thomas Campbell, she remembered how, during that period:

> My industry and perseverance were indefatigable. That I had strength and courage to get through all this labour of mind and body, interrupted too, by the cares and childish sports of my poor children who were (most

unwillingly often) hushed to silence for interrupting my studies, I look back with wonder.³

Her working mother's guilt lay just below the surface, even then.

As the Siddons settled into their more comfortable life in Bath, and Sarah established herself as a hugely talented tragic actress, she began to create a network of aristocratic patrons and to forge several friendships which would last her for the rest of her life. As an actress her social status was ambiguous. Many well-known actresses of the time were illegitimate by birth and had started their working lives as prostitutes or street sellers. But if they were talented and spoke well, losing any trace of an accent which gave this away, they were accepted into polite society. Sarah's pride at her early friendship with Henrietta Boyle demonstrated her social ambitions. With her striking good looks and her beautiful voice, she was able to move up the social ladder with relative ease. She soon got to know the infamous Georgiana, Duchess of Devonshire, who came frequently to see her perform. The romantic poet Anna Seward, nicknamed the Swan of Lichfield, made Sarah's acquaintance, as did Hannah More, the religious writer. Both the diarist Hester Thrale (who later became Hester Piozzi) and Fanny Burney, the novelist with royal connections, came to see Sarah perform in Bath. She would get to know them both later in life. Sarah also made friends with the heiress Sophia Weston, who changed her name to Penelope Pennington when she got married, and who would play a significant role as Sarah's two eldest daughters, Sally and Maria, reached adulthood.

Sarah met one of her greatest lifelong friends, the Reverend Thomas Sedgwick Whalley, at this time. He and his first wife, Elizabeth, lived in Royal Crescent and at Langford Court, the manor house in the village of Lower Langford, near Bristol. Although Whalley was notionally the rector of a village in Lincolnshire, it was considered an unhealthy location, so the local bishop made it a condition of the role that Whalley would never live there. For fifty years Whalley's duties were discharged by a curate instead. Meanwhile, he dedicated himself to the enjoyment of a rich and varied cultural life. Whalley was very tall, handsome and thin, with the delicate, affected air of a confirmed aesthete. Fanny Burney mocked his habit of forever expressing his feelings, holding forth extensively on matters as trivial as the way the wind whipped around Royal Crescent, but Sarah empathised with Whalley's style, fresh as she was from playing tragic heroines on stage every night. Whalley wrote a couple of plays, which were moderately well received, but he did not force his writing on Sarah, never pressuring her to appear in anything he had written, unlike others she would encounter. He loved art almost as much as he loved the theatre. Sir Joshua Reynolds painted him with his lapdogs, and Sarah wrote affectionately about their shell-pink ears and amusing habits. The Whalleys were to prove a constant support to Sarah from now on.

Sarah's social status was intricately bound up with her professional life. The Irish theatre impresario, Thomas Sheridan, came to see her perform and was soon an influential and helpful supporter. His son Richard Brinsley Sheridan also came to see her, bringing with him his first wife, Elizabeth. She was a member of the talented, musical Linley family, and her father, Thomas Linley, was another of the new owners of Drury Lane. Someone else who met Sarah at this time, and who was professionally involved in the theatre, was the playwright Samuel Jackson Pratt. Like Whalley, he came from a wealthy family and was notionally a clergyman, but he had spent much of his life acting and writing both plays and poetry. At the time he owned a bookshop in Milsom Street, in the centre of Bath. Sarah's relationship with Samuel Pratt would not be as easy as her friendship with Whalley.

As Sarah's professional reputation rose, the memory of her disastrous first season in London began to fade. She had been young then, and under pressure. What if she got the chance to try her luck in London again? In 1780, two years after she had first arrived in Bath, Richard Brinsley Sheridan made his first offer. He and his father had seen her perform at the Old Orchard Street Theatre. But Sarah refused. The Siddons had found security in Bath and were enjoying their new, settled family life. It must have felt too much of a gamble to throw all this certainty away, wagering everything on the hope that Sarah might find the success which had previously eluded her.

Two years later, in the summer of 1782, Sarah received a second offer from Sheridan. This time it was a formal, financial one. If she joined his Drury Lane company, she could earn ten guineas a week (£1,373 today), considerably more than John Palmer was paying. Yet even then Sarah hesitated. 'After my formal dismissal from thence, it may be imagined that this was to me a triumphant moment,' she wrote as an old woman, in her notes for her biographer.[4] It should have been a triumphant moment, she explained, but perhaps it did not feel quite like that. The stakes were just too high. For his part, John Palmer failed to match the London management's financial offer. He had benefited from his leading lady's popularity, using the extra box office receipts to make improvements to his theatre and put up the ticket prices. Yet he was not prepared to increase Sarah's salary.

Rumours abounded. Would Sarah stay or would she go? Her friend Thomas Sedgwick Whalley jumped the gun and wrote a poem congratulating her on joining Sheridan's company before the deal was even done. Sophia Weston wrote that she felt it was a pity Palmer had failed to realise the value of his leading actress. He should have listened to the rumours. Eventually Palmer did decide to offer Sarah the financial increase she had been asking for. The Bath newspapers printed his statement that he was doing his best to secure Sarah's services for another year. But it was too late. She had already accepted Sheridan. No longer was she the tongue-tied, nerve-wracked, too-young mother, fearful of falling into poverty. Instead, she was the successful and confident Bath tragedienne, determined to put right her past failures.

Sarah had not only improved her performance skills in Bath. She had also learned the vitally important lesson that her reputation was something which needed careful handling. She would never forget the poor notices she had received in the newspapers during the Garrick season. If she gave a good performance, of course, she would expect to receive a flattering review. But beyond that she now knew that she needed to manage her own image. Her Bath audiences were influential. It was important to present in the best possible light her decision to desert them and head to London for a second time. To argue that she wanted to make more money would not be acceptable. Nor would her followers be particularly sympathetic to her being motivated by hoping to right past wrongs.

On 21 May 1782 the Old Orchard Street Theatre presented a production of Ambrose Phillips' play *The Distrest Mother*, starring Sarah in the lead role. It told the story of Hermione, a faithful widow who prioritised her love for her son above everything else – a classic Siddons tragic heroine. In the play Hermione threatens to commit suicide rather than consummate a marriage into which she has been forced against her will. William Siddons had placed a piece in the local paper, advertising the special evening. After the play, it stated, Sarah would 'produce to the Audience THREE REASONS for quitting this Theatre.'[5] She would seek to explain to them her motivation for heading to London and absolve herself from any reputational damage in the process.

After the play was over and the lighter theatrical piece which traditionally followed the main event had also been performed, Sarah faced her audience, walking alone onto the stage. She had changed into her own clothing so she could appear as herself, albeit as a curated version. Her audiences would have been accustomed to seeing her on stage alone at the end of a play, while still in character, to speak the epilogue. But this was different. This time Sarah began to recite a poem of her own composition. She never had ambitions as a writer in the theatre, but here she knew that she needed to express herself in her own words. The poem she had written was deliberately simplistic and heartfelt. This was Sarah herself, appealing to her audience not as the famous tragic actress but as a young woman.

She was not here, she stressed, to demonstrate her intellectual credentials. Her motivation, as she put it, was 'honest gratitude, at whose request /Shamed be the heart that will not do its best.'[6] She had decided, she explained, to accept

Sheridan's offer to perform in London. It was important that she conveyed to them her reasons for doing so:

> The time draws nigh when I must bid adieu
> To this delightful spot – nay, even to you –
> To you, whose fostering kindness reared my name,
> O'erlooked my faults but magnified my fame.[7]

Her reputation as one of the most promising actresses in the country, she acknowledged, was due to her success in Bath. Here her loyal audiences had overlooked her faults. They had magnified her fame. And yet she had decided to leave them.

In a kind of show-and-tell, Sarah explained that she had three reasons for doing so. She walked to the wings of the stage and led out her three children – her three reasons – holding the toddler Maria in her arms, with 8-year-old Henry and 7-year-old Sally either side of her, shepherding them downstage to face the audience. Henry and Sally had appeared on stage with their mother before, but always playing stage roles, never simply as themselves. They stared unblinkingly out at the faces before them. Sarah was also eight months pregnant. A mere two weeks later she would give birth to another daughter, Elizabeth Anne. Her 'Three Reasons' could easily have been four, but it was thought indelicate to allude to actresses' pregnancies. The proud mother explained her reasoning for heading to London:

> These are the moles that bear me from your side,
> Where I was rooted – where I could have died.
> Stand forth, ye elves, and plead your mother's cause.[8]

The poetry might have been doggerel, but the sentiment was heartfelt. Sarah stood before her audience as a pregnant working mother, the sole breadwinner of the family, arguing that it was the future of her children which had led her to take this decision. The famous tragedian was playing yet another role – that of the dignified matron working to support her family.

The evening then concluded with Sarah taking the part of Nell – 'by particular desire' as the playbill puts it – in Charles Coffey and John Mottley's comic ballad opera, *The Devil to Pay*, a simple girl who longs to better herself socially.[9] Again, the message was clear. The evening as a whole – a benefit night for Sarah – brought in £145 18s (£19,080 today) and was deemed a huge success. Two weeks later Sarah gave birth to Elizabeth Anne, and two weeks after that, she repeated the evening, including her 'Three Reasons' speech, in Bristol, earning herself a further £106 13s (£13,880 today). There were rumours that some in the company were critical of her attempt to argue her case in this way. The sense was that the Siddons had overdone it, protesting Sarah's virtue when in fact her reasons for leaving were largely venal. Two actresses in the company jokingly announced that they planned to hold a benefit in which 'they would produce reasons for continuing on the Bristol stage,' rather than leaving it.[10] Unlike Sarah, they would stay loyal to John Palmer.

This was the first time Sarah endeavoured to control her own public image in this way. It would be the first of many. She now understood the perils of celebrity, where her reputation might be lost at any time. As a result, she was prepared at this moment to push her children into the limelight and use them for her own devices, a 'mommy-diva' as one academic has described her.[11] She would always seek to portray herself as the supremely virtuous mother. At a time where many actresses used their sexuality as part of their attraction, Sarah played down her own sex appeal. Her self-image was that of a motherly, even at times queenly figure. Many of her contemporaries on the stage took lovers openly, had children out of wedlock and divorced their husbands. She emphatically did none of these things. Her position as a respectably married woman and devoted mother was something her upbringing had taught her to value highly. It was vitally important to her. As one of her fans famously phrased it: 'One would as soon think of making love to Mrs Siddons as to the Archbishop of Canterbury.'[12]

Her four years in Bath had given Sarah the confidence she needed to accept Richard Brinsley Sheridan's offer and risk her reputation in London a second time. The Bath years had provided her small family with some hugely valued security, a permanent home and a steady income. This, in turn, had allowed Sarah to find her real strengths as an actress. Now she knew that it was as a tragic heroine that she excelled. She had also learned the vital skills of managing her own image, to protect herself from unwanted publicity. She had shown she could conquer the provinces and succeed in the fashionable city of Bath. But the real prize, that of success as a performer in one of London's two royal theatres, still eluded her. The first time aged only 20, she had failed. Now, aged 27, a married mother of four, she was prepared to take that risk for a second time.

Chapter 5

Triumph

'She was Tragedy personified.'[1]

The next few weeks completely changed Sarah's life. She had met with acclaim in Bath, but she was still simply a jobbing member of a provincial theatre company. Her opening performance at Drury Lane turned out to be one of the greatest nights ever to take place on the London stage. That was followed by a triumphant season where Sarah was lauded in each of the different plays she performed. From now on she took the art of performance to a whole new level. She became a superstar, a game-changer, beautiful and accomplished, mobbed by fans wherever she went.

Two days after she had held her benefit at Bath and recited her 'Three Reasons' speech, Sarah gave her very last performance there as part of John Palmer's company, playing Mrs Belville in Hugh Kelly's comedy, *The School for Wives*. Mrs Belville is a character role, not even the lead. While she worked for Palmer, Sarah still occasionally played subordinate comic characters. Never someone to shun the chance of extra work, she then travelled with the company and performed in Bristol throughout July, having given birth in the interim. She next took an engagement in Cheltenham for the month of August, sending William and her children to the seaside resort of Weymouth to enjoy a summer holiday while she worked on. She would eventually join them there.

Yet Sarah was still feeling exceptionally nervous about this new move to London. She studied her lines to steady herself. In Weymouth she and William even began to question whether they should defer her arrival. They wrote to Thomas Linley, Brinsley Sheridan's father-in-law and one of the three owners of Drury Lane, but he was adamant that this was not possible. It was too late to turn back. The Siddons were forced to agree to his terms. Anxiously they made their way to London. In late September 1782, Sarah, William, their children Henry, Sally, Maria and the baby Elizabeth Anne, all settled into their new London lodgings at 149 The Strand, a stone's throw from the magnificent Drury Lane Theatre.

This time Sarah's salary was more than double what she had been paid by Garrick six years earlier – ten guineas a week (£1,373 today). Playbills had already started appearing, alerting audiences to her imminent arrival: 'Mrs Siddons (From the Theatre Royal, Bath) will shortly make her appearance at this Theatre in a Capital Character in Tragedy.'² Sarah was to wait two nerve-wracking weeks before her first night. Recalling this time, she wrote about her extremely nervous state and that 'my own fate and that of my little family hung upon it.'³ During that time she had only two formal rehearsals for the role.

After much discussion it had been agreed that Sarah should make her debut playing the title role in Thomas Southerne's play *Isabella, or The Fatal Marriage* (see Appendix 2). Thomas Sheridan was instrumental in this decision. He had seen and admired Sarah's performances in Bath. Now he played a fatherly role for her, helping the anxious actress make the right decision over the choice of play, whereas under Garrick she had gone so wrong in agreeing to play Portia on her debut. Thomas Sheridan knew that Sarah was at her most powerful when she acted a role which was characterised by pathos. He saw that *The Fatal Marriage* would give her this opportunity. Sarah would have preferred to have played the part of Euphrasia in Arthur Murphy's play *The Grecian Daughter*, but Thomas Sheridan was adamant that for her opening night Isabella was the right role. Sarah's old supporter, Tom King, who had recommended her to Garrick when he saw her at Cheltenham six years earlier, was now acting manager at Drury Lane. Seeing Tom King again must have grounded Sarah as she prepared for the biggest professional night of her life.

Thomas Sheridan had chosen well. The character of Isabella in *The Fatal Marriage* betrays all the classic hallmarks of the great Sarah Siddons heroine. When the audience first meet her, she is widowed and has fallen on hard times, stoically bringing up her only son with very little money. Her husband has reputedly been a casualty of war. She asks for pity from her father-in-law, but he will only support her if she gives up the custody of her son to him and accepts that she can never see the boy again, something she is not prepared to do. And so, reluctantly, she agrees to marry a nobleman, who has always been in love with her. No sooner is the marriage consummated than Isabella's first husband reappears. She is plunged into torment at the fate which has befallen her, through no fault of her own. In the final act, unable to see a way through for herself, Isabella commits suicide by plunging a dagger into her own heart. As one contemporary writer explained:

> For anyone gifted with the tragic powers of tenderness, greed, rage, nothing better could have been chosen.⁴

Sarah's own little boy, Henry, was to take the part of Isabella's son.

During the first rehearsal, Sarah had asked an ally to stand at the back of the auditorium. She needed to be confident that this time her voice could be heard by her audience. After all, even once she had begun to do well in the regions, friends had advised her that her voice would never be powerful enough to carry sufficiently on the London stage. Initially, she admitted, she was so overcome with nerves she merely whispered. Then she gained confidence enough to project her voice. Delighted, her friend confirmed that everyone throughout the whole theatre would be able to hear her. Seemingly, one ghost from the disastrous Garrick season had been laid to rest.

Sarah's son Henry, just turned 8 years old, also helped her during rehearsals, albeit unwittingly. He was so overcome by the action of the play and was so convinced by Sarah's method acting that he thought his mother might be dying. During the first rehearsal he burst into floods of tears. Ever the showman, Brinsley Sheridan could immediately see the advantage publicity-wise of the little boy's response. He ensured that the story of Henry's reaction appeared in *The Morning Post* on the morning of the first performance. Sarah's son's tears, wrote the journalist in *The Morning Post*, had 'struck the feelings of the company in a singular manner.'[5] This was going to be something special.

The second rehearsal was scheduled for 8 October, but Sarah woke that morning so hoarse she was unable to speak. She could not rehearse. That evening she went to bed wretched. Maybe her voice would be her undoing yet again. But the next day she found to her relief that she was able to speak properly. As if in solidarity, the sun also shone. Sarah wrote:

> I hailed it though tearfully, yet thankfully, as a happy omen and even now am not ashamed of this (as it may perhaps be called) childish superstition.[6]

A final rehearsal had been planned for ten o'clock that morning, but her family had decided not to wake her after her anxious night, so she slept until one o'clock in the afternoon and failed to make it into the theatre.

Thursday 10 October 1782 was scheduled for Sarah's first appearance. Again, the day dawned bright and sunny. Regardless, she spent the day worrying about how the evening's performance would turn out. Her father Roger arrived at the family's lodgings to escort his daughter to what she described as 'my fiery trial'.[7] For his part, William kept away. Perhaps the couple felt his nerves on her behalf would only make things worse. Once she arrived at Drury Lane, Sarah allowed herself to be dressed without saying a word to her attendant. The only sound she made was the odd deep sigh, a habit of hers which she described as one of 'my desperate tranquillities (which usually possess me under terrific circumstances)'.[8] Her dressers must have wondered to themselves how the actress would perform once she was on stage, given her melancholy mood. As Sarah made her way onto the stage she passed her father, awkwardly hovering in the wings to wish her well. And then, finally, she faced the packed house, an experience she wrote later that she would never, ever forget.

Her performance proved to be a triumph. Her tenderness in the role and her exquisitely sweet voice went to every heart. This time it did not fail her. The men in the audience were described as being moved to tears, particularly when Sarah asked her young son if he could ever forgive her, while the women, according to contemporary observers, were in hysterics. Her early biographer, James Boaden, who was in the audience, described a 'peculiar *wildness*' in her.[9] When the moment came for the character of Isabella to stab herself with a dagger, Sarah emitted a laugh which 'seemed to electrify the audience; and literally the greater part of the spectators were too *ill themselves* to use their hands in her applause.'[10] One woman went into convulsions and, according to the newspapers 'continued in that miserable state for a considerable time after the curtain dropped.'[11] In the final act the audience anticipated Sarah by breaking into spontaneous, tumultuous applause before every single one of her lines. It even crossed Sarah's mind that the cast might not be able to bring the play to an end. She had come to London from Bath 'to found a new religion', as James Boaden put it.[12] An epilogue had been planned, written by Sarah's acquaintance from Bath, Samuel Pratt, but she was so overcome with emotion at her reception that she did not perform it. She felt compelled to write to their mutual friend, Thomas Sedgwick Whalley, to apologise a few days later. Instead, that night she left the theatre 'half dead'.[13]

Sarah returned home to the family's lodgings in The Strand, exhausted, unable to shed tears of emotion, or even to speak a single word. There, she had a simple supper with her husband and father. The three ate in silence, interrupted only occasionally by William's exclamations at his delight over how the evening had turned out. Once Roger, now 61, had finished eating, he put down his knife and fork, threw back his silver hair and wept with happiness, his tears plopping onto his plate. Never could he have imagined such a triumph for his beautiful, talented, oldest daughter. Despite all his anxieties for her, his attempts to give her the chance of a life away from the stage, her marriage to someone he felt unworthy of her, and the ignominy of her first season at Drury Lane, this was now all behind them. She had banished her past. She had scaled the heights. Her life would never be the same again. When Sarah eventually went to bed, she was unable to sleep for a whole hour, while she went back over the evening's events. But when she finally fell asleep, she slept so soundly that she did not wake until the middle of the next day, totally restored and ready for her next performance.

Over the next three weeks, Sarah appeared as Isabella eight times. The production would then be revived a further sixteen times throughout the rest of the season. The management knew they were onto a good thing, selling every seat in the house each time Sarah appeared as Isabella. She was accorded the honour of being moved from an inconvenient upstairs dressing room and permitted to use Garrick's stage-level dressing room instead. She pronounced herself delighted at the gesture. All memories of her suffering under his management were now conveniently forgotten. The owners of Drury Lane also gave her a monetary gift of 100 guineas (£13,730 today).

Any nervousness Sarah had felt initially now disappeared completely. Every night she found herself responding more easily to the play and to the audience. A couple of old men stationed themselves outside the theatre and waited all night to secure tickets, playing chess to keep themselves occupied. The cream of London society packed the theatre. Richard Brinsley Sheridan himself sat in one of the boxes along with his father-in-law and fellow owner of the theatre, Thomas Linley, and wept at Sarah's performance. As a journalist writing in *The Morning Chronicle* described it:

> she wore her sorrows with so much persuasive sincerity, that she ... made the audience her advocates, and ... created an universal and a melting sympathy all around.[14]

One of the newspapers wrote that on a Siddons night, Drury Lane looked more like a meeting of the House of Lords than a theatre. Her benefit book – where those who had paid money towards the evening wrote their names – was described as the court guide: the list of all those favoured by the king. Fashionable society had taken the girl from the provinces to their hearts.

Sarah's second role in that triumphant season was as Euphrasia in Arthur Murphy's *The Grecian Daughter* (see Appendix 2). Boaden described the play itself as 'splendid pantomime', far more clichéd than *Isabella, or the Fatal Marriage*.[15] And yet, when he saw Sarah perform the role of Euphrasia, he approved of what she did with it. He described Sarah's imposing stage presence, how:

> The commanding height and powerful action of her figure, though always feminine, seemed to tower beyond her sex.[16]

The role allowed Sarah to stretch her voice in a way she had never been able to do before now on the London stage – the same voice which had caused her such unhappiness in her past, but which, as her confidence increased, was to become one of her greatest assets. She would perform the role of Euphrasia eleven more times that season.

The play had been written for Ann Crawford, an actress some twenty years older than Sarah, who had made it her own. Staging *The Grecian Daughter* was a particular tactic of the Drury Lane management. They were keen to snatch Ann Crawford's crown and Sarah managed this effortlessly. Ann Crawford was in Ireland at the time, having quarrelled with the London management. But the rival theatre of Covent Garden had decided to stage its own production of *The Grecian Daughter*, with Sarah's old fellow-actress, Mary Ann Yates, who had caused her such unhappiness at Drury Lane, in the role of Euphrasia. The Covent Garden production opened nine days before Drury Lane's and boasted John Henderson, with whom Sarah had worked extensively in Bath, playing the part of Euphrasia's father. But Sarah's Drury Lane production was generally acknowledged to be the better of the two.

At Drury Lane the actor William Brereton was cast opposite Sarah as her imprisoned, dying father. In the play Euphrasia has abandoned her husband and child to protect her father and at one moment in the play she even breastfeeds him (offstage!), so great is her daughterly love. Brereton burst into tears at Sarah's performance in the second act one night and found it hard to complete his lines. Gossips noticed that he was falling in love with Sarah as the production went on, a relationship that would have serious consequences over the next few years. The writer Hester Thrale, who had first seen Sarah perform in Bath and would later become a close friend, described her in the role of Euphrasia at Drury Lane as one of 'the noblest specimens of the human race I ever saw.'[17]

On 8 November Sarah opened in her third role of the season, playing the part of Jane Shore in Nicholas Rowe's tragedy of the same name (see Appendix 2). Thomas Campbell, her official biographer, described her performance in this production as being both terrible and perfect. Unusually for a Siddons role, Jane Shore is someone who has previously strayed from the high moral ground. She was the married mistress of King Edward IV, and he has died before the play begins. The plot follows Jane's decline as she is hounded by her enemies and falls into such extreme poverty that she cannot even find food to keep herself alive, while repenting her previous actions and behaving with enormous dignity throughout. It would be difficult for us today to connect to the character, who reads as self-righteous and humourless. But Sarah's audiences were bowled over by her performance. In the final act, Jane Shore is driven to death by starvation. Somehow Sarah transformed herself so that those who saw her in the role believed completely that she was starving to death.

The writer Anna Seward, who had made Sarah's acquaintance during her years in Bath, described how difficult it proved for her to get a seat at Drury Lane that season. *The Whitehall Evening Post* had reported that the huge crowds pressing to see Sarah were 'near suffocation'.[18] Hester Thrale wrote to her friend Fanny Burney that there was 'such a Crowd! I confess myself frighted, as I had no Taste to crush my Limbs into Fractures and Cancers.'[19] She decided not to risk it. But Anna was determined. She arrived in London on 25 March 1783 in the late afternoon and was told that it would be impossible for her to get in to see the show that night. A few nights later she attempted to secure a seat in one of the boxes, but instead had to fight her way through the crowds to sit in the pit.

Anna also saw Sarah appear as Calista in Nicholas Rowe's *The Fair Penitent*. Calista has fallen in love with the dishonourable Lothario and eventually stabs herself to death out of remorse for her actions (see Appendix 2). *The Morning Chronicle* was ecstatic about Sarah's performance in the role. She 'united the genius of Garrick and Cibber', it claimed, deliberately connecting her in their readers' minds with two of her most famous male predecessors.[20]

After having seen Sarah perform, Anna did manage to exchange a few words with her friend, but she was so overawed by Sarah's new-found celebrity that she confessed she was embarrassed at her own reticence. Nevertheless, having managed to acquire tickets for two plays, she was now determined to see all Sarah's repertoire that season. On one night an usher allowed her into an unoccupied seat in the fifth row of the front boxes, just as the curtain went up. Tradition dictated that if the person who had bought the seat failed to appear by the end of the first act, then Anna as the newcomer would be allowed to stay there. She had no sooner tipped the usher with a shilling, thinking herself safe, than the rightful occupier arrived, furious that his claim was in vain because he had arrived just a moment too late.

So what was the recipe for Sarah's success as a performer at this moment in her career? Aged 27, she made a striking figure, tall, slim and dark. She was not classically beautiful by the standards of the time, with a prominent nose and chin, but her unusual looks meant that she was particularly memorable for those lucky enough to see her perform. Her deep brown eyes were noted for their piercing brilliance. Sometimes her gaze was said to be 'so full of information, that the passion is told from her look before she speaks.'[21] But when she did speak, now that she had found her confidence, her famous voice came into its own. She had a very particular delivery – stressing syllables idiosyncratically – which rendered her interpretation of individual lines unforgettably distinct. She studied for her roles with enormous care, and, once in character, she inhabited the part completely, in a deeper, more intense manner than any of her predecessors or contemporaries. She was very *method*, we would say today. Whereas Garrick would often come out of character and engage in badinage with the audience, once Sarah took on a part, she immersed herself wholly in it. She stopped being Sarah Siddons and became whichever tragic heroine she was inhabiting.

Perhaps most important of all, Sarah had the gift of making those who saw her empathise with the character she was playing. She emoted like no-one else, and her audiences emoted right back to her. When she was up, they were up.

When she was down, they sobbed along with her, or broke into unprompted hysterics. Her friend Tom Erskine noted that she was:

> the greatest Favourite of the Public that has appeared upon the Stage since the death of Mr Garrick (and yet) she receives less visible applause during the *performance* than very inferior actors receive.[22]

This he attributed to the fact that her audiences were just too moved by the action to stop and applaud her. 'Siddons fever' became a phenomenon of the time.[23] In an era when sensibility was all the rage, Sarah's ability to convey emotion was a game-changer.

After her triumphant opening season, Sarah slipped into a routine of playing at Drury Lane from autumn to spring, taking the lead in a series of tragic roles, and then touring elsewhere during the summer months when the London theatres were closed. This pattern continued for the next ten years, until Drury Lane was shut permanently for refurbishment and the company, which by now was under the management of Sarah's brother John Philip Kemble, moved to a temporary home at the King's Theatre, Haymarket. Sarah was sometimes criticised for appearing too often at Drury Lane, but her audiences loved her. The theatre was mobbed whenever she appeared. The newspapers began to write about every aspect of her private life. She was fêted wherever she went. Anyone who was anyone wanted to get to know her. She had achieved true celebrity status.

Sarah herself gave an account of one evening which serves as a telling example of how her new-found fame would impact on her life from now on. Mary Monckton, a bluestocking hostess of the time, whom Dr Johnson had described as a goose, invited Sarah to visit her one Sunday evening. Mary claimed that there would be at most half a dozen of her other friends with her that evening. She specifically requested that Sarah bring along her young son, Henry, who had acted with his mother in *Isabella, or The Fatal Marriage*. Failing (and later regretting) to reply that she would have preferred to spend some time alone with her family on a Sunday night, studying for her next role, Sarah took Henry with her and arrived at Mary Monckton's wearing a very simple, unglamorous dress. After chatting with a small group of Mary's friends, seated on the sofa, she hoped to take her leave. Instead, there were repeated thunderous knocks at the door until, bit by bit, the entire room filled up with a whole variety of people, all anxious to have their time with the celebrated actress.

Eventually there were so many crowded into the room that the people at the back began standing on chairs, to see Sarah all the better. Everybody had a question for her. Someone even pushed forward a little girl in a white frock to recite poetry to the famous performer. Sarah was overpowered. This was not what she had intended. The novelist Fanny Burney was there, as was Hester Thrale. Fanny noted that Hester commented to her, acerbically: 'This is a leaden goddess we are all worshipping!'[24] The proprietor of *The Observer* newspaper was also there and did not hold back in his criticism of how Sarah had dealt with all this attention, writing:

> The truth is, Mrs Siddons was rather 'touchy' and impulsive, and always too vehement in fancying offence was meant.[25]

Sarah could not win. Worse, *Parker's General Advertiser* concluded that:

> to her own merit, she owes much; but to the tide of fashionable fancy, she stands much more indebted,[26]

that her success on stage was because she was the darling of polite society, rather than her own skills as an actress.

From now on Sarah would indeed be 'the darling of polite society', but the journalist was maligning her when he said this had nothing to do with her skills as an actress.[27] She excelled as the leading tragedienne of her age. No-one could match her when it came to bringing the popular series of tragic stories to life. Her opening night at Drury Lane as Isabella had opened a floodgate. Her audiences wept buckets at the action or dissolved into hysterics at the fate of her characters. Sarah touched a chord in them in a way that no-one else had ever done before her. As life was changing in Britain from the eighteenth-century so-called Age of Reason, where intellectual thought was all, to the period of Romanticism, where feelings triumphed, Sarah's timing was perfect. The emotions she unlocked in her audiences became an enormous phenomenon. And this inevitably resulted in great personal fame for Sarah herself, along with vast earnings. Suddenly she was a household name, painted by the greatest portrait artists of the day and written about in all the newspapers, a celebrity whose every move was scrutinised, every decision called into question.

Chapter 6

Lady Macbeth

'The effect was sublime'[1]

Sarah enjoyed huge success over the next few years. She moved her family to a new house in Gower Street and, for the first time, she was able to afford her own carriage. The greatest artists of the time started painting her. When William Hamilton first showed his portrait of Sarah playing the part of Isabella in *The Fatal Marriage*, carriages blocked the street in front of his house, full of people desperate to see the painting. Several ladies even burst into tears when they saw it. Sir Joshua Reynolds, the first president of the Royal Academy, painted her as *The Tragic Muse*, the epitome of tragedy, and exhibited his canvas, to enormous acclaim. Sarah had the honour of now being able to number the king and queen among her greatest fans. Her fame was not limited to London. She had undertaken two tours of Ireland, which were not without controversy (see Chapter 7) and had also been well received in Scotland. She had reached the milestone of her thirtieth birthday and gave birth to her second son, George, at the end of the year.

It was in this context that Sarah took on the role for which she was most celebrated and with which, more than any other, her name would always be inextricably linked in the minds of her contemporaries – that of Lady Macbeth in Shakespeare's tragedy. She first played the part in London on 2 February 1785, some two and a half years after her triumphant return to Drury Lane. As Byron expressed it, it was impossible to imagine Lady Macbeth as anyone other than Sarah Siddons. Or as William Hazlitt wrote, as Lady Macbeth, 'she was Tragedy personified.'[2]

Sarah had played the role in the provinces while she was still honing her skills. It was a feature of the way she worked that she always prepared for a new part in immense detail, reading and re-reading the text, whispering the words to herself. Perhaps this was in part an attempt to make up for her lack of a more formal education. She always loved the part of Lady Macbeth because of the moral ambiguity which the character displays. Her husband and children were all asleep one night in their house in Axford's Buildings in Bath, while Sarah stayed up late studying the character of Lady Macbeth. Sitting alone in the darkness, she got so deeply into the part that she spooked herself. Heading up to bed, she found that she was holding a candlestick, just like Lady Macbeth herself, to light the way. Fortunately, she explained, she restrained herself from murdering the sleeping bodies upstairs.

Now, on Wednesday 2 February 1785, Sarah made her London debut in the role. In her preparation, she went to see how real people walked and talked in their sleep, just as Lady Macbeth does in the final act. Gentleman Smith, who was largely known for playing the lighter lover roles in comedies, was her Macbeth on this occasion. She totally eclipsed him. Soon afterwards the role was taken by her brother John Philip Kemble. He became her usual Macbeth from then onwards. On this first night William Brereton, who had played opposite her in *The Grecian Daughter* and was rumoured to have fallen in love with her, played Macduff.

For the famous sleepwalking scene, Sarah had chosen a different costume from the usual elaborate evening gown. Hers was designed by Sir Joshua Reynolds and consisted of clouds of white drapery, as if she were encased in a shroud. The elite of London society were there, eagerly anticipating her performance. Edmund Burke (the Conservative politician and philosopher), Charles James Fox (the prominent Whig statesman, who had been Foreign Secretary in the previous government), Edward Gibbon (the author of *The History of the Decline and Fall of the Roman Empire*), and Sir Joshua Reynolds himself were all in the front row on the opening night. Everybody in the audience sensed that theatrical history would be made that night.

It was the tradition at the time that famous actresses 'owned' a particular role. In taking on the part of Lady Macbeth, Sarah had to contend with the legacy of Hannah Pritchard. Some forty years older than Sarah, Hannah had been the most famous Lady Macbeth of the previous generation. In October 1783, sixteen months before Sarah played Lady Macbeth, she was taken by Hester Thrale to meet the elderly Samuel Johnson. He immediately brought up the subject of Hannah Pritchard. In real life, he declared, Pritchard was 'a vulgar idiot' but as soon as she appeared on stage, she 'seemed to be inspired by gentility and understanding.'[3] Emboldened, Sarah then asked him what he thought of Hannah Pritchard's interpretation of Lady Macbeth. Dr Johnson was critical. He told Sarah that Hannah Pritchard had only ever read the sections of the play in which she appeared. She had, he contended, never read to the end of *Macbeth*. Samuel Johnson was not alone in his criticism. Sarah's brother John Philip Kemble would go on to liken David Garrick and Hannah Pritchard in the respective roles to a butler and a housemaid quarrelling over a carving knife. Yet, despite these words, Sarah knew that in interpreting the character of Lady Macbeth for the Drury Lane audience, she was treading in Hannah Pritchard's hallowed theatrical footsteps.

As a retired actress, many years later, Sarah wrote some notes about her interpretation of the character of Lady Macbeth. She felt, she wrote, that Lady Macbeth should be portrayed as fair and feminine, a seductive presence for her husband, displaying:

> a charm of such potency as to fascinate the mind of a hero so dauntless, a character so amiable, so honourable as Macbeth, to seduce him to brave all the dangers of the present and all the terrors of the future world.[4]

She knew her readers would probably disagree with her over this emphasis on Lady Macbeth's femininity and seductive power, she wrote in her notes. Yet she saw Macbeth as fundamentally a good man, led astray by the ambitions of his wife. She pointed out that Macbeth often expresses his tender love for her, but that she never reciprocates.

Sarah also wrote that she believed Lady Macbeth sees Banquo's ghost in the banquet scene, just as Macbeth does. Nothing in the play's text gives any indication as to what Shakespeare intended. As a woman, wrote Sarah, Lady Macbeth was able to control her feelings at that moment, and to hide the fact that she saw the ghost whereas her husband, as a man, could not. It was the repression of these feelings, in support of her husband, which then in turn, Sarah believed, caused the emotional damage which characterises Lady Macbeth's actions later in the play. Sarah even visited a lunatic asylum as part of her research for the role. As Sarah interpreted the famous scene with Banquo's ghost, Lady Macbeth behaves as the gracious hostess throughout, anxious to keep her guests happy, despite her husband's collapse at the ghost they both see. Professor George Joseph Bell, who saw Sarah perform the role, wrote that in the banquet scene she:

> Descends in great eagerness; voice almost choked with anxiety to prevent their questioning; alarm, hurry, rapid and convulsive as if afraid Macbeth should tell of the murder of Duncan.[5]

She was magnetic in the role.

Sarah also explained to Thomas Campbell, her official biographer, that it was her belief that Lady Macbeth decided that they would need to murder Banquo and his son at the same time as her husband began plotting to do so. So her evil intention was equivalent to his. In Sarah's mind, although Lady Macbeth had many fewer lines in the play, she was just as important as Macbeth himself. Lady Macbeth was, in Campbell's words, Macbeth's 'evil genius, his grave-charm'.[6] In later life, Sarah would perform an evening of dramatised readings to an invited audience. Reading from *Macbeth*, she was said to be at her most powerful when she uttered Macbeth's lines, rather than those of Lady Macbeth. But for now, it was the wife rather than the husband whom she portrayed, and she endowed the character with enormous dramatic weight.

Audiences described Sarah's huge burst of energy when she delivered the line as Lady Macbeth to her husband:

> Glamis thou art, and Cawdor – and shalt be
> What thou art promised...[7]

She deliberately placed the emphasis on 'shalt be', to chilling effect. One audience member wrote about Sarah's delivery of her line '*We* fail!'– when she is urging on Macbeth to commit his first murder. She noted how Sarah was superb in deliberately:

> modulating her voice to a deep, low, resolute tone, which settled the issue at once, as though she said, "If we fail, why, then we fail, and all is over" ... The effect was sublime.[8]

Audiences also remarked on Sarah's intensity when she entreated Macbeth to give her the daggers so that she could smear the murdered victims with their own blood. They found themselves chilled by the manic, even demonic, quality in which Sarah delivered Shakespeare's famous lines.

Sarah's greatest innovation in her interpretation of the role, though, was in the sleepwalking scene in the final act. Lady Macbeth enters, holding a candle, and she remains asleep throughout the scene. Hannah Pritchard had always delivered the lines uttered by the sleeping Lady Macbeth: 'Out damned spot! Out, I say!... Yet, who would have thought the old man to have had such blood in him?' while holding the candlestick.[9] But Sarah chose to put the candlestick down and to rub her hands together with enormous vigour, as if she were trying as hard as she possibly could to wash out the 'damned spot' of the murdered victims' blood from her nightdress.[10] The effect was electric. Hester Thrale commented elsewhere about Sarah's ability to express emotion like no-one else:

> By her countenance alone, she could signify anger, revenge, sarcasm, sorrow, pride, and joy, so perfectly, that it was impossible to misunderstand her, though she had not spoken a word.[11]

Here Sarah was employing all these skills in a scene where Lady Macbeth has relatively few lines of dialogue, all of which are uttered as she walks in her sleep.

She found a way for her audience to empathise with Lady Macbeth which differed dramatically from any previous interpretation.

Just before Sarah was about to go on stage for her opening night's performance, she was interrupted in her dressing room by the theatre's owner and manager, Richard Brinsley Sheridan. Hannah Pritchard had never played the sleepwalking scene this way, he argued. She had not put down the candlestick and attempted to wash her hands clean of the blood. He absolutely did not want Sarah to break with tradition. She was to hold firm to the candlestick throughout the scene. Altering this way of playing it would be considered a 'presumptuous innovation'.[12] Sarah was overwhelmed. But her mind was made up. As far as she was concerned, it was too late to change.

Looking back on that evening, many years afterwards, Sarah said that her respect for Brinsley Sheridan was such that, if she had been able to make this last-minute alteration, she would have done so. She had observed that sleepwalkers enact the content of their dreams in just this way, as part of her research for the role, and yet she respected Sheridan enough to want to please him. But she could not change her plans without jeopardising the entire scene. She then went on stage to play the part. Her performance, but above all her innovative interpretation of the sleepwalking scene, was an overwhelming success. To Sheridan's credit, he came backstage as soon as the play was over and congratulated Sarah on her determination to stick to her own interpretation. She had been right.

Another story Sarah always told, when she was describing those moments after her first triumphant performance in the role, was that while she was standing in front of the mirror in her dressing room, taking off her costume, she continued to mull over the appropriate tone and action for the line from the play: 'Here's the smell of the blood still!'[13] She could not tear herself back to real life. Her dresser, seeing Sarah perturbed, could not help remonstrating with her:

> Dear me, ma'am, how very hysterical you are tonight; I protest and vow, ma'am, it was not blood but rose-pink and water; for I saw the property-man mix it up with my own eyes.[14]

The poor, beleaguered dresser was struggling with this most *method* of actresses. The play was over, and they were left with rose water, not blood, but Sarah did not see it that way.

Immediately, Sarah Siddons' interpretation of the role of Lady Macbeth became definitive. In Shakespeare's play she had the chance to play a tragic heroine with so much greater depth and intensity than the various heroines in the many other tragedies she had already made her own. Lord Byron, who came to see her perform the role as a young man, could recall her voice uttering every line, a voice 'whose tones were superhuman, and power over the heart supernatural.'[15] For him, she was the 'beau idéal of acting', worth all other famous actors put together.[16]

The poet William Hazlitt wrote a piece in *The Examiner*, having seen Sarah perform Lady Macbeth much later in life. After her formal retirement, she agreed to give a performance of the role for the benefit of Princess Charlotte. William Hazlitt regretted her decision. She had been regarded in the past, he wrote, almost as a goddess, or a prophetess from the gods: 'her face has shone as if an eye has appeared from heaven.'[17] Overall, Hazlitt felt that Sarah should not have played Lady Macbeth at that late stage, but in recalling her glory days playing the character, his review contains probably the most famous comment ever made about Sarah:

> Power was seated on her brow, passion emanated from her breast as from a shrine. She was Tragedy personified. She was the stateliest ornament of the public mind.[18]

She was matchless. No-one else could play tragedy like her.

It is simplistic to think that from this moment on Sarah's professional life was merely a triumphant one. She was a working actress and was expected to learn and perform new roles all the time. Gradually it became clear which were her most successful, among the great variety she was expected to perform. Her Shakespearean roles at Drury Lane included Constance in *King John* and Katharine in *Henry VIII* (neither of which are performed very often today and both of which roles she would play more and more as she got older), together with Isabella in *Measure for Measure*, Hermione in *The Winter's Tale* and Cordelia in a bowdlerised version of *King Lear*. Other favourites included Mrs Beverley in Edward Moore's *The Gamester*, which tells the story of the havoc wreaked by addiction to gambling; Lady Randolph in John Home's *Douglas*, another tragedy centring around a lost family member who returns to disastrous consequences; and Zara in William Congreve's *The Mourning Bride*, an exotic queen, captured by her enemies (see Appendix 2 for synopses of these plays).

Only a couple of months after her triumph as Lady Macbeth, when her reputation might have been thought to protect her from any bad reviews, Sarah received a poor reception for her performance as Rosalind in Shakespeare's *As You Like it*. She had made the mistake of choosing for herself a costume which broke with the traditional one for the part. Perhaps she was nervous about appearing in a breeches role, now she was a 30-year-old matron. Sarah was always painfully aware of 'the scrupulous prudery of decency', according to Anna Seward.[19] The unflattering costume made it look as if she were wearing a gardener's apron when seen from the front and a petticoat when viewed from behind. It was incongruously paired with hussar's boots. The critic George Colman referred to Sarah as 'a frisking Gog' in the role, while her biographer, James Boaden, described her as 'a stricken deer.'[20] Notably, Sarah copied down in one of her notebooks a poem which an admirer had written to her about her playing the role of Rosalind so soon after appearing triumphantly as Lady Macbeth:

> ... The same soul-searching mind
> Which late, so true, Macbeth's storm Queen portrayed
> Th'unnerving eye of nature still will find
> Mid' the warm colouring of the love-sick Maid.[21]

Perhaps she needed to remind herself that someone at least thought she would perform the part of 'the love-sick Maid' Rosalind well. The general view, though, was that Sarah came across as too majestic for the role and was already too elderly to be disguised as a boy.

Comedies never really worked for Sarah. Perhaps she was just too intense, too involved with the characters she portrayed, to allow her audiences to relax into the conceit of her playing comic heroines. Journalists soon described her as The Tragic Muse, Melpomene, and artists portrayed her as such. Her comic equivalent soon emerged in the person of the actress Dora Jordan, who was described as the Comic Muse, Thalia, counterbalancing Sarah's Melpomene. When Dora came to London, like Sarah she had huge success, playing Peggy in *The Country Girl* (adapted by Garrick from William Wycherley's *The Country Wife*) in 1785, the same year that Sarah first played Lady Macbeth. James Boaden wrote of Dora that 'She seemed as if formed to dry up the tears which tragedy had long excited.'[22] Sarah sat in the box of Dr James Ford, one of the three owners of Drury Lane, to watch Dora's performance and even she admitted that Dora was a phenomenon.

Dora's life was very different from Sarah's. She soon became the mistress of Richard Ford, James Ford's son, having already given birth to an illegitimate child. She then went on to have a long relationship with William, Duke of Clarence, son of George III. They had a large family together, but he eventually deserted her, knowing that he was likely to become king on the death of his childless brother. She died alone and in poverty, in France. This passionate, scandalous life could not have been further from the matronly respectability Sarah always strove to maintain, the happily married woman with several legitimate offspring.

In time, Dora's success in comedy meant that Sarah was not forced into such a punishing schedule. The two very rarely appeared together, so Sarah could have an evening off whenever Dora held the stage. Sarah was able to give informal supper parties to friends at home instead – always her favourite way of entertaining. Even with Dora taking some of the strain, Sarah would normally perform anywhere between fifty and a hundred times during the six-month London season, excluding the performances she gave either for her own benefits or for those of other actors. And once the London season was over, she would set off on tour.

Sarah's interpretation of the character of Lady Macbeth cemented her reputation as the Queen of Tragedy, the tragic muse of her generation. Lady Macbeth proved the perfect role for her, a flawed heroine whom she brought to vivid life for her audiences, notably in her revolutionary portrayal of the scene where Lady Macbeth walks in her sleep. It was true to Sarah's immersion in any role she took on that she studied real-life sleepwalkers before she played the part. Yet even The Tragic Muse sometimes had to play other roles, and occasionally these were met with criticism, very different from her notices as Lady Macbeth. Sarah never did prove herself as a comic actress. But from her triumphant season in 1782 onwards, she was a huge star, a household name, a celebrity. And with that new fame came attendant dangers.

Chapter 7

Ireland

'a sink of filthiness'[1]

Although she performed in Ireland, Sarah never had the success there that she experienced elsewhere. Irish blood flowed through her veins, and yet she never felt at home across the Irish Sea. Despite the enormous success she had made of her triumphant 1782 Drury Lane season, she was still vulnerable. The two Irish summer tours she made in 1783 and 1784 demonstrated that her future life would not be entirely problem free. She might be the darling of the London stage, but Ireland was far less welcoming.

Ireland itself was suffering political unrest at the time. The Anglo-Irish aristocracy were seen as being out of touch with the problems of most ordinary Irish people. The Lord Lieutenant of Ireland, who ruled on behalf of the monarch, was an unpopular figure. Sarah had an entrée into aristocratic society here through her old friend, Henrietta Boyle, now married to an Irish nobleman. News of Sarah's runaway success in London had reached Ireland. Prior to her arrival Lord Inchiquin, an English-supporting Irish peer who sat in the House of Lords, had made a toast in Dublin to 'the matchless Siddons' and sent her a ring with a miniature portrait of herself created out of diamonds. She could win the hearts of the upper classes, but to succeed she needed to appeal to the masses as well.

Just four days after her triumphant London season closed in 1783, Sarah set off with William for their agreed engagement in Ireland, leaving their children behind. She made sure to fit in an evening's performance in Liverpool before taking the boat from Holyhead to Dublin. Sarah's brother John Philip had been the leading actor in Richard Daly's company at Dublin's Smock Alley Theatre for the past couple of years, and the Siddons were keen to join him there. The travelling party consisted of Sarah and William; Sarah's sister, Frances Kemble; the Irish actor Francis Aickin; the English actor William Brereton, whose feelings towards Sarah were already dangerously out of control; and Brereton's young wife, Priscilla Hopkins (whose father had been the man to tell the Siddons they were not needed after their unhappy Drury Lane season back in 1776).

They arrived in Dublin very early in the morning of 16 June 1783. At first customs detained them, locking them up in a small room. Once released, they suffered the further indignity of having to wander the streets in the pouring rain, unable to find anywhere to stay. As Sarah wrote to her friend Thomas Sedgwick Whalley, 'there is not a tavern or a house of any kind ... that will take a woman in.'[2] After her recent triumph in London, this must have felt like very rough treatment. With the help of William Brereton's father, they persuaded Brereton's landlady, albeit reluctantly, to allow the women of the party to stay there, just for that first night. This experience turned Sarah against the city from the very beginning. Dublin, she declared, was 'a sink of filthiness'.[3] What's more, she formed a visceral dislike of the Irish people, claiming that:

> They are all ostentation and insincerity, and in their ideas of finery very like the French [not that Sarah had been to France] but not so cleanly; and they not only speak but think coarsely.[4]

By the time she wrote these words to Whalley, she had been in Ireland for nearly a month, and her judgement had not altered from her first night's impression. She was sufficiently distracted that she forgot to pay the postage, so her letter to her friend, with all its indiscretions, was opened and its contents read and made public. Her words did not endear her to the Irish people.

On a personal level, Richard Daly, who ran the Smock Alley Theatre, did not get along with Sarah's brother John Philip Kemble. Daly had dared to complain that John Philip's performance in one of his comedies was not sufficiently energetic, and the two had resorted to a duel to settle their differences. Neither of them had been injured, but the memory lingered. It quickly became clear that Richard Daly liked the sister just as little as he liked the brother. Both Sarah and John Philip's habitual shyness was often taken for arrogance. In addition, Sarah was already in the process of securing a three-year contract for John Philip to return with her to Drury Lane. This cannot have endeared either of the siblings to their Irish manager.

Among the cast in Dublin was a singer named Anna Maria Philips, who was already romantically attached to John Philip. He was forced to deny rumours swirling around that the two of them were engaged. Also in the cast was the now widowed Elizabeth Inchbald, still very much in love with John Philip, and the actress Priscilla Brereton, whose husband's mental instability was causing her concern, and who would also be romantically linked to John Philip in time. Such a heady mix would not have been easy for Sarah, with her focus on the importance of respectability.

For a single actress, the culture of the Smock Alley Theatre was one fraught with danger. The future Dora Jordan, still using the name Dorothy Francis at the time, had been in the company up until the previous summer, playing the female leads opposite John Philip Kemble. But she had been sexually assaulted by Richard Daly, and, realising she was carrying his child, had fled to England. Elizabeth Inchbald had also reported that Daly had tried to assault her in Dublin, but that, after refusing him, she had only been given insignificant acting roles. As a married woman, Sarah had some protection, but she could not escape Daly's dislike.

Sarah opened the season playing Isabella in *The Fatal Marriage*. The night went well, and the theatre was besieged by people wanting tickets. She was being well paid. She was to make £600 over her twelve performances in Dublin, with £60 deducted for expenses (£69,160 overall today). But she did not warm to her Irish audiences. The stardust which surrounded Sarah in London did not seem to work its magic in Ireland. Sarah's rival, Ann Crawford, the actress for whom Thomas Murphy had written *The Grecian Daughter*, was playing at the rival Crow Street Theatre at the time. Twenty years older than Sarah, Ann had made herself unpopular by getting married for a third time, to a man much younger than herself. Yet the audiences who came to see her were rather larger than Sarah's at the Smock Alley Theatre.

A satirical piece soon appeared in the Dublin press and was reprinted back in England, mocking Sarah's general style. Hundreds had crowded in to see Sarah at the Smock Alley, its anonymous author wrote, but thousands more had been turned away, because Sarah 'was nature itself – she was the most exquisite work of art.'[5] Several people supposedly fainted even before the curtain went up, such was Sarah's power. The violinists in the audience blubbed like hungry children and the bassoon player's tears ran down in such showers that they choked his finger stops, claimed the satirist. The pit of the theatre had become a briny pond and those in the stalls were compelled to sit ankle-deep in tears. And yet, reported the piece, Sarah was hissed at on her second night. It was true that Garrick had 'pronounced her below mediocrity' and that the audience in London had not liked her: 'But what of that?'[6] Sarah's past continued to haunt her.

Various awkward moments made Sarah come across badly in the press. *The European Magazine* reported that an Irish merchant's wife had asked for an introduction, but William had found various lame excuses to prevent it, saying he did not know how to 'break the matter' to her.[7] The Dublin-based portrait painter, Robert Hume, wanted to paint Sarah, but she was reported in both the Irish and English press as having refused him, claiming she hardly had time to sit for Sir Joshua Reynolds back in London. The fact that this was not true and that she did sit for Hume was not reported. Then Sarah was asked to perform for the benefit of the Dublin City Marshalsea Debtors' Prison. She could not fit in the time for a performance before she left for Cork and sent a contribution instead. While this was acknowledged by the Irish press, her treatment of the prison would come back to haunt her when she returned to Dublin the following year.

Despite these problems, Sarah played the role of Belvidera in *Venice Preserved* at the Smock Alley Theatre to an illustrious audience headed by the Lord Lieutenant, for which she received glowing reviews. She then went on to perform several of her favourite other roles that summer, including Euphrasia, Jane Shore, Zara and Calista. Having played the agreed twelve nights, she next did six benefit performances, after which she proceeded to Cork, in a tour organised by Richard Daly, which included her erstwhile rival, Elizabeth Younge, along with the infamous Anna Maria Phillips and the actor West Digges.

Irish audiences tended to heckle more than those in London. One night, when Sarah took the part of Lady Randolph in *Douglas* at the Lord Lieutenant's request, she was jeered so much that the audience could not hear the action. On another night, in Cork, Sarah froze when someone shouted out to her during a performance: 'Sally, me jewel, how are you?'[8] As an actress who immersed herself totally in whichever role she was playing, she could not engage in the sort of repartee which was necessary to work well with these kinds of houses. Overall, having spent ten weeks in Ireland that summer, she came back to London having earned £1,000 (£128,100 today) and must have felt relatively pleased. There had been problems, yet she had done well financially at least. But things would deteriorate disastrously on her return the following year.

A successful second season at Drury Lane followed in 1783/84, in which Sarah had the bonus of playing opposite her brother John Philip. Next, she travelled to the Theatre Royal Edinburgh to play for ten nights, followed by a charity benefit evening and a benefit for herself. She would leave the city some £1,000 wealthier (£128,100 today), after a relatively short time there. Huge crowds flocked to see her, some travelling across from the rival city of Glasgow, just to watch her perform. Dibdin's *Annals of the Edinburgh Stage* described some 2,557 people applying on one day for just 630 seats. A mob would gather at midday to be let into the theatre at three. People passing by in the street told the papers that they were swept up by them. Pickpockets reportedly even travelled up from London, so good were the takings. The Scottish General Assembly was forced to change its working hours to allow its members to get to Sarah's performances, and the church elders saw their congregations diminished.

In Ireland, Sarah had thought the audiences over-familiar. In contrast in Scotland, she found the silence with which the audiences there received her performances initially very disconcerting. As she put it: 'She had been used to speak to animated clay; but she now felt as if she had been speaking to stones.'[9] One evening she was caught murmuring to herself: 'Stupid people, stupid people.'[10] On another she steeled herself to give an especially powerful performance as Belvidera, despite the frosty response. She got to the end of a particularly dramatic speech and was pausing for breath, when out of the deafening silence a voice shouted: 'That's no bad!'[11] The whole auditorium shook with laughter, and then broke into long, deafening applause. The ice was broken. From then on, Sarah relaxed, and her audiences relaxed with her. The heat of the unventilated theatre and the crowds packed tightly together to see Sarah caused some audience members to faint. The term 'Siddons fever' was first coined here in Edinburgh, plagiarising the term 'Garrick fever' which had been deployed about the Dublin audiences' response to the actor some forty years earlier.[12] Notably, Sarah Siddons and David Garrick were the only actors who were ever described as having elicited a fever among their passionate fans.

Sarah performed in two Scottish plays here: Shakespeare's *Macbeth* and John Home's *Douglas*. In the latter she took the part of Lady Randolph, whose husband and only son have been lost in battle and who has since remarried. Her son returns as an adult, and Lady Randolph is caught up in the tragic repercussions as he is then tricked into killing her second husband and goes on to die in her arms. Unable to cope with the grief, she throws herself off a precipice. Lady Randolph is a classic Siddons heroine, morally virtuous and fatally compromised (see Appendix 2 for more detail). John Home himself came to see her perform his play. Several years earlier, the Scottish church had objected to the plot. Suicide was still a criminal offence and the church disapproved of displays of emotion such as Lady Randolph's. As a result, Home had been forced to flee to London. Now he was back home to see an English actress perform the role. In Scotland, where the desire for a distinct cultural identity was very powerful, Sarah symbolised both English power over Scotland and at the same time, Scottish independence. It was a complex and intense message.

Here Sarah managed the complex situation with great éclat. She pronounced herself delighted by her reception in what she called 'dear Edinburgh' and told her authorised biographer, Thomas Campbell, 'never can I forget the private no less than public marks of their most gratifying suffrages.'[13] She was presented with a silver tea vase, inscribed with the words 'As a Mark of Esteem (for) Unrivalled Talents'.[14] She left Edinburgh on 15 June 1784. The Reverend Dr Mackenzie of Portpatrick reported that she sighed at the wildness of the sea she would have to cross to reach Ireland. So loud was her lament, apparently, that the people of the town rushed out to see what was wrong. Her real life was being written up as if she were one of the characters she played on stage.

Although Sarah's Dublin fee remained the same as for the previous season – £50 per night (£6,508 today) – she was engaged for twenty performances rather than twelve. A letter to a friend admitted that she was already longing for an easier time. She had suffered more as a result of ill health that previous winter, she confessed, than ever before. Her schedule here in Ireland was due to be punishing. Yet, despite this, the season started well. The Siddons settled immediately into a house at 28 Dawson Street, near St Stephen's Green, and Sarah's opening performance, as Belvidera in *Venice Preserved*, met with excellent reviews, along with her new part as the title role in Robert Dodsley's *Cleone*. A Dublin newspaper, *The Freeman's Journal*, described her as 'the greatest star in the theatrical hemisphere'.[15]

Sarah's other piece of good fortune was that she was reunited with her friend Henrietta Boyle, now Henrietta O'Neill, who was living at beautiful Shanes Castle, on the shore of Lough Neigh. Sarah was delighted by the visit she paid to her friend and overawed by her luxurious, aristocratic life. She particularly admired the table settings at dinner:

> The sideboards were decorated with adequate magnificence, on which appeared several immense silver flagons containing claret. A fine band of musicians played during the whole of the repast.[16]

When it came to dessert, guests were led into the conservatory to pluck exquisite fruit for themselves from the trees. Sarah was always quick to notice domestic details, and this way of life was finer than anything she had previously encountered.

At Shanes Castle, Sarah met Lord Edward Fitzgerald, 'the most amiable, honourable, though misguided youth I ever knew,' as she described him.[17] Fitzgerald had fought on the British side in the American War of Independence a few years earlier and had the right to sit in the House of Lords in London, but he was now embracing the cause of Irish independence from Britain. Sarah seemed not to realise the implications of becoming involved with someone who was openly hostile to British rule. Later in the season, Sarah stayed with Fitzgerald's mother, the Dowager Duchess of Leinster. The duchess had scandalously married her lover, her children's tutor, who was several years younger than her, as soon as her first husband died. Sarah enjoyed being driven into Dublin from her lodging at the Dowager Duchess's house to attend rehearsals. The two women remained close after the visit. Sarah wrote to her a few years later, when they were both in London, in terms of exquisite politeness, expressing herself delighted to be invited to call on the duchess:

> I return your Grace a thousand, thousand thanks for allowing me the happiness of waiting on you and will do myself that honour about two o'clock.[18]

When it came to aristocratic friends, Sarah was always at her most solicitous.

By contrast, Sarah's audiences at the Smock Alley Theatre were by now openly supporting democratic reform and an independent Irish republic. On 9 July there were cheers from the gallery when someone in the audience called out in support of the United States of America, recently freed up from British rule, and there were claps for 'Independence for Ireland'. The following night there was uproar when Sarah played Lady Randolph in a command performance in front of the Lord Lieutenant, the Duke of Rutland. The moment Rutland appeared in the viceregal box, the audience shouted they would rather sing *The Volunteers' March* than *God Save the King*. The curtain went up to a chorus of whistles and groans, making it almost impossible for Sarah to perform. No-one could hear a word she said, and she suffered the indignity of being pelted first by an apple and then by a potato. She wrote that she 'came away in a terrible fright.'[19] In truth, she had been somewhat naïve in ignoring the political undercurrents.

At the same time, Sarah's relationship with the theatre manager, Richard Daly, was deteriorating. Despite – or maybe because of – the reports of assault on various actresses in his company, Daly saw himself as a ladies' man. He was surprised when he failed to have the desired effect on Sarah. They were in rehearsal for Shakespeare's *King John* (he was playing the part of Falconbridge) when she made the mistake of suggesting that he change the blocking. Although Daly agreed to the suggestion, Sarah reported that he seemed furious that he should be positioned so far from the audience.

These, though, were lesser worries. Up until now Sarah had managed to maintain her desired image of being honourable and supportive to others, a selfless wife and mother. Now two separate incidents would damage her reputation and she would find herself being accused of selfish and mercenary behaviour as well as a lack of compassion.

The first concerned William Brereton, who was again part of the company in Dublin. Rumours continued to swirl that he was in love with her, and that he was mentally unstable. The terms of Brereton's engagement were that he would perform for no money for the entire season in Dublin but that a benefit would be held in his honour there. He would be allowed to keep all the proceeds from the benefit night, without any of the other actors or the theatre itself taking a cut. Brereton had been unwell the night of Sarah's own benefit in Dublin, so Sarah made it clear that she would now be unwilling to perform for nothing at his. After all, she was the main attraction. Rather than her usual nightly fee of £50 (£6,508 today), she would normally charge £30 (£3,905 today) for someone else's benefit night. For Brereton, she offered to reduce this further to £20 (£2,603 today). He had no option but to accept. But then Sarah became ill. She had been suffering from ill health the whole year and was exhausted. She went down with a bad cold, a sore throat and a violent fever, and was forced to take to her bed for two whole weeks.

William Brereton saw this as malingering. So too did Richard Daly, who had his own reasons to be displeased with Sarah. They began leaking stories to the press accusing her of pretending to be ill to get out of acting for Brereton. His benefit was delayed. And then it was delayed again. The season was ending, and Sarah was due to leave for her tour of Limerick and Cork. That could not be pushed back. Eventually there simply was no time left in Sarah's calendar. It was impossible for her to appear in Brereton's benefit. He took this very badly indeed and even attempted to take his own life. It felt as if Sarah was implicated, although the reasons for Brereton's suicide attempt were far more complex than simply his delayed benefit. The following year he would be certified as insane and, two years later, he would die in Hoxton Asylum. For the moment, though, there was bad blood between him and Sarah. A letter appeared in the newspapers signed *Laertes*, but probably written by John Philip, arguing Sarah's case. 'Mr Brereton and his wife have an ample salary at Drury Lane Theatre,' it started:

> They cannot receive less than *five hundred pounds* per annum [£65,080 today]. Mrs Siddons performed for the benefit of Mr Brereton only a few months before … Could he be, therefore, an object of such necessity as to require a *gratis* performance?[20]

Public opinion clearly felt that he could and should.

The second scandal also involved another member of the cast and Sarah's performance at his benefit. Early that summer, the Irish actor West Digges suffered a stroke on stage, rendering him permanently paralysed. The word went out that Sarah had insisted on her £50 (£6,508 today) fee if there were to be a benefit. In fact, it was Sarah herself who had suggested that they hold a benefit for Digges and initially there seemed no suggestion that she should receive a fee. She proposed a special performance of *Venice Preserved*, in which she would play Belvidera. Time was short, though, and Sarah's absence due to illness made it even shorter. Sarah and William worked hard to get a company together for Digges' benefit night. The only possible evening clashed with Sarah's prior engagement to appear at the City Marshalsea Debtors Prison, whom she had let down the year before. She would, she said, regrettably have to miss West Digges' benefit. There was a furious response, not least from Richard Daly, who accused her of malingering yet again. Hurriedly, Sarah changed her mind. But she said she would need to be paid. The evening was quickly cobbled together. Sarah rose from her sickbed, but she had not even met the cast until they appeared on stage opposite her. As she rationalised it:

Poor Mr Digges was most materially benefited by this most ludicrous performance; and I put my disgust into my pocket, since money passed into his.[21]

Both sides were left dissatisfied by events.

Sarah then headed off on tour, 'unconscious,' as she later told Thomas Campbell, 'of the gathering Storm.'[22] She had been due to appear in both Cork and Belfast, but the *Belfast Newsletter* wrote a piece criticising her for being indisposed and failing to appear. She was beginning to gain a reputation for falling ill whenever it suited her, and for not turning to and helping those less fortunate than herself, if required to make any financial sacrifice of her own. As one journalist wrote in the *Hibernian Journal*:

> This enriched actress gave no sign of doing a benefit for any private or public charity, nor would she lend to Heaven, where the interest is so long delayed.[23]

She had made over 3,000 guineas that summer (£410,000 today).

The Siddons returned to London in September 1784 and moved into the new house they had leased in Gower Street. Sarah's salary for the coming Drury Lane season was agreed at £24 10 shillings per week (£3,189 today), compared to John Philip's of ten guineas per week (£1,367 today). For this she was contracted to appear at least three times each week. On top of this were the considerable amounts she would expect to make from her own benefits. On the face of it, she was now a powerful force. Yet word of the Irish benefits scandals had reached London and Sarah feared how her public would react. She was right to be concerned.

The Drury Lane season opened on 30 September. Although Sarah was not due to appear that night, the manager, Tom King, gave a prologue in which he praised her in her absence, and even referred to her 'living worth'.[24] The audience howled. Earlier that day a letter, written by William Siddons, had appeared in several newspapers, in which he had sought to exonerate his wife from any scandal. William wrote that Sarah had never taken any money from West Digges. Indeed, Digges had written a polite note to Sarah, but she had destroyed it. William's letter also gave a fuller explanation of the Brereton affair but concluded that the accusations against his wife were unfounded. He accepted the fact that newspapers used their critics to evaluate Sarah's professional performances. But, he wrote, he reserved the right to defend her against attacks on her private conduct, which would lower her estimation if unanswered.

If the Siddons thought this would dampen the flames, they were wrong. On Sunday 3 October, William published a letter from Brereton in which Brereton claimed that 'to the friends I have seen I have taken pains to exculpate her [Sarah] from the least unkindness to me in Dublin.'[25] But the tone of Brereton's letter came across as churlish and curt. It failed to carry any conviction. Brereton, it was suggested, was envious of John Philip's beginning to take lead roles in the coming season opposite Sarah. A note at the bottom asserted that William Siddons expected to receive a similar letter from West Digges 'that will entirely confound the artful schemes of her detractors.'[26] But Digges' promised letter did not arrive.

William pushed Brereton to write a second letter, which appeared in the press on Tuesday 5 October – the day of Sarah's first performance of the season. The letter stated that Brereton thought it necessary to repeat that his failure to have a benefit in Dublin was not due to Sarah. This was not strictly true. Her being unwell had delayed things until there was no time left. Throughout his own illness, wrote Brereton, Sarah had been both friendly and supportive to him. It is easy to imagine the Siddons pressuring the mentally fragile Brereton to put pen to paper for a second time, suggesting phrases to him, editing what he wrote. Today we would call that bullying, given Brereton's mental state.

That same night, Brereton was on stage with Sarah and her brother John Philip in a performance of Edward Moore's play *The Gamester*. The evening was one of the most dramatic Sarah ever experienced in the theatre. She took the part of the virtuous Mrs Beverley, whose husband's gambling leads to tragedy (see Appendix 2 for more details). For forty minutes after Sarah's first entrance, she tried to withstand the hissing and hooting that greeted her. Eventually someone in the audience called out that she should not degrade herself by giving an apology, 'impelled by benevolence and manly feeling.'[27] Sarah's notes for Campbell about the evening indicate that she was unhappy with James Boaden's account of events in the unauthorised biography he wrote about her life. He had been in the audience that night. All those years later, it was still important to Sarah to ensure that her own account got an airing. The heckler was silenced – both accounts agree – and the shouting continued, until John Philip came on stage and led Sarah to the wings, where she immediately fainted. She was glad, she wrote, that her persecutors had not witnessed this sign of weakness.

While William Siddons revived the fainting Sarah, John Philip insisted to Brereton that the two of them should go back on stage and exonerate her. But Brereton refused to do so. Instead, Sarah was compelled to face her audience alone. After all the noise, she was struck by the profound silence which greeted her entrance. Her speech was simple and dignified. The words had been written for her beforehand, in anticipation of the audience's response, by John Philip and Richard Brinsley Sheridan. The stories against her, Sarah told her audience, were calumnies. There was no reason for 'having deserved your censure.'[28] Sarah's courage in facing them and giving her account changed the mood. The audience were impressed. The curtain fell and Tom King came forward to ask for a few minutes 'while the gallant actress was recovering herself.'[29] Then the action continued. From that point on, the evening was a triumph.

But Sarah's troubles were not over. On Thursday 7 October an anonymous letter appeared in the *General Advertiser*, addressed to William Brereton, asking whether it had been he or William Siddons who had really written his second letter. The public, apparently, believed that Brereton only '*scratched* and then *signed*.'[30] They may have been right. On 22 October the long-promised letter from West Digges finally appeared and was printed in *The Morning Chronicle*. The windy weather had apparently delayed its arrival from Ireland. Rumours spread that Digges had been too unwell to put pen to paper and that in reality this had been the work of his son. In the letter, Digges asserted that Sarah had not been paid anything by him and repeated that she had destroyed the original letter he had written to her confirming this. But it felt as if this was simply too little, too late. And, of course, it was not entirely true. Sarah had indeed been paid a fee for appearing in West Digges' benefit. In late October yet another letter appeared in *The Morning Chronicle* from William Brereton, stating for a final time that he did not pay Sarah. The public, though, had stopped concerning themselves with details. They had already made up their minds about the famous actress.

From now on, Sarah was portrayed as money-grabbing and stingy. She earned herself a new nickname, Lady Sarah Save-All. She 'would as soon part with her eye tooth as with a guinea,' it was reported.[31] She was said to be the most parsimonious actor in the green room, always reluctant to help others at their benefits yet determined to make as much as she could for her family when it came to her own benefit nights. In addition, she was described as loitering behind in church at one point, supposedly to listen to the organ, but really to avoid having to put money into the offering plate.

A cartoon by James Gillray in 1784 (Illustration 18) shows Sarah's new public image. She is portrayed as the Muse of Tragedy, Melpomene, trying to release funds from a money bag, looking like testicles, suspended from the devil's pitchfork. A poem alongside the cartoon mocks the 'Three Reasons' speech Sarah had given when she left Bath to seek her fortune again in London. It reads:

> Famished and spent relieving others woe
> Your Poor devoted suppliant only begs
> This morsel for to buy a bit of Bread.[32]

She is a glamorous actress, it implies, and yet she talks as if she were a beggar. Money is her primary motivation. And the cartoon also sexualises her. For Sarah, who had always taken pains to come across as the most deliberately asexual of actresses, this was a further indignity.

The whole experience had a profound effect on Sarah. The worry and stress threw her into yet another depression. She retreated from the world, reading and studying for hours by herself. Her fellow actors now found her unresponsive when they worked with her. She looked pale and thin to those who saw her perform. Lord Hardwicke had loaned her the memoirs of Pericles, and she could see in them a powerful connection with her own situation. She wrote to him that she sympathised with the classical hero, who had been the favourite of the mob one year and degraded by them the next. She had too. She even considered giving up the stage entirely. William Siddons wrote to his friend Sir Charles Hotham that, although his wife was obliged to continue for her children's sake, she admitted that acting would never be as pleasant and as charming as it had been in the past. By the spring of 1785, though, she felt able to write to Thomas Sedgwick Whalley that her spell of unhappiness was now over. Like many a celebrity, Sarah had weathered a scandal which had attached itself to her name.

The truth was that Sarah would never again be able to rescue her reputation entirely. What was done could not be undone. She would be forced to endure what her critics wrote about her, however unfair their accusations seemed to be. And to make things all the worse, despite her protestations, Sarah was not entirely innocent over what had happened in Ireland. William's role, endlessly negotiating for as strong a financial share as possible for his wife, had not helped the situation. But Sarah had also played her part in creating the mess which resulted from West Digges and Brereton's mismanaged benefit nights.

As so often with celebrity scandals, at its core there was a germ of truth in what was written about Sarah. Money was indeed very important to her. She had a family to support. Many of her contemporary actresses relied on rich, aristocratic lovers to provide income. But Sarah did not have any other source of wealth. Whatever she had was thanks to her earning power. She would never forget the tough times she had experienced early on in her life. She would always be motivated by the desire to provide her family with the stable, financial security which she had not herself received. She was proud of being able to do so. But her ability to earn unprecedented sums could tip over into what appeared to be grasping avarice which did her reputation no good at all.

Chapter 8

Behind the Scenes

'the tender Mother and the blameless Wife'[1]

Sarah's personal life was always very important to her. Her married status gave her the respectability she and her parents had always craved, making her distinct from most of her female contemporaries on the stage. Yet her marriage was not always easy, not least because Sarah was the sole earner. Being a good mother was also hugely important to her. She was proud and protective of her growing family. While she herself was a household name, she mainly tried to keep her children out of the spotlight. Her family were demanding of her, and she was forever struggling to juggle the professional and the personal.

Now the couple had achieved their longed-for financial security. Sarah could command fees that made the Siddons wealthy beyond their wildest dreams. William continued as the house husband. He operated as Sarah's manager, but in negotiations he tended to alienate people and confuse matters. He also began to make some unwise investments, losing the couple money, notably by speculating on the new Sadlers Wells Theatre in Islington. Although Sarah earned all their income, William owned everything, according to the laws of the time. William was always keen that Sarah continued to take on work, so the cash would keep rolling in. He often failed to pay attention to the fact that her health was suffering as a result.

After the disastrous time following her second Irish tour, Sarah wrote to the Whalleys that the drama there had taken its toll. She and William had sacked their servant Mary, who had drunk too much and had begun gossiping about the state of the Siddons' marriage. The rumours were that William was petulant. He nagged her. Sarah reassured her friends that 'all the scandalous reports of Mr Siddons' ill-treatment of me originated entirely in [Mary]'; it was all the fault of their disgraced servant.[2] Nothing was wrong. But gossip has a habit of lingering.

A friend, John Taylor, described dropping into the Siddons' home in London to find Sarah sitting by the fire, destroying some old letters of hers. She had sent them to a poet who had just died, and who had at times been critical of her and at other times supportive. John Taylor saw that the papers included a poem that had been printed in *The St James Street Chronicle* and which was disparaging of her. As he helped her, the two of them began talking. She admitted that the poet had once indicated that William had a mistress who was living in Chelsea. It was this, John Taylor believed, which caused Sarah to throw letter after letter into the fire so doggedly.

William had been handsome as a young man and kept his looks. The few of his own letters that survive give a strong sense of his personality. He comes across as cheerful and energetic. He enjoyed life with his family. He would often take the children away on holiday, while his wife performed. But he was not the most sensitive of people. He was always a lover of action rather than emotions, determinedly masculine, a sort of John Bull figure, proud of his country's military might.

William saw himself as a man of finance, interested in how his investments were faring and how the war against France was progressing. In a letter to the Siddons' friend Hester Piozzi in June 1794 from Rectory Cottage, Nuneham, the house the couple rented for a few years in Oxfordshire from George and Elizabeth Harcourt, he devotes much of his letter to describing the extensive local celebrations at the news of the victory in a recent naval battle. He does mention his wife's swollen ankles – she had only recently given birth – but only in passing.

In another letter to Hester later that same summer, he refers to Sally and Maria, his eldest two daughters, as 'the two matronly Babies'. The real new baby, their daughter Cecilia, he reports as simply feeding and sleeping:

> Tomorrow she is to have a little cold Water thrown on her face and Then you know we are To hope it will cry – or it will not live long – and that will be a pity for 'tis a nice Baby enough.[3]

Few fathers today would dare to appear so disinterested in their offspring. But William's letter is couched in terms of a fond joke with Hester that he is someone for whom feelings are the preserve of his famous actress wife, while he concentrates on the more masculine domain of thoughts and facts.

As time went on, William's health deteriorated. He suffered from pain in his feet – due to gout, rheumatism or sciatica – and used crutches, wherever he went. Hester began speculating that he would soon leave 'dear lovely Siddons' a widow. In 1792 the 37-year-old Sarah discovered that her unfaithful husband had now given her a form of venereal disease. She began by thinking that the symptoms she was suffering were 'Nerves and Nerves only', but in October she got the definitive diagnosis from her doctor.[4] As Hester Piozzi wrote to their mutual friend, Penelope Pennington:

poor Mrs Siddons's Disorder that we have all been at such a stand about, turns upon close Examination to be neither more or less than the P[ox] – given by her Husband. What a World it is![5]

Sarah was possessed by 'an indignant melancholy', consumed by resentment at the harm William had wrought on her.[6] Three years earlier Hester had noted in her diary:

I think Mrs Siddons, though beautiful, and endowed with Talents not to support only, but to enrich her Family – is a woman by no means particularly beloved either by Parents, husband, Brother or Son.[7]

The couple seemed to patch up the problems in the relationship. In 1793, leaving their children with Sarah's sister, they set off together on Sarah's next tour of Ireland. Friends reported that Sarah appeared to be in better health, and she returned in January three months pregnant. As Hester put it on her return:

Everybody worships that admirable creature except her own family – to *them* She is no Heroine – though contented to make herself Valet de Chambre.[8]

Their final child, Cecilia (the baby whom William had described as being 'a nice Baby enough') was born that July. Sarah was 39 years old. The labour was long and exhausting. Only a month after giving birth she performed at a benefit for her sister-in-law. She had to rest for an entire week afterwards, thanks to severe back ache. The whole family then went to Margate for a holiday. She wrote wistfully that she wished she could simply stay at home to rest with the baby.

Sal and Sid's first child to survive into adulthood had been their son Henry, who was twenty years older than his youngest sister, Cecilia. When the Siddons came to London, they sent Henry to Dr Barrow's Academy in Soho Square, but after a few months, at the recommendation of Queen Charlotte, they enrolled him at Charterhouse public school. Henry had ambitions as a writer. Aged 15, he wrote a short play, which was performed at his uncle Stephen Kemble's benefit. Sarah wanted Henry to enter the church, just as her parents had hoped John Philip would become a priest. But history repeated itself. Henry had other ideas. He wanted to act.

Sarah could see that Henry did not have sufficient talent to make a good living as a professional. She warned him against the life of a professional actor. In Durham, when mother and son appeared together in *Macbeth*, she even subdued her own performance, to bring down his boisterous acting style. If he were only able to resolve his character faults, she wrote, he might become a good actor. She later admitted that he repented many times at not taking her advice.

Nevertheless, once Henry had decided to act professionally, Sarah, ever the tiger mother, began campaigning on his behalf to persuade John Philip to accept him into the company at Covent Garden. The family friend Elizabeth Inchbald also pulled strings. In 1801 Henry was articled on a three-year contract at Covent Garden, at a starting salary of £6 per week (£497.80 today). Sarah wrote to her friend Charlotte Fitzhugh, professing herself anxious that Henry should be a success and proud that he had made it this far, ignoring the nepotism that had been at work. Henry was cast as Hamlet. In Sarah's words it was 'a tremendous undertaking for so young a creature'.[9] But it immediately became evident he did not possess the acting skills to carry it off. John Philip could not hide his irritation at his untalented nephew.

The following year Henry Siddons married Harriet Murray, the daughter of a lawyer. Sarah was touring Ireland at the time, so was unable to attend the wedding. During the service Henry was so nervous he went deathly pale and started shaking from head to foot. He even got the timing wrong for his most important line, 'I will' – all his experience as an actor forgotten in the moment. Harriet had as little talent as her husband as a performer, but the marriage did prove to be extremely happy.

By 1808, it was evident Henry needed to find work outside London, and in a different capacity. He was not making enough to support himself as an actor, and his (by now widowed) mother was funding him and his family. Sarah wrote to the influential novelist Walter Scott asking him to help secure Henry a place not as an actor but instead as the manager at the Edinburgh Theatre Royal. She had already, she let slip, written to the Duke of Buccleuch on the same subject. Scott was sympathetic. He told Joanna Baillie, the Scottish playwright: 'Siddons is a good lad and deserves success.'[10] The good lad was by now a 34-year-old father of two. But he got the post and took it up that year. Having helped Henry secure the role, Scott was disparaging about his attempts as a playwright. Nevertheless, Henry did make a go of management, which suited him better than acting.

But Henry died of tuberculosis, aged only 41. A weakness in the lungs was something to which the Siddons' children were all susceptible. Campbell described Henry's death as 'a severe shock' to Sarah.[11] She wrote to her friend Charlotte Fitzhugh that her eldest son's death 'seems to have laid a heavier hand on my mind than any I have sustained.'[12] Henry had not been entirely successful in his career, but his marriage had been very happy, she consoled herself. That autumn, Sarah came out of retirement to appear for ten nights in Edinburgh, so she could raise money for her son's widow and their children.

Sarah's next child, Sally, was born in 1775, in Gloucester, just before Sarah's disastrous season with Garrick at Drury Lane, and her sister Maria in 1779, in Bath. The two sisters were very different from each other both in looks and temperament. Sally was demure and virtuous, like her mother, while Maria was far more impulsive and tempestuous. When they were aged only 11 and 7 respectively, Sarah had written to Thomas Sedgwick Whalley that Sally 'is an elegant creature and Maria is as beautiful as a seraphim.'[13] There was never any question of either Sally or Maria working for a living, let alone going on the stage. They were sent to boarding school in Bath and then to a finishing school in Calais. Back in London, they lived the lives of aristocratic young women of the time, socialising and waiting for marriage. Yet neither enjoyed good health. Their mother worried constantly that they would be unable to cope with the strains of married life. Both would go on to be linked romantically to the artist Thomas Lawrence, who was especially close to their famous mother. Maria died, aged 18, in 1798, from tuberculosis, and her sister Sally five years later, aged 27, from emphysema brought on by asthma. (Chapters 14 and 15 give a fuller account of the ends of both their lives and Lawrence's role in their stories.)

Sarah lost several other children at an even earlier age and suffered a series of miscarriages, while continuing to appear on stage. Her daughter Elizabeth Anne, 'fair as wax, with very blue eyes, and the sweetest tuneful voice you ever heard,' died aged 6 in 1788, only two weeks after Sarah had had yet another miscarriage.[14] Sarah went to stay with her friends, the Greatheeds, at Guy's Cliffe to recuperate but was nevertheless back on stage only ten days later. The death of children was a common occurrence at the time but must still have been heartbreaking.

There was therefore a gap of six years between the birth of Maria and that of the Siddons' next child to make it to adulthood, their second son, George. He was born in 1785, the same year his mother had first triumphed as Lady Macbeth. Sarah also appeared eight months pregnant playing The Tragic Muse in yet another revival of Garrick's *Shakespearean Jubilee*. By now Sarah had become a firm favourite of the royal family, and King George III and Queen Charlotte sent a box of medicinal powders for her to use during her confinement. Sarah joked in a letter that the new baby looked like King George, but that she had not been unfaithful to William. Perhaps she named the baby George as a patriotic tribute. From the beginning he was a robust child, 'healthy and lovely as an angel'.[15]

A letter to Hester from Rectory Cottage, Nuneham, in 1793, gives an account of a near-accident which typified George's childhood. The Siddons children were in a donkey cart with their father when the shaft broke and frightened the horse. Everyone else jumped out as the horse reared and bolted, but the

7-year-old George stayed where he was, and 'was left Safely Smiling at the Sport upon the very verge of the grave.'[16]

George did not pursue a career on the stage. Instead, like many second sons at the time, he was sent abroad to serve in the British empire, in the Bengal Civil Service. The Prince of Wales secured him the post in India, and he took out with him royal letters of recommendation. England was at war with France at the time, so perhaps this was also a means of evading active service in the army in Europe. Even so, it meant that George created a life for himself on the other side of the world, far away from his parents. Before departing for India in 1803, he went to stay with his mother – who was on yet another tour of Ireland – for two weeks. At the end of the fortnight, he left without saying a formal goodbye, to avoid causing her too much pain. George married in India, without a single member of his family in attendance. He and his wife had several children, who were sent back to England to school and who enjoyed their visits to their famous grandmother. George outlived his mother.

The Siddons' final child, Cecilia, or Cecy as she was nicknamed, was a bonny 'lumping baby', instantly adored by her much older siblings.[17] A friend of Sarah's wrote 'the baby is all a baby can be, but Mrs S laughs, and says it is a wit and a beauty already in her eyes.'[18] Cecy was only 4 years old when her sister Maria died. She had been kept out of the way, to give her invalid sister some peace. After her sister Sally's death, there was even more parental anxiety about Cecy, as the only surviving daughter. Hester Piozzi, after whose daughter Cecy had been named, wrote that the Siddons' youngest daughter grew up 'sick and spoiled, and fretful and fragile ... they are fearful that She will *not live*.'[19] Sarah wrote to Hester, expressing her constant anxiety about her youngest daughter's health:

> she has that cruel tendency in her Constitution that has already cost me so many Sighs and grounds and tears – these will never cease to flow.[20]

The adult Cecy lived with her retired mother, and their companion, Patty Wilkinson, until Sarah's death. She married a phrenologist a couple of years afterwards and died childless many years later.

The Siddons' family life took place in a variety of venues. Once Sarah's career was established, they always kept a home in London. From their initial lodgings in The Strand, they moved to 14 Gower Street, where Sarah bought her own carriage, and later to 28 Gower Street, where they acquired the lease. In 1790 they moved to 49 Great Marlborough Street. William wrote to Thomas Sedgwick Whalley that the new house was 'not so pretty as Gower Street but more among our friends ... with plenty of closets, which the ladies in general seem fond of.'[21] But Sarah also always longed for a country retreat, a place where work did not need to dominate. She wrote to the Whalleys in March 1785, confessing her plans to amass £10,000 in savings (£1,348,000 today) and buy a country cottage where she could retire. She had been distracted, she wrote, but:

> Now I'll begin my cottage again: it has been lying in heaps a great while, and I have shed many tears over the ruins; but we will build it up again in joy.[22]

The Siddons' friends, the Harcourts, rented them Rectory Cottage, in their estate village of Nuneham Courtenay, from 1791. Sarah began her hobby of sculpting there and made busts of at least two of her children.

In 1795 the Siddons bought their own country retreat, 'a little nutshell upon Putney Heath'.[23] But Sarah was too busy and then too caught up in the tragedy of losing both Maria and Sally to make much use of this second home. After Sally's death the Siddons rented Capo di Monte Cottage in Hampstead instead, yet another attempt to create their dream retreat. In time the Siddons' marriage would come to an end (see Chapter 17) and, at that stage, Sarah gave up Great Marlborough Street, which she confessed had sad memories for her, and moved into lodgings in Hanover Square.

Sarah then began looking for a more formal country house for herself, and in 1805, aged 50, she bought Westbourne Farm, near Paddington, which at the time was surrounded by countryside yet was convenient for London. Her landlord from Hanover Square helped her fit out the new house, creating an additional room as her studio and laying out a garden with a shrubbery. Sarah wrote to a friend that 'it is the prettiest little nook in all the world.'[24] William thought it rather small. He wrote to Hester describing it as 'her little Box, which she continues to think is very pretty.'[25] He liked the air but thought the house was too close to 'the great Brick kiln called London.'[26] He felt, he wrote, that Sarah would need 'a snug House in Town for the damp and dreary months'.[27] After Sarah's retirement she also rented 27 Upper Baker Street, looking north into Regents Park, so that Cecy and their companion, Patty Wilkinson, could attend parties more easily. Sarah enjoyed giving magnificent lunch parties there. In time she gave up Westbourne Farm and spent winters in Upper Baker Street and summers visiting friends in their country homes. She died in Upper Baker Street in 1831.

Sarah's career meant that her mothering was often conflicted. She made up for the fact she could not always be with her children by expressing her love for them passionately, glorying in the time they did have together and taking immense pride in all their achievements. On tour in Leeds, she wrote: 'My ... children are ... well, clever and lovely.'[28] Living a happy family life was hugely important to her. She always remained close to her own parents. Her mother even came to live with the family once her father had died. The family loved their pets too, and their dog Trudge was a particular favourite. Sarah adored cooking for the whole family. Her receipt book is full of recipes for legs of fowls forced, gingerbread made with caraway seeds, mulligatawny soup, raspberry cakes, potato pudding and what she calls 'blamange' [*sic*]. She always enjoyed her food. The family butcher confided in the painter, Benjamin Haydon, 'never was such a woman for chops!'[29] There were medicinal recipes in Sarah's receipt book too, for rheumatism – 'put to it a large bullock's gall (fresh). Rub it on the part two or three times by the hour' – and (heartbreakingly) for consumption.[30] She had also read that tapioca, newly imported from Portugal, might help the patient. But she could do nothing to prevent three of her adult children dying from diseases of the lung.

Throughout her life Sarah had a simple, unshakeable Christian faith. Her notebooks were full of poems she had copied, and jottings from the sermons she had heard in church on a Sunday. Inevitably the deaths of her various children preyed on her mind. She made a note of the words from a gravestone in Abington, near Winchester, in memory of an entire family who, like hers, had had two sons and three daughters. She was very fond of Byron, whom she knew, and copied down several poems of his about loss. She also made a note of the inscription on a sundial she had come across: 'I come and go with each revolving day/Thou must ere long, for ever stay away.'[31] The ritual of religious services always gave her comfort. Dealing as she did with so much personal suffering, it reassured her to listen to sermons telling her that a life existed beyond the grave, where she would be reunited with her loved ones.

Sarah's punishing work regime inevitably took its toll on her own health. Several times during her life, she suffered from what she termed 'a miserable nervous disorder'.[32] When she was under pressure, she tended to lose weight quickly. Conversely, as an older woman she would put on weight in stressful times. By the age of 32 she was already cutting back on her punishing work schedule, due to her ill health. She had earned enough money even at that age to work less, but she began to suffer from what the doctors diagnosed as 'Scorbutic Humours', for which they prescribed mercury.[33] She endured painful headaches and aching limbs, probably the beginnings of the rheumatism which she suffered in later life. In 1787, William wrote to his friend, Sir Charles Hotham, that Sarah had had a violent fever for some time but was now beginning to do much better and was sleeping through the night again, in contrast to the previous eighteen months. She had finally begun to put on some weight. By now she was under the care of the royal physician, Sir Lucas Pepys, and he encouraged her to swim in the sea.

In 1790, aged 35, Sarah had another bout of ill health. She only performed seven times during that entire London theatre season. One journalist wrote that her physical state improved her performance: 'this languor gave a deeper interest to the illusion, by making it more perfect.'[34] In truth, Sarah was suffering from the venereal disease William had given her, but this was still undiagnosed. The following summer she decided not to embark on her usual tour of the provinces. By now Sir Lucas Pepys was telling her she might never be cured from her complaint. He had probably guessed what was wrong. At his suggestion she went to Harrogate to drink the waters, and this improved her health to some extent. That October, while staying with the Siddons, Hester let slip in a letter to their friend Penelope Pennington that Sarah's problem was now confirmed as a venereal disease, given her by William. Sarah's daughter wrote to Penelope at the same time, claiming that her mother was cured. This, though, was simply a daughter seeking to reassure herself that all was well with her parent. Hester was right.

After the birth of Cecilia there was even a rumour that Sarah had gone mad. She wrote to a friend in February 1796: 'You will perhaps see some tale about my illness in the Papers, but it is only a pain in my head and face which is more tiresome and dangerous than you know.'[35] At least three of the national newspapers had indeed reported it. For the next few years, Sarah ignored most of her own symptoms, as she struggled with the usual demands of her career and the weakening and eventual deaths of her two eldest daughters.

In 1801, after Maria's death but before Sally's, Sarah wrote to her friend Charlotte Fitzhugh: 'My face has been very much enflamed but is getting well by the aid of a Dr Ferrier.'[36] She had begun, it was reported, to suffer from erysipelas, an infection on her lip which caused her burning pain. Erysipelas is a bacterial skin infection of the surface layer of the skin. It presents as a bright red rash, accompanied by a fever and vomiting. Sarah certainly had a scab around her face, which she picked at continuously, and she did run a fever and vomit. She also described having a recurring dream that all her teeth fell out while she was on stage. She had started taking laudanum for her condition, which perhaps explains the nightmares. Erysipelas often recurs and can develop into a more serious bacterial infection. But Sarah's symptoms are very similar to those from syphilis. With syphilis, the patches around the mouth are white rather than red, but there is no record of the colour of Sarah's skin infection. Perhaps she was editing the truth, to save her own reputation. Other than once saying something to Hester, Sarah herself never acknowledged that William had given her a venereal disease.

When Sarah was nearly 50, she suffered yet another bout of extreme ill health. She began to be tortured by sciatica, which spread from her hips to her toes.

As a result, she lost the use of her left side and was confined to bed. She and William were staying together at their cottage in Hampstead at the time, and William was suffering from painful rheumatism. William had heard of a new quack remedy, an electrical treatment, which he recommended. When she agreed to try it, Sarah described feeling as if burning lead were being poured into her veins. Her cries of pain were so loud that William wrote that he expected crowds to rush into the house, thinking she was being murdered. Syphilis is known to have four stages, and my own instinct is that this was second stage syphilis. Ill health and general exhaustion were certainly a factor in Sarah's decision to retire, aged 56, in 1812. She then lived nearly twenty more years, but her own health was always a concern to her. The official line when she died, aged 75, was that complications from the erysipelas had killed her. But the real cause may well have been fourth stage syphilis (see Chapter 17).

Despite the tragedies of losing children, the sadness of her marriage being less successful than she had hoped, and her own ill health, Sarah's letters show her to be someone who enjoyed life. A large part of this happiness derived from her friendships, mainly with other women. Her letters to Hester Piozzi show her as a warm and supportive friend, despite the fact the two women were very different from each other. Hester had inherited wealth, while Sarah always worked for her living; Hester was perceptive and at times acerbic, while Sarah tended towards the sentimental; Hester was intellectual while Sarah was instinctive. Another female friend was Charlotte Fitzhugh, the wife of a Conservative MP, whom Sarah often visited at her home, Bannisters Lodge, near Southampton. Sarah was also a frequent visitor to Guy's Cliffe, the home of Bertie and Ann Greatheed, where she had worked as a servant in her early years. A friendship with the gay bluestocking sculptress, Anne Damer, who lived at Strawberry Hill, was the catalyst for Sarah taking up sculpture as a hobby.

While she was celebrated by her contemporaries as the greatest tragic actress of her generation, behind the scenes Sarah's life was an exceptionally full one. Her marriage was long and had its share of complications. Five of her children lived to adulthood, though only two survived her. She lost children as babies too and suffered various miscarriages. For her, death was part of life. Perhaps these tragedies shored up her instinctive Christian faith. She herself suffered from a series of illnesses for many years, both mental and physical. And yet, despite all this, she was a proud and energetic mother, a committed wife, and supportive friend, while at the same time continuing her acting career, enjoying triumphant London seasons, and then setting out most summers on tour. She could never have achieved all this without astounding energy and enormous physical strength.

Chapter 9

Celebrity

'A strange capricious master is the public.'[1]

In her private notebook Sarah kept a copy of a letter from a male admirer. He wrote: 'you have been the cause (paradoxical as it may sound) at once of my happiness and my ruin.'[2] The writer had fallen on hard times, living on just one meal a day, and spending all his spare money on tickets for the theatre. When he heard a rumour that Sarah was due to appear in Dublin, he followed her across the Irish Sea, even going so far as to sell the buckles from his shoes so he could see her perform every night there. His landlady evicted him, but he wrote to Sarah that, in watching her and knowing that he would probably never see her perform again: 'I forgot my cares, and in imagination ate my dinner and I can safely say I never experienced bliss so near my idea of heaven as seeing your play.'[3] Sarah's fame brought with it huge power and huge responsibility.

Sarah was famous. But she was also a celebrity. While the term 'celebrity' only appeared after Sarah's death, in 1869 according to the *Oxford English Dictionary*, the concept existed during her working life. Celebrity is a transient status, something which has been won but which also has the potential to be lost. Celebrities – unlike the merely famous – are flawed. Their fans judge them. What is more, they fear that their personal actions will cause them to lose their magic. They are dependent on their audience, so their source of power can potentially disappear at any time. They need their strong fan base at all times. And they will often seek to control their own narrative, partly in response to this danger.

The historian Stella Tillyard describes London at the time as 'the crucible of celebrity'.[4] Sarah's celebrity status needs to be seen as part of this wider trend. Various contributing factors all came together to create a very particular heat. The decline in organised religion, along with a loss in a sense of the divine right of the monarchy, left people looking for something to believe in. A more powerful, corrupt parliament, an emerging public sphere and an increase in the printed press resulted in a society where critical voices were becoming ever louder. Weak and ineffective libel laws meant anything was fair game. And an increase in wealth and leisure time allowed people to pay more attention to the lives of the rich and famous. All this added up to a toxic mix.

An audience of a few hundred well-connected, influential individuals might see Sarah perform in one of the two official London theatres, and experience 'Siddons Fever', as they connected emotionally to the heroic figures she portrayed.[5] Then newspapers would review her performances, disseminating word of her power. As *The Morning Post* phrased it: 'we boldly venture to affirm, no age, and country, ever produced a more eminent actress.'[6] London's newspaper readership at the time was approximately 3,000–4,000. News about Sarah then spread even further. Reputation was all, as she learned to her detriment during her first disastrous London season and the reaction to her two first Irish tours. When the London theatres were closed and Sarah performed in the English regions, in Ireland and in Scotland, she increased her currency among her fans.

Whereas Sarah's male contemporaries dreamed of acquiring fame through military glory, political life or success in the arts, her female contemporaries – actresses, writers and even aristocrats – might better be described as seeking celebrity rather than fame, promoting their own personal brand. It was no coincidence that this huge increase in the phenomenon of celebrity came about in the years when women had first started appearing on the London stage. Sarah's celebrity meant that her audiences wanted to possess her. As *The Rambler's Magazine* described the situation in February 1783: 'no mantua-maker or milliner is now employed who has not studied to cut and make every branch of their profession *a la Siddonne*.'[7] Sarah's most fanatical fans were largely female. They would delight in poetry praising her, or they would read novels in which the fictional heroes and (more often) heroines attended the London theatres and saw Sarah perform one of her famous roles. A sort of licensed same-sex attraction from Sarah's female fans was accepted. The interest often became obsessive. Sarah was frequently disturbed in her own home by strangers knocking on her door and forcing themselves into her drawing room so they could look at her in person.

Anecdotes of experiences in Sarah's life were carefully curated to give the right impression to her supporters. At the beginning of her second London season, in October 1783, Hester Thrale took her to meet the famous, elderly Dr Samuel Johnson. Hester was Johnson's young, literary protégée at the time. When Sarah entered the room and found there was no chair for her to sit on, Johnson made an entirely characteristic remark that 'you who so often occasion a want of seats to other people, will the more easily excuse the want of one yourself.'[8] The entire event felt staged and written, not spontaneous and relaxed. Sarah knew just what to say when Johnson asked her which was her favourite Shakespearean role. Knowing he liked *Henry VIII*, she replied that it was Queen Katharine. Johnson promised to come and see her play the part, even though he was too elderly ever to do so. He did, however, let Hester know that he felt Sarah had 'behaved with great modesty and propriety.'[9]

Now she was famous, Sarah sat for portraits by celebrated artists such as Sir Joshua Reynolds and Sir George Romney. These portraits were then reproduced as engravings, and circulated, rather as powerful photographs of a celebrity become iconic images online today. Mass-produced representations, which had in the past been reserved for monarchs or saints, were now widely available. They added a touch of glamour to the lives of those who saw them. Sarah's admirers could also purchase merchandise to keep her in their lives – a porcelain figurine, a miniature depicting her face, a snuffbox with her image on its lid, a fan showing her profile or a screen reproducing one of her portraits.

Sarah's admirers identified with her. They wanted to emulate her. Amateur theatrics were increasingly in vogue. The same tragedies in which Sarah excelled – *The Fatal Marriage, Venice Preserved, Jane Shore* – were put on in private homes. Amateur actors who had seen her perform could now impersonate her in one of her famous roles. As the letter from her impoverished male letter-writer demonstrates, Sarah's fans felt a very strong connection with her. It was as if they really knew her. Suddenly a private life such as Sarah's could become a public commodity. Sarah might have to accept that her husband William kept all her earnings, but her fame was something she herself possessed and could trade in her own right.

Sarah's fans also wanted to see her in the flesh rather than just owning an engraving or reading about her. The development of a system of mail coaches connecting different parts of Britain during Sarah's working life meant that it was far easier to travel out to the provinces than it had been even during her parents' careers. She could tour the nations and regions of Britain in the season when the London theatres were closed – to York or Manchester or Bristol or Glasgow – and perform for just a few nights in those cities, to huge acclaim. Her appearance at a venue would be the highlight of the cultural calendar wherever she went. Normal life was suspended. Box offices were besieged. And, of course, Sarah herself, along with the management of the theatres where she performed, made huge profits, often at the expense of the actors based permanently in one of these regional theatres.

Sarah actively fuelled her own celebrity status. She was not a passive recipient. In choosing the roles she played, she was creating a fiction about herself, that she was noble, morally righteous, prepared to put aside her own needs to protect her family. This fiction then played out in her own personal life. She was not alone in this. Other actresses too confused their public identity with their costumed performances. Dora Jordan, for instance, always played the innocent coquette, sexually appealing without threatening in any way. Sarah's image was that of the noble wife and mother, sacrificing herself for the sake of her loved ones. Inevitably, she saw her own private life through this same fictional prism. When she played Euphrasia in *The Grecian Daughter*, James Boaden, her unofficial biographer, wrote that:

> Her spectators *here* inferred…that in any signal crisis of her own life, she would be found indeed the noble creature she appeared to be on the stage.[10]

As her friend Joseph Farington put it, she was 'always a Tragedy Queen: always acting a part even among her own relations.'[11] Marriage to William must have had its challenges, but Sarah's attitude to him at any point was in part at least informed by the role she had played the night before.

Sarah's audiences related to her portraying extreme emotions, and they in turn experienced strong feelings themselves. When writers described audience members – and particularly female audience members – affected by Sarah, they often did so in terms of illness. It was as if her audiences felt her effect so strongly that they made themselves unwell. Sarah started playing the part of Mrs Haller in Kotzebue's melodrama *The Stranger* when she herself was struggling with the personal problems of a dying daughter and a difficult, unfaithful husband. The play tells the story of a husband and wife whose marriage had fallen apart but who are reconciled for the sake of their children. Sarah's own daughter, Sally, described her mother often returning from playing the role in a very low, tearful mood. Her performance was informed by her own experiences, but the role she played in turn impacted on her personal life. The tragic heroine onstage became the tragic heroine offstage as well.

Busy as she was with her career and family, Sarah had limited time to socialise. She was careful to select the occasions she attended for their maximum impact. She admitted to Sir Charles Hotham 'the necessity of being a little mysterious sometimes.'[12] Her friendships with aristocrats were extremely important to her. Other actresses had relationships with members of the aristocracy. Elizabeth Farren had a long affair with, and then married, the Earl of Derby. Dora Jordan was the mistress of the Duke of Clarence. But Sarah's connection was not sexual. She was respectful of the niceties of rank, but she nevertheless saw herself as the equal of her aristocratic women friends. Her success in her own right, and the moral position which the roles she played bestowed on her, meant that she was almost an aristocrat herself. As her contemporary, Thomas Davies, observed 'she looks, walks, and moves like a woman of superior rank.'[13]

Sarah admitted in her notes for her official biographer that she was 'an ambitious candidate for fame,' making sure that she had time to sit for the best portrait painters of the day.[14] It was David Garrick who first understood the importance of portraiture as a way of enhancing an actor's status. The two London art galleries, the Royal Academy and the Society of Artists, were very close geographically to Drury Lane and Covent Garden. Every year the Royal Academy held its annual exhibition, and a key component of its success was the chance for those who attended to star-spot. The latest portraits of actors and actresses were on display and the subjects themselves attended the exhibitions. Commercial galleries did not exist at the time, so artists relied on their paintings being shown there to enhance their reputations. The system benefited everybody.

Sarah admitted that she had little time to attend parties and concerts but: 'As much of my time as could now be "stolen from imperious affairs" was employed in sitting for various Pictures.'[15] Once a portrait was finished, an artist's assistant would make copies for circulation. Then prints were made. Sarah took a great interest in the quality of these prints. She insisted that Sir Joshua Reynolds' portrait of her as *The Tragic Muse* be copied using the fashionable new stipple process, rather than simply as a standard mezzotint. She urged Reynolds to employ a particular engraver to ensure the copies were of a high standard. She also loved distributing the prints to her friends and admirers, just as if she were a 1930s Hollywood star. As a contemporary wrote of her in the press: 'Perhaps she has given greater exertions to the pencils of the artists than any lady in the dramatic world.'[16]

In May 1783, after Sarah's first successful London season but before she had made her mark as Lady Macbeth, Sir Joshua Reynolds began working on his famous portrait of the 27-year-old, known as *The Tragic Muse* (see Illustration 9). The previous year's exhibition at the Royal Academy had not been particularly fruitful for the 60-year-old Reynolds and he was determined to improve the outcome the following season. There had already been grumblings in the press that an image of this beautiful new actress had not so far appeared in one of the Royal Academy exhibitions, 'but yet such faint and inadequate Resemblances of her as stated in Front of Sixpenny Plays and Magazines, should excite some of our artists to do her ampler Justice.'[17] Reynolds took up the challenge.

Reynolds' studio at the time was in Leicester Fields (today's Leicester Square) and Sarah was in temporary lodgings nearby. His large and beautifully decorated house had an extensive gallery where potential purchasers could come to view his works. Reynolds encouraged a very broad social spectrum of visitors to his studio, so aristocrats would often be there at the same time as actors and actresses. Any one portrait would require up to fifteen or sixteen sessions with the subject. Life models or plaster casts were used, and Sir Joshua's assistants would paint the draperies worn by his subjects, while he concentrated on the face and body. Grasping the opportunity presented by Sarah's new-found fame,

Reynolds planned to exhibit *The Tragic Muse* in the following year's Royal Academy exhibition.

Much of Reynolds's reputation as the best portrait painter of his era depended on his excellent people skills. Self-made, like Sarah, and exceptionally cheerful by nature, he knew just how to make his clients feel at ease. Visitors would wander in and out during the different sittings. The sculptor John Flaxman and the American artist Gilbert Stuart both came to the studio while Reynolds was painting Sarah. Stuart remarked on how agitated Reynolds seemed as he worked on the portrait, with his wig askew and his stockings loose. Reynolds knew that exhibiting Sarah's painting at the Royal Academy exhibition would increase the number of visitors to his studio. Even if he did not sell the painting, he would have rationalised to himself, then he could keep it in his studio, unsold, to attract future clients.

The whole experience of being the subject matter for a Reynolds portrait was quite theatrical. The artist performed for his clients but they in response became part of this performance. Reynolds would always put a mirror close to his subject's face, to allow them to see exactly how the painting was progressing. It was a prescribed process and yet Reynolds kept the whole experience very spontaneous. He enjoyed an exceptional level of interaction with his subjects, so that both parties had a sense of intimate involvement. This was not dissimilar from the way Sarah worked with her adoring audiences in the theatre. For Sarah, Reynolds had placed a raised seat, like a throne, in the centre of the room, as if she were on stage, performing for an audience. Little wonder then that the two instantly connected. Yet, ironically, Reynolds admitted he was not a huge admirer of Sarah's acting, that she 'never made Him feel' when he saw her perform.[18]

In her description of the first sitting, Sarah wrote in her notes for her official biographer, Thomas Campbell, that Sir Joshua took her by the hand and asked her to ascend the makeshift throne he had in place, to give him a sense of what might be the perfect pose. She sat down and he was instantly delighted with the position she took. Her contemporary, the poet Samuel Rogers, gave a different, less flattering account. As he described it, Sarah simply slumped herself down in the seat and Sir Joshua was satisfied. She might have wanted her public to feel that she was instrumental in the choice of pose, but it seems more probable that Sir Joshua had some idea of what he wanted before she arrived. The attitude she had struck gave him the chance to capture her very individual profile, with her distinctive long nose and strong jawline. She held up her left index finger, looking upwards and parting her lips, as if she were about to speak – a typical attitude for a subject to strike in contemporary portraits.

Reynolds' *The Tragic Muse* is not dissimilar from a painting by Thomas Stothard of Mary Ann Yates, Sarah's rival from her unhappy first season at

Drury Lane. Stothard too painted the actress as The Tragic Muse. At the time Sarah came for her first sitting with Sir Joshua, both she and Mary Ann Yates were playing the same role, that of Jane Shore, in the two rival London theatres. Sarah's reviews had been surprisingly mixed. Perhaps Sir Joshua had seen them both perform. The association would not have been a happy one for Sarah, which is perhaps why she so pointedly gave her own account of how it was she who chose her pose. Both the position and the garments worn by Sir Joshua's sitter were also like another painting of his, a portrait he had painted of Maria, Duchess of Gloucester, nine years previously. He kept prints of past paintings in a folder in his studio. Sarah would have liked the aristocratic connection.

Reynolds could have portrayed Sarah as herself, just as Gainsborough would do a couple of years later. Yet at this point she had only just rebuilt her reputation. Her triumphant appearance as Isabella in *The Fatal Marriage* – the part which changed her life – had taken place only just over six months earlier. So, instead, Reynolds chose to paint her in character, as *The Tragic Muse*. It was as if he was creating a theatrical piece of his own. The famous actress was performing in his painting. This idea of what the muse of tragedy might look like was then mediated by Reynolds' own ideas about how Sarah should appear in the portrait, what expression she should use, and which costume she should wear. At once the piece felt both contemporary and classically timeless.

Sir Joshua depicted her with the twin figures of Pity and Fear at her shoulder, both key emotions in the cathartic effect experienced by Sarah's audiences as they watched her perform a tragedy. Although he kept her pose the same throughout, he made various other key changes while painting the portrait. Sarah is surrounded by clouds, but initially Reynolds painted a cherub kneeling at her feet, holding a scroll. He decided to dispense with the cherub at some point during the sessions. Perhaps it felt too lightweight. At first the allegorical figure of pale Melancholy appeared alongside Sarah. Reynolds had progressed quite far with painting this sad figure, when he decided to increase the drama, changing the figure to one of screaming Horror instead. He used a pencil drawing of himself as the impromptu model for the new shape. So now both Sarah and Sir Joshua himself appeared in the portrait. Reynolds also made the decision to change Sarah's costume from something low-cut and creamy to a far more dramatic gold, edged with fur. He was adapting and improving his ideas as the painting progressed.

In the final sitting Sarah reported that Reynolds now seemed to be afraid to touch what she termed his 'unequald [*sic*] glorious work'.[19] Her account for Thomas Campbell emphasised her own artistic involvement in the piece. She was not just the passive sitter. Reynolds thought he might like to heighten her colour, but she begged him not to, apologising for being so presumptuous as to give him this input. Her pale colouring, she explained, gave her more of a sense of melancholy. He thought about what she had said and then he agreed. When the picture was finished and framed, he thanked her for arguing he should keep her skin pale. He then signed the hem of her skirt in the painting, explaining: 'I have resolved to go down to posterity on the hem of *your* Garment.'[20] Others might have sat for him, was the implication, but Sarah's portrait was extra special. Little wonder that Sarah made a note of his words for Thomas Campbell to include in his biography. All this was invaluable to her.

When the portrait was exhibited at the Royal Academy in 1784 it was an instant success. It was hailed as not simply a picture of Sarah but as a work of art in its own right: a masterpiece. By allowing Sarah to be involved in every element of the process, Reynolds had captured 'the character as well as the features' of the young actress who was 'among the most inspiring objects of genius', wrote contemporary journalists.[21] The two were inextricably linked. Sarah would live up to Reynolds' portrait for the rest of her life. Sir Thomas Lawrence, who succeeded Reynolds as president of the Royal Academy, described the painting to his students several years later, in 1824, as 'indisputably the finest female portrait in the world'.[22] Soon after the Royal Academy exhibition, Sarah used the distinctive costume and make-up, together with the pose she adopted, in a tableau in honour of Garrick. After she had retired and was giving public readings of Shakespeare's plays, her brother John Philip noted that she looked just like the painting. Reynolds too was bound to Sarah from now on. Whenever he came to see Sarah perform, he would sit in the orchestra, looking up at her just like those who gazed up at his portrait of her when they came to see it on display. From now on, he would often be involved in her choice of costume and make-up for a new role.

The other most famous portrait of Sarah is by Thomas Gainsborough (Illustration 10). By the time Gainsborough painted her in 1785, the 30-year-old Sarah had sealed her reputation in her bold portrayal of Lady Macbeth. Yet rather than choosing to paint her as an actress in one of her many roles, Gainsborough instead portrayed Sarah as herself, a classic beauty, in a blue striped gown, brown muff and a black hat. By now she had dispensed with wearing a wig when she appeared onstage and her audiences could see for themselves her distinctive auburn hair, which was how Reynolds had pictured her a couple of years earlier. Yet Gainsborough kept the powdered wig, as if he wanted her audience to see her as a member of the aristocracy rather than an actress, however celebrated. She looks composed in Gainsborough's painting, fashionably dressed and remarkably beautiful, even seen through today's lens. As her contemporary, the historian Catherine Macaulay, wrote, she was in 'the prime of her glorious beauty' at this point in her life.[23] Yet Gainsborough found

Sarah's face difficult to capture, complaining: 'Confound the nose, there's no end to it!'[24]

By contrast, William Hamilton preferred to paint Sarah playing the roles for which she had become so famous. Hamilton, who was younger and only establishing his career at the time, chose to record her performances faithfully for posterity rather than using her theatricality to create an imagined character, as Reynolds had done. He painted five portraits of Sarah in all, four of which show her playing theatrical characters. Since we have no recording of Sarah's actual performances, Hamilton's portraits are invaluable. Together, they form a valuable part of her legacy. The wisdom of her using her celebrity to promote her own brand can be said to have been vindicated.

The most famous of Hamilton's paintings of Sarah shows her as Euphrasia in *The Grecian Daughter* (Illustration 11). The part was a very physical one. Sarah told friends that it often exhausted her, as if she had been beaten up on stage. Yet rather than showing this violence, Hamilton concentrated on the heroic. He also painted Sarah as Isabella in *The Fatal Marriage*, the virtuous mother, sorrowful and veiled, with her son Henry beside her. Sarah was in Bath for much of the time Hamilton was painting her as Isabella, while he was in London. She may have sat in his studio for a sitting or two, but Hamilton also made a life-size sketch of her head, which he could transport easily to his studio in London, and he then used a model for the body. One Siddons fan explained to a friend how she first saw Hamilton's portrait of Sarah as Isabella. This then prompted her to go and see the only portrait Hamilton had made of Sarah not as a theatrical character. And then, as a result, she was encouraged to go and see Sarah act, first as Isabella (since she had seen Hamilton's portrait) but then as Calista in *The Fair Penitent*. Hamilton's strategy had worked, but so had Sarah's. His pictures of her helped both enhance his reputation and increase her audiences.

Sir George Romney painted a striking oil sketch called *The Siddonian Recollections* some time after Sarah's triumph as Lady Macbeth. It shows her expressing three separate emotions: pain, fear and horror. Romney also painted Sarah as Melpomene, The Tragic Muse. He started by planning a full-length portrait, but later cut it down to merely head and shoulders. Sarah was particularly fond of the portrait and made a point of going several times to sit for Romney, who was known as being shy and reticent. The painting was based on an ancient statue Romney had seen in Italy, and Sarah was keen to encourage this connection to a Greek heroine. She had been at William Hamilton's house when she had noticed a statue of the goddess Ariadne, and stopped to study it, aware of its striking resemblance to herself. She quickly checked herself, aware that it looked as if she had conceded that she had goddess-like beauty. Later in life Sarah would take up sculpture, partly so she could create self-portraits.

She knew the value of her own physicality. Not that she was always pleased with the results of artists' portraits of her. They were 'horrid daubs', she once wrote to her son George, but, on the other hand, she did not have 'any taste for publishing libels against my own person.'[25]

By far the closest association Sarah developed with a single portrait painter was her relationship with Thomas Lawrence. She had first met Lawrence as a child when she stopped at The Black Bear Inn in Devizes, which was run by his father. When the Siddons were living in Bath, the Lawrences moved there too, and Lawrence drew Sarah in a black velvet hat, as well as depicting her as Euphrasia in *The Grecian Daughter* and as Zara in *The Mourning Bride*. In 1787, aged 18, he came to London to set up his studio. Sarah was in her thirties by this time and she and her family all welcomed the talented young artist. The two became all the closer as Lawrence went on to fall in love first with Sarah's eldest daughter, Sally, and then with her second daughter, Maria (see Chapters 14 and 15). Yet despite these complications, Lawrence and Sarah retained an exceptionally close relationship. He continued to paint her as the signs of her aging began to show.

Inevitably, visual images of her beauty became more difficult for Sarah to use to promote herself as she grew older. This was an era where physical appearance was particularly important. By allowing herself to be painted later in life, Sarah laid herself open to ridicule and even disgust. Lawrence painted Sarah in 1804, aged 49, no longer slim but a middle-aged matron. When she was aged 62, George Henry Harlow exhibited a group portrait at the Royal Academy of several of the Kemble family in the trial scene from *Henry VIII*, with Sarah central as Queen Katharine. And Henry Perronet Briggs painted her the year before she died, looking old and tired, alongside her vivacious young niece, Fanny Kemble. Even then Sarah's status meant her inclusion in the painting ensured it would be a commercial success, while at the same time flattering Fanny.

Like any celebrity, Sarah did not always get a good press. Not everyone bought into the image of Sarah as virtuous wife and mother, who never stepped out of line. Although she deliberately steered away from promoting her sexuality on stage, the fact Sarah had such a large family drew attention to her active sex life. A degrading caricature, *The Rival Queens of Covent Garden and Drury Lane Theatres*, published during her triumphant Drury Lane season in 1782, showed Sarah bare-breasted, fighting it out with Mary Ann Yates as to who was the true leading lady (Illustration 13). Besides the occasional bad review, she was also lampooned in the press for her supposed meanness and apparent coldness towards other people. In truth she was shy, but this often came across as haughtiness. She was also criticised for lacking a sense of humour. This was not helped by her distinctive voice, so that even when she ordered something in a shop it sounded as if she was performing a tragic role on stage.

As someone celebrated and successful, Sarah sometimes got into trouble with friends and acquaintances. Samuel Pratt had been a friend when she lived in Bath, and he remained close to Thomas Sedgwick Whalley. The Siddons loaned Pratt money, perhaps as much as £500 (£64,040 today). At the same time Pratt started making unwanted advances towards Sarah's sister, Fanny. He then asked Sarah if she would champion a tragedy he had written, to ensure it was performed at Drury Lane. She had a carefully phrased response to these kinds of requests, which she always used, where she explained she would not read unsolicited plays but would be happy to help once they were accepted by the theatre's management. In Pratt's case this went down extremely badly. He threatened to publish a poem of his entitled *Gratitude*, in which he portrayed himself as a ladder which Sarah had climbed up in the past but which she was now kicking away. Later, when he let it be known he wanted to be reconciled with her, she refused.

A further problem arose with Bertie Greatheed, whom Sarah had taken care of when he was a boy at Guy's Cliffe, and with whom she was now on good terms socially. He too had written a play, *The Regent*, and pressed Sarah to read it and champion it. She confessed in a letter to Thomas Sedgwick Whalley that she was extremely disappointed in the wooden characterisation of the character Bertie had proposed she should play. She was anxious that he should never find out that she had criticised his work. She even asked Whalley to burn her letter (which he did not do). The following year, *The Regent* was indeed staged at Drury Lane. On the second night Sarah was forced to withdraw, having suffered a miscarriage. The piece was already playing to a near-empty Drury Lane and, as a journalist writing in *The Ipswich Journal* described the situation, 'the audience strongly expressed their disapprobation.'[26] Sarah's part was recast, and the play ran for a few more nights but it was generally thought that the story in the press became about Sarah's indisposition rather than about the poor quality of the play itself.

Once she became famous, Sarah used her celebrity status to control her image among her public. James Boaden described her as 'exquisitely chaste and dignified in her exterior,' a mirror 'in which our noble youth did dress themselves'.[27] Those who went to see her on stage or in paintings felt themselves especially connected to her, or as Boaden expressed it, they 'became *related* to her look, to her deportment and her utterance.'[28] She was a hugely influential role model, symbolising virtuous domestic respectability. As she aged, she even acquired a grandeur which felt regal. Like the celebrity she was, she fought to contain the fallout from any scandals which threatened to taint her, and to work on building her brand in her defence. In the deadly serious game of reputation, Sarah was a powerful player.

Chapter 10

Royalty

'I had certainly often personated queens.'[1]

For most of Sarah's life, George III ruled as king. Sarah's success meant that she came into close contact with both the king and his wife, Queen Charlotte. The royal couple enjoyed seeing her perform and then invited her to Windsor, where they asked her to take up an honorary role, reading aloud to them. Sarah was instinctively patriotic and a great supporter of King George. And on a personal level too, Sarah and the royal couple had much in common. Just like the Siddons, King George and Queen Charlotte saw their marriage as hugely important to the image they wanted to project to their public. They too had a large family, in whom they tried to instil their own values and about whom they worried constantly. Stability and respectability were guiding principles for both couples. George III's son succeeded his father in the final ten years of Sarah's life. Sarah's relationship with George IV was rather different, but she remained a loyal monarchist.

The connections between Sarah and Queen Charlotte were particularly striking – and the similarities helped enhance Sarah's reputation. Charlotte was totally supportive of her husband throughout their long marriage and bore him thirteen children. Like Sarah, she was praised as an exemplary mother. Like Sarah, she was a largely asexual figure, her sexuality only ever expressed in terms of her fertility. And like Sarah, she was promoted as a great role model. When the king recovered from his first serious bout of mental illness in 1789, nearly a quarter of the 700 loyal addresses composed by his grateful subjects, who were all relieved that he was well once again, were specifically addressed to Queen Charlotte. One newspaper wrote: 'No female ever more justly deserved it. She is a pattern of domestic virtue which cannot be too much admired.'[2] These were exactly the sorts of words used to praise Sarah.

As soon as Sarah started to have her huge success at Drury Lane, King George and Queen Charlotte came to see her perform. They enjoyed the theatre, although the king tended to prefer comedies to the tragedies Sarah played. As James Boaden, Sarah's unauthorised biographer, explained, going to see a performance of a comedy 'associated more naturally with the joyous occasion, which gave the sovereign and his family to the grateful welcome of his people.'[3]

Comedy sat better with the concept of royalty at the time. But King George and Queen Charlotte were immediately much taken by Sarah.

The royal couple had been in the audience at Drury Lane and observed Sarah as an actress during her disastrous Garrick season, but now she had become such a huge success they came to see her once again, firstly on 2 January 1783, as Euphrasia in *The Grecian Daughter*. Here she played the Greek princess who heroically supports her doomed, imprisoned, royal father. That week the king and queen were criticised in the press for choosing to go to the theatre at a time of political crisis and yet, ignoring this criticism, a week later they went to see Sarah for a second time, this time as Belvidera in *Venice Preserved*. She played the noble daughter of a senator, who is punished for taking a moral stance. Clearly the royal couple liked what they saw. Over an eight-day period, they came to see Sarah three more times, playing the roles of Calista, Jane Shore and Isabella. She had touched a nerve. The queen even sent Sarah a gift of £100 (£13,080 today). King George and Queen Charlotte had joined the ranks of Siddons' supporters.

When the following season opened at Drury Lane, the royal couple again came to see Sarah, this time once more performing Euphrasia in *The Grecian Daughter*. Their first experience had been a good one and they connected to its heroine. On 8 October they even brought three of their children to see her perform Isabella in *The Fatal Marriage* for a second time. In this play, Sarah's character refuses to give up her son to her controlling father-in-law as it would mean that she, as his mother, would be denied access to her child. Perhaps the king and queen felt their children would benefit from seeing such a powerful tale of parental love. This time the king and queen's box had been built out to project forwards into the auditorium, so the audience could get a better look at the royal personages. King George and Queen Charlotte sat under a specially constructed dome, covered with crimson velvet and embroidered in gold leaf. George, Prince of Wales, the 20-year-old heir to the throne, sat under a similar blue velvet and silver-embroidered dome, while two of his sisters, 16-year-old Princess Charlotte and 14-year-old Princess Augusta, shared a third dome of blue satin, sporting a silver fringe. The press paid much attention to the royal party's clothing. King George wore a plain suit, like a Quaker, but with gold buttons. Queen Charlotte's dress was of white satin, with a head-dress of diamonds, while both her daughters also wore diamonds in their hair. The Prince of Wales sported a suit of blue Geneva velvet. The theatricality of the royals easily equalled the splendour on stage.

Queen Charlotte was so moved by Sarah's performance on this occasion that she turned her back to the audience, to hide the fact she was crying. It was, she pronounced in her German accent, 'doo desagreble [*sic*]'.[4] Her husband looked at Sarah through a single opera glass but found his tears were flowing so fast that he was prevented from seeing the action properly. He liked Sarah's stillness, he explained, which he pronounced very different from Garrick's fidgety acting style. He praised her fulsomely to Fanny Burney: 'I am an enthusiast for her, quite an enthusiast. I think there was never any player in my time so excellent.'[5] Fanny herself was less enamoured with the tragic actress. That night Sarah had been unwell and had even considered cancelling the performance, but had gone ahead, out of loyalty to her royal patrons. By the end of the play, she was so exhausted she had to be helped to her dressing room.

The royal command performances continued throughout Sarah's time at Drury Lane. In December 1783, at the king's request, Sarah played the role of Constance in Shakespeare's *King John*. Constance is the ever-loyal mother of her flawed son, the king. The connection between Queen Constance onstage and Queen Charlotte offstage cannot have been lost on the spectators. While the royal family maintained a studied theatricality in their dress whenever they attended the theatre, the onstage queen Sarah was becoming ever less formal and less constrained. As Constance she gave up the tradition of wearing hoops. Instead, her costume consisted of a simple black satin skirt with a petticoat. The audience loved it. Later Sarah would also stop wearing powdered wigs, preferring to show her own naturally auburn hair instead.

When Sarah played Lady Macbeth to huge acclaim, within five nights of her debut she was giving a command performance of Shakespeare's play to the king and queen. The play might tell a story of regicide, but the royals were relaxed enough to know that they wanted to see Sarah in the role, regardless of how their critics might respond. The king's enthusiastic applause was noted by the press.

Sarah had introduced a new role into her repertoire: that of Mrs Beverley in *The Gamester*. The play tells the tragic story of Beverley, an inveterate gambler who prioritises his debts to his supposed friend over the bonds he owes his family, with tragic consequences. Sarah played his virtuous wife. The actor William Macready described how, in the final scene, when Mrs Beverley came across her dying husband in a dungeon, Sarah 'uttered a shriek of agony that would have pierced the hardest heart, and rushing from them, flung herself as if for union in death, on the prostrate form before her.'[6] King George and Queen Charlotte stayed away, not because they were hard of heart but because they had their own problems. Several of their sons had fallen prey to the craze at the time for gambling, as well as to alcoholism and promiscuity, but two of them – George, Prince of Wales, and Ernest Augustus, Duke of Cumberland – did come to see the play. They both wept openly at Sarah's performance. Clearly it spoke to them personally.

Soon after Sarah's Drury Lane triumph, now that the royal couple had become frequent visitors to see her onstage, she was invited for the first time to the royal home, Buckingham House. In her account of this first audience, Sarah explained that she was required to wear a particular dress which was not commonly worn elsewhere at the time, a 'sack' with 'hoop and treble ruffles'.[7] She felt extremely uncomfortable in it. First, she was shown into an antechamber, where there were some ladies she knew slightly, and then in time the king himself came in, pulling his young daughter, the 3-year-old Princess Amelia, on a cart. Sarah always had a strong affinity with small children, and she was delighted when the young princess came over to look at the flowers in her cleavage. She confided in one of the ladies with her that she longed to embrace the little girl. Instead, the princess put out her hand so that Sarah could kiss it. Sarah was struck by how the formality of royal etiquette had been learned at such a young age.

Once the queen arrived, Sarah began to read aloud to the royal party, as she had been requested to do. Thanks to her awkward dress her movements were restricted. To keep reading without a break for such a long stretch was not easy. She was offered refreshments in a room next door, but she could not turn her back on her royal hosts. She would have had to reverse out of the audience chamber. The floor was highly polished and slippery, and she feared catching the hem of her dress. So she refused any food or drink for the entire evening. The queen remarked on Sarah's being so composed. As Sarah put it: 'I had certainly often personated queens.'[8] The onstage queen knew how to behave in front of offstage royalty.

The satirist John Wolcot, who often lampooned the royal family, wrote:

> Poor Mrs SIDDONS she was ordered out –
> To wait upon their Majesties to spout –
> To read old Shakespeare's *As You Like It* to 'em;
> And how to mind their Stops and Commas, shew 'em – [9]

According to Wolcot, one of the princes remarked that Sarah might be happier sitting down. Etiquette demanded that no-one could sit in the presence of royalty in audiences such as these. The royal couple reportedly went next door for a few minutes, so that, finally, Sarah could sit and rest.

The session went sufficiently well, despite these various accounts of its social awkwardness, for Sarah to be offered an honorary role as Preceptress in English Reading to the princesses. From now on she would come back often to read aloud to the royal family, both in London and at Windsor Castle. King George and Queen Charlotte showed her several acts of kindness over the years. Charlotte secured a place for Sarah's oldest son Henry at Charterhouse School, for instance.

George once sent a personal message to Sarah, urging her not to use white paint on her face in case it harmed her skin. (He had presumably concluded she must be artificially whitening it, since she was always particularly pale. In fact, she never used paint. She was indignant that she should be 'suspected of this disgusting practice.'[10])

Sarah also encountered the royal couple via her friends, George and Elizabeth Harcourt, who owned Nuneham Courtenay, the estate where Sarah rented Rectory Cottage and often spent her leisure time. The royal family came to visit the Harcourts while Sarah was there and enjoyed themselves so much, they sent back to Windsor for extra changes of clothing so they could prolong their stay. Sarah read the part of Hamlet aloud to the house party. She was pregnant at the time. When Sarah's son George was born, the royal couple sent her kind messages of congratulations, urging her not to hurry back to work. Sarah confessed to her friend:

> These very superior honours, as you may suppose, create me many enemies; but it was always so, and I must bear their malignity with the best grace I can.[11]

She was accustomed to evoking envy in others and to dealing with the consequences.

The following year Sarah wrote to her friend Thomas Sedgwick Whalley. She was unsettled, she confessed, by the news of the very close relationship that had developed between George, the Prince of Wales, the heir to the throne, and Maria Fitzherbert, a twice-widowed Roman Catholic, and as such deemed an unsuitable wife for him. Sarah did not spell out in her letter that George had gone through a secret, illegal marriage with Mrs Fitzherbert the previous month. She was careful not to be too judgemental. She noted that Mrs Fitzherbert was 'an example of propriety' – like Sarah herself. She approved of the fact that 'everything goes on with the utmost formality; provision made for children, and so on.'[12] Reaction to the news seemed to have been mixed but 'I have not heard what his mother says to it.'[13] Again, Sarah empathised with Queen Charlotte. Perhaps she was recalling her own mother's reaction to the news of her attachment to the young William Siddons. The whole royal family seemed to have been ill, she noted. She knew at first hand the effect of these emotional disturbances.

Fanny Burney was present when Sarah visited the Royal Lodge at Windsor in August 1787 to read Colley Cibber and John Vanburgh's play *The Provoked Husband* to Queen Charlotte. Although their paths had crossed previously – Fanny had been present, for instance, the evening at Mary Monckton's when the large crowd gathered simply to stare at poor Sarah – the two women had never been introduced or spoken to each other before now. Fanny wrote in her diary that she had heard Sarah was keen to make her acquaintance, but instead she had found the actress rather distant and solemn. Fanny had expected Sarah to be excited, even elated, by the honour the royal family were showing her. Instead, she seemed to take the chance to read to the royal family as a matter of course, as if this were a natural result of her great celebrity. By now Sarah must have been accustomed to being summoned for these readings. Perhaps she was less enthused about meeting Fanny Burney than Fanny was at the prospect of meeting her.

Sarah was able to slip easily from the life of being a royal courtier, with all its infinite rules of etiquette and petty snobberies, to that of the London stage, with its harsh critics and demanding audiences. Fanny, while aspiring to be a stage writer, found this far more difficult. Some eight years later Sarah appeared in a play Fanny had written called *Edwy and Elgiva*, which proved to be an unmitigated disaster. The audience laughed throughout, even when Sarah's character was dying on stage, not helped by her being brought out from behind a hedge, lying on an elegant sofa, to play one of the scenes. There was a popular drink at the time, sold in taverns, called a bishop, so the laughter became even more raucous when one of Fanny's lines for a character was 'Bring in the bishop.' As Sarah described it to Hester Piozzi, who knew them both: 'The Audience were quite angelic and only laughed when it was *impossible* to avoid it.'[14] The play had just one performance.

In 1791, one of King George and Queen Charlotte's sons, William, Duke of Clarence, started a relationship with the queen of stage comedy, Dora Jordan. Dora already had three illegitimate children by two different men, so she could never be accepted by the royal family. In the same way that Sarah had given her 'Three Reasons' speech to her loyal audience in Bath, explaining her decision to leave them to seek her fortune at Drury Lane, now Dora gave a speech to the London audience justifying her relationship with Clarence. Both women were seeking to control the message by talking directly to their fans. Dora and Clarence lived happily together for many years, with their large, growing family. Sarah, as the queen of stage tragedy, had always kept her distance from Dora. She was a potential rival, after all, and their professional and personal styles were very different. Dora's new life as the mistress of a member of the royal family now meant that Sarah was even more careful to keep her at arm's length, lest she alienate Clarence's parents. Both actresses had lived in Gower Street for four years, just a few doors apart, while Dora was still the mistress of Richard Ford. Yet Sarah never mentioned Dora in her letters or in later accounts of her own life. The royal patronage Sarah received was too valuable to risk.

As her career developed, Sarah increasingly often took the role of a queen on stage. As well as playing Constance in Shakespeare's *King John*, she also played Katharine of Aragon in another Shakespeare play rarely performed today, *Henry VIII*. This was another perfect Siddons role, that of the virtuous queen who has had wrong done to her through no fault of her own, but who bears her misfortune with enormous grace and forbearance. Sarah's brother John Philip's director's notes for the production reveal that he changed the action in the play for Sarah's trial scene to make her seem even more regal. Shakespeare has Katharine enter while the other actors simply kneel. But John Philip made much more of the moment. The other actors bowed as Sarah came in. She then knelt to say her prayers, with the entire cast standing and waiting in rapt silence until she rose from the cushion. Yet another favourite role, which Sarah played with 'undisputed supremacy' in James Boaden's words, was Volumnia, the hero's mother in *Coriolanus*, persuading her warlike son not to attack his enemies in Rome.[15] Later in life she delighted her fans by playing Hermione in *The Winter's Tale*, another queen who is badly treated by those close to her but who behaves with dignity despite her misfortunes. For Sarah's supporters it was evident that she was queen of the stage, and, as a loyal Briton, reflected the glory of the real king and queen.

Sarah was the first person, it transpired, to have an inkling that the king's mental health was beginning to suffer. Alone in a room with the king one day at Windsor Castle, she was surprised to find that he handed her a sheet of paper which was totally blank, apart from his signature at the bottom. The implication was that she could fill in whatever demand she wanted at the top, and whoever received it would believe there was a royal command to comply. The ever-loyal Sarah, with great presence of mind, said nothing to the king, but instead immediately took the paper to the queen, who thanked her profusely. Sarah made sure to include this anecdote in the notes she made for her authorised biographer, Thomas Campbell.

Historians have diagnosed George's illness as acute hepatic porphyria, a physical disease with mental side-effects, but today it is thought more likely that he was bipolar and at this stage was beginning to suffer a psychotic breakdown. Whatever its cause, the king's illness was to precipitate a constitutional crisis. Political parties were split as to whether his unpopular eldest son should now take over, while across the channel the French Revolution was beginning to rage and the monarchy there was proving dangerously unpopular.

Sarah, ever supportive of King George, played a key role in the celebrations at his recovery in 1789. She was fundamentally apolitical. But George's illness politicised her instinctive loyalty. Richard Brinsley Sheridan, who owned and managed the theatre where she worked, was far more interested in his own political career at Westminster than in the theatre at Drury Lane. And he was closely allied with the interests of the Prince of Wales rather than with King George. So now the king had recovered, Sheridan needed to demonstrate his continued loyalty to the crown. He arranged a gala evening, with a concert, a supper and a ball at Brooks' club, to be repeated later at the King's Theatre, Haymarket. The centrepiece of the gala was Sarah, whom he cast as Britannia. She recited an ode, written by a self-declared 'furious zealot of liberty', in which she voiced the wish of many of his loyal subjects that 'long may [the king] rule a willing land,' but also 'oh! forever may that land be free!' – unlike, by implication, the neighbouring country of France, where there had just been a revolution.[16] The applause for Sarah's ode was ecstatic, even more so when she sat down, copying exactly the pose in which Britannia is depicted on the British penny piece. She repeated her performance at a thanksgiving service at St Paul's Cathedral. The royal couple, genuinely relieved that the king had returned to normal, went weekly to the London theatres that spring, and Sarah, Dora Jordan and Elizabeth Farren played to full houses every night.

In August of the same year, the royal couple were holidaying in Weymouth. The Siddons were also at the seaside resort, since Sarah was not in good health and had been encouraged by her doctor to take some sea air. But during the visit to Weymouth, the royal family asked Sarah if she would put on a performance for them as Lady Townley in Cibber and Vanburgh's *The Provoked Husband*. On the day of the play, the king and queen decided to take a boat to Lulworth Castle, but a strong wind meant they could not get back to Weymouth by the time the performance was due to start. Loyal as ever, Sarah waited, along with all her cast and the entire audience. Finally, at ten o'clock that night, the royal party returned. Their servants were sent hurriedly to fetch their evening wigs, and the play began. It was out of the question that Sarah should refuse to perform so late at night.

On the same trip, Sarah wrote to her friend, Elizabeth Harcourt, that the queen had gone out of her way to compliment Sarah on her 4-year-old son George, saying that he was 'a very fine little boy and so civil'.[17] Sarah admitted that the maid had taken George onto the esplanade and that she herself would not have dared to do this when the king and queen were likely to be there, as George tended to be boisterous. The only time he was subdued, apparently, was when he went for a swim in the morning. Here, as always, there appeared to be no relationship at all between the royal family and Sarah's husband, William. Sarah guarded her personal connection with royalty; it was very much her preserve, a perk she enjoyed because of her fame.

Sarah may have instinctively felt more empathy towards King George and Queen Charlotte, but she was always careful to maintain good relations with their son, the future George IV. When, in 1798, she was invited by George, who was Prince of Wales at the time, to dinner at Brighton Pavilion, along with his latest mistress, Lady Jersey, the cause of the most recent of the scandals which always seemed to surround him, Sarah hesitated but then reluctantly agreed to attend. She was on tour at the time, but desperately anxious about her daughter Maria, who was terminally ill. The prince had insisted and, as Sarah rationalised it to herself 'nothing but death or deadly sickness will excuse one from obeying.'[18] Death and deadly sickness were very much in her mind.

In 1808 George, who was now the Prince Regent, came to open the New Covent Garden Theatre, where Sarah and her brother John Philip Kemble had been based for a few years. It poured with rain that day and Sarah wore a plume with black feathers in honour of the occasion. She also included in her private notebook at the time a prayer for the prince, in the hope that he might be able 'to vanquish and overcome all his enemies and difficulties which so awfully surround him in his personal life.'[19] She might be the ever-loyal subject, but Sarah knew enough of the Prince Regent's personal circumstances to be aware that he did not enjoy the stable family life which she herself valued so highly.

Sarah often played the part of queens, and her general demeanour was seen by her contemporaries as supremely regal. She was stage royalty. Her friend Hester Piozzi, for instance, wrote of her:

> At times, in private company, she gave one the notion of a wicked, unhappy Queen, rather than of a purely well-bred gentlewoman.[20]

Unsurprisingly, the royal family numbered among her fans. They liked to see her perform roles to which they could connect and became unashamed admirers of the Queen of Tragedy. The entire royal family forged a close relationship with Sarah, not only often coming to see her perform but also giving her an informal, unpaid role reading aloud. King George and Queen Charlotte went out of their way to show kindness and concern towards their great actress. For her part, Sarah was always totally loyal and sympathised with the problems the king and queen experienced with their oldest son. Their relationship benefited both parties.

Chapter 11

Revolution and Society

'Until then so noble a figure and a countenance
so expressive never stood before me.'[1]

Theatre always plays an important role in serving as commentary on what is happening in the real world. As someone who was always careful to avoid being controversial, Sarah had no personal desire to critique what was going on in society at the time. And yet she had a very particular relationship with her audience. They invested emotionally far more strongly in her than in anyone else on stage. She became a sort of vessel into which they poured their feelings and desires. As she grew older and more established, she was increasingly seen as a national treasure, someone who embodied the allegorical figure of Britannia, personifying the country itself. She represented traditional, patriotic, British values. By contrast, *Macbeth*, in which she played her most celebrated role of Lady Macbeth, came to be seen by her contemporaries as something subversive, as both a celebration of political revolution and a critique of it, inextricably linked in audiences' minds with what was happening just across the channel, in France. Inevitably, the subject matter resonated. Of course, as simply an actress rather than a theatre manager, Sarah had no role in programming which plays were to be put on at any time. And yet, paradoxically, she came to be seen both as someone who embodied establishment values and as someone who challenged them.

France was going through a bloody revolution, ridding itself of its monarchy and creating an entirely new form of government during the years when Sarah was at the height of her career. In time, once Napoleon seized power, France would declare war on Britain itself. At home, Britain was recovering from a disastrous war in America, where it had been forced to allow the rebel states across the Atlantic to declare independence. The balance of power between the monarch and parliament was shifting, and the king's debilitating bouts of illness were threatening to destabilise the status quo.

Sarah's stage persona as the tragic, noble heroine, patiently accepting the trials heaped upon her, made her a role model for many in her audiences. The artist Benjamin Haydon wrote that going to see Sarah had 'something of the feeling of visiting Maria Theresa.'[2] Sarah's unauthorised biographer, James

Boaden, wrote about how William Pitt the Younger had become Chancellor of the Exchequer aged just 23, in 1782, at the same time as Sarah, aged 27, took London by storm. Pitt became a powerful force in reconciling the various political factions after the fallout from the American War of Independence, and Boaden claimed that Pitt had taken his inspiration in the way he rose to the occasion from Sarah herself, 'our transcendent actress'.[3] Her dignity and nobility was something Pitt sought to emulate. And others in society followed his lead. Sarah served as a sublime example for all that was best in Britain.

Not that Sarah's reputation was always unblemished. She did not always lead the way to greater feeling, as if she were some higher being. If she became too closely linked to fallible politicians, then she exposed herself to satirical criticism. Early in her career, a cartoon entitled *The Orators' Journey* (Illustration 23), was critical of the 29-year-old Sarah, who is portrayed in her newly triumphant role of Lady Macbeth, as being too closely linked to Edmund Burke and to Charles James Fox, two of the leading politicians at the time. All three are seen riding a horse on the way to perdition. The cartoon's powerful message is that they are all doomed. Just as Lady Macbeth leads her husband to his eventual destruction, so here Fox and Burke are leading the country in entirely the wrong direction. And in so doing, so the cartoonist claims, they are aided and abetted by Sarah. As someone in the public eye, Sarah could never escape criticism entirely. She might like to be seen as a sublime tragic heroine, but even taking that stance, she was still sometimes fair game for satirists.

In general Sarah was careful not to express her own views politically. By contrast Richard Brinsley Sheridan was consumed by politics, to the detriment of Drury Lane, the theatre he owned and where Sarah worked. He was far more interested in promoting his own political career than he was in his company of actors, who often went unpaid as a result. In time he had so little interest in Drury Lane that Sarah's brother John Philip was made the manager, though Sheridan still controlled the purse strings. Warren Hastings, the first governor-general of Bengal, was accused of mismanagement and personal corruption during his time in Calcutta and was impeached by the British parliament in 1788. Sheridan gave the most powerful speech of his career in Westminster Hall as part of the trial, a speech which lasted four days. Sarah sat next to his wife throughout. She was moved to tears and even fainted at one point. As Catharine Macaulay, the Whig historian wrote: 'There Siddons ... looked with emotion on a scene surpassing all the imitations of the stage.'[4] Sometimes real life was more dramatic than the theatre.

As her career developed, Sarah increasingly played the role of queens who were almost exclusively noble and exalted. The essayist William Hazlitt wrote of her that she seemed to be almost godlike, of a different order from the rest of mankind, as if she had simply dropped down from heaven. Her image of queenliness was a sort of fairy-tale fantasy. When she portrayed a queen, that queen was nothing less than a sublime being. When George III's illness had looked as if it might mark the end of his reign, Sarah famously took on the role of Britannia in a nationalistic tableau, to give thanks for his recovery. In doing so, she was playing an important part in reassuring her audiences that all would be well.

These kinds of patriotic gestures became even more important when Britain found itself at war with France. 'The Siddons', as she became known, played characters with strong moral fibre – the noble mother as Isabella in *The Fatal Marriage*, the devoted daughter as Euphrasia in *The Grecian Daughter* or the supportive wife as Belvidera in *Venice Preserved* (see Appendix 2 for more details). In so doing Sarah was holding her audiences to a firm patriotic standard. Her onstage heroines, and as a result her offstage persona, came to embody the very best qualities which Britons felt they represented – fairness, bravery, stoicism, kindness. Revolutionary ideas might be swirling around, it was implied, but Sarah's strong female role models would shield her fans from them. As Archibald Hamilton, who saw Sarah perform in 1784, wrote to his friend Sir Charles Thompson:

> I trust and am persuaded that even these momentary impressions have a great and good effect even in so corrupt a society as ours.[5]

Sarah's stance was conservative (with a small 'c'). In some sense she kept female behaviour constrained, presenting a model of virtue which her audiences were encouraged to emulate. Today we would probably see her patriotism as jingoistic. But at a time of political turmoil, it was extremely powerful. The moral fibre of the characters she portrayed served to reassure her audiences, nervous at the threats from abroad and at the revolutionary ideas fermenting at home, that Britain would always remain safe.

The British theatre, in which Sarah had so central a part, played a vital role in creating a new kind of patriotism during these years. This was a deliberate attempt to counter the violent radicalism going on in France. The actors at Drury Lane almost became part of a national company, playing for and on behalf of the British people. It was not by chance that Sir Joshua Reynolds, as the first president of the Royal Academy, began encouraging a growing vogue for history painting at the same time. He wanted to encourage a portrayal of the story of Britain as something totemic. And Sarah began to be painted portraying historical characters such as Katharine of Aragon. She played a vital part in promoting this resonant story. As she grew older, increasingly, admiration for Sarah Siddons became almost a patriotic British institution.

Politically, perhaps the most important role Sarah played was that of Lady Macbeth. Across the channel, the French Revolution was raging. So the play came to be seen as a powerful fable of the dangers of conspiring to overthrow the reigning monarch and create a new form of government. And yet, as we have seen, Sarah's Lady Macbeth was not simply a portrait of evil. Sarah sought to understand what motivated her character. Her audiences were encouraged to empathise with a woman who was willing to sacrifice everything to further the ambitions of her husband. In the real world, outside the theatre, many people sympathised with the revolutionaries in France. Romantics such as the poet William Wordsworth and political thinkers such as the writer Mary Wollstonecraft travelled to France to experience the revolution for themselves. The Drury Lane productions of *Macbeth* gave people in theatrical form a way to respond to the social and cultural effects of what was happening to their neighbouring country and to the ripples which this had caused back home, regardless of where they themselves stood politically.

It feels surprising that, in 1790, only a year after the Storming of the Bastille, the Siddons decided to send their two eldest daughters to a finishing school in Calais. They were perhaps rather naïve. But many people in England failed to predict the years of violence and destruction that would follow the early stages of the revolution. When Sarah visited her daughters there in 1791, with William and a friend, Bridget Wynne, she seemed more concerned about her own health than about any physical danger from the political situation. In a letter to her friend Elizabeth Harcourt, she praised the simplicity and truth of Anglicanism as set against the Catholicism she had witnessed in France. But she also professed her support for the French people in their quest for a new form of government:

> the idea of so many millions throughout that great nation, with one consent, at one moment (as it were by Divine Inspiration), breaking their bonds asunder, filled one with sympathetic exultation, good-will and tenderness. I rejoiced with them from my heart, and most sincerely hope they will not abuse the glorious freedom they have obtained.[6]

She might have personified something proudly British on stage, but she could identify with her French hosts regardless. By 1793 the situation was too incendiary. The Siddons withdrew Sally and Maria from their finishing school and dropped plans to place their eldest son Henry in a school in France.

The execution of Queen Marie Antoinette the same year was viewed as deeply shocking by the public in Britain. No royal woman had died in this way in Europe since the unjust killings of Henry VIII's wives. Sarah – aged 38, just one year older than Marie Antoinette – was in Liverpool at the time and then in Dublin, both cities where there were many Catholic residents and great sympathy for the fate of the French queen, who was seen as an innocent victim. People read in the newspapers about how Marie Antoinette's trial had been rigged. The stories that she was grand and remote – the infamous 'Let them eat cake' remark – had not yet reached England and Ireland.

Sarah returned to London, pregnant with Cecilia, and the renovated Drury Lane Theatre reopened with her playing Lady Macbeth opposite her brother. The reverberations from France must have been upmost in the audience's mind as they watched Sarah playing a flawed queen who would do anything for her husband. She also played two other queens that season, Hermione in *The Winter's Tale*, and Katharine of Aragon in *Henry VIII*. She may often have been identified in the audience's mind with the plain, stiff, dutiful Queen Charlotte, but now she was also linked to the beautiful, romantic, tragic French queen, Marie Antoinette.

Sarah later owned a lace veil, nearly five yards long, which had belonged to Marie Antoinette. She only ever wore the veil on stage when she appeared in the trial scene of Hermione (herself a queen) in *The Winter's Tale*. It was lost in a fire when Covent Garden Theatre burned down in 1808. Sarah wrote to her Scottish friend, James Ballantyne, that it was probably worth at least £1,000 (£82,790 today) 'but that's the least regret. It was so *interesting!*'[7] She had been collecting clothing and jewellery for over thirty years, ever since the Siddons became financially secure during their time living in Bath, and she lost her entire collection that night. Yet it was the loss of the Marie Antoinette veil she felt most poignantly. Here was something previously owned by a beautiful, doomed royal, and purchased in turn by a stage royal. Sarah felt herself connected at a deep, personal level with the tragic French queen.

More generally, the new Romantic movement was also bringing about a greater freedom of expression in British society. The Age of Reason of the early eighteenth century was giving way to a much stronger emphasis on the power of feeling, of sensibility, as it was generally called at the time. David Garrick, actor/manager of Drury Lane in the generation before Sarah's, had ushered in a more naturalistic style of acting. But Sarah upped the emotional tempo on stage. She was not afraid to express violent, overwhelming emotions for her audience. And they then experienced the same emotions along with her. They cried, they screamed, they fainted, and they even sometimes vomited at her passionate portrayal of her tragic heroines. Sarah herself regularly fainted as she came off stage, so great were her exertions. In a society where expressing emotions was increasingly seen as laudable, Sarah was reflecting her age. But she was not simply passive. She was also leading the way. She was encouraging a sea change in people, away from thought and reason and towards feeling.

A further element to Sarah's make-up, which critics noted at the time, and which feels relevant both to the society she lived in and to how she should be seen today, is that she seemed to draw on both the masculine and feminine within herself. On the face of it her behaviour was almost invariably remarkably conventional. Women at the time were often described as timid, helpless creatures who relied on men. Sarah never thought of taking the lead in managing a theatre or writing or directing plays. Her marriage to William also appeared to operate along strictly conventional lines. And yet, when it was needed, she could call on what James Boaden called 'a male dignity'.[8] He used these words to describe how she stood on stage in front of the baying crowd at Drury Lane after her tour of Ireland. This male dignity 'raised her above the helpless timidity of other women.'[9] As for the men behind the scenes that night – her husband, Sheridan, Brereton and her brother John Philip – they left it to Sarah, 'this NOBLE BEING' as Boaden described her, to 'assert her innocence and demand protection.'[10] Describing another performance of Sarah's on a different night, Boaden noted that:

> The commanding height and powerful action of her figure, though always feminine, seemed to tower beyond her sex.[11]

To Boaden she epitomised the strong woman. She could maintain her femininity but balance that with a powerful masculinity.

Only a few years earlier any association with the theatre had been seen as tainting a woman's virtue. Frances Abington, who had been one of Garrick's theatrical company during Sarah's disastrous season at Drury Lane, had started her professional life as a courtesan. Yet the emphasis on respectability had been drummed into Sarah from an early age. When she did emphasise her femininity on stage, it was normally as a mother rather than a lover. Her ability to manipulate how her audiences saw her, so she came across as both masculine and feminine, as gender-blended, gave her a means of escaping, for the most part, any potentially scandalous sexual suspicion such as often dogged other actresses. It was known that Sarah studied hard when she was learning a new role. Being bookish was seen as a male virtue. Again, Boaden praised her for being able to put aside the cares and vexations of domestic life which meant, he explained, that she 'shews a mental firmness of the highest value' – as if she were a man, concentrating on the outside world rather than getting bogged down in domesticity.

Sarah might not have recognised herself as a political being, but she played an important and unique part in the society in which she lived. She was a role model to many of her fans, often taking the part of idealised queens. When Britain became embroiled in a dangerous war with France, she represented all that was best in being patriotically British. And yet, while she was known for being ultra-loyal to king and country, she was able at the same time to convey an enormous variety of emotions like no other performer.

With the emphasis the Romantic movement was beginning to place on the importance of feelings and in the power of sensibility, Sarah was very much a woman of her time. Her famous Lady Macbeth gave her audiences a chance to process their often conflicted reaction to the French Revolution, which was going on nearby. The play felt like a fable for the dangers of upsetting the political status quo and Sarah's empathetic performance meant that her audiences could live through Lady Macbeth's tragic trajectory along with their heroine. Sarah could also combine a tender femininity with a masculine bravery and strength which even her contemporaries noted as being particular to her alone. Understanding all these elements helps us grasp more fully the nature of Sarah's power.

Chapter 12

The Kembles

'My sister is married...and I thank God she is off the stage'[1]

Sarah had been born a Kemble, and her early training – after her false start in 1776 – had proven vital to her success. Although she became the leading tragic actress of her age, her birth family continued to play a central part in her life. Her great friend, the artist Thomas Lawrence, told their mutual friend, the diarist Joseph Farington, that Sarah was 'naturally a very grave character, but among her family she is easy, yielding and unaffected.'[2] And this closeness was not simply personal. Her siblings were all carving their own careers in the same profession at the same time as her. Several of them would play an important part in her career. Best known was her brother John Philip, just eighteen months younger than her, who not only acted alongside his older sister, but also managed Drury Lane and then Covent Garden. Her two other brothers, Stephen and Charles Kemble, also performed with her for many years. Her relationship with her sisters, both on and off stage, was not so straightforward.

Although John Philip Kemble's parents' wish for him was that he entered the Roman Catholic priesthood, he soon realised that his vocation was in the theatre. As we have seen, it was probably thanks to his sister that he was recruited by Drury Lane in 1783. Sarah tended to lobby for members of the Kemble family to join whichever company she was part of at the time. John Philip made his London debut, aged 26, playing the role of Hamlet. His performance was noted for its tenderness, in striking contrast to the far showier interpretation which David Garrick had favoured. John Philip's felt just the right Hamlet for a time when Romanticism was beginning to blossom.

John Philip was tall and imposing, like his sister, and he played the Shakespearean classical roles, notably Coriolanus (he had a Roman nose), to great acclaim. He was always a scholar-actor, fascinated by the text and dedicated to bringing it to life for his audiences. His maternal grandfather had had a special interest in preserving the integrity of Shakespeare's writing and John Philip inherited this mantle. It was largely due to his efforts that Shakespeare's plays continued to be performed during this period. John Philip always had a very notable pronunciation, never losing his Welsh lilt. The word 'virtue', for instance, he pronounced as 'varchue'.

John Philip's relationships with women were always complex. Elizabeth Inchbald and he had a particularly intimate friendship throughout his professional life. Early on, when Elizabeth was married to Joseph Inchbald, it was evident to those who knew them that she and John Philip were in love. Both shared a Catholic faith so it was expected that John Philip would propose as soon as Elizabeth's husband died. But instead, when that happened, John Philip contented himself in writing a Latin inscription on Joseph Inchbald's tomb, and addressing a blank verse ode to his memory but failing to propose to his widow. Elizabeth admitted to him many years later that she would have jumped at the chance of marrying him, but perhaps the very fact they were such firm friends dissuaded him. Elizabeth was his intellectual equal, and he always showed a lively interest in her various writing projects. He also relied on her to advise him whenever he was taking on a new role. When he was preparing to play Sir Giles Overreach in Philip Massinger's play *A New Way to Pay Old Debts*, for instance, he wrote asking her advice on his costume, admitting:

> I shall be uneasy if I have not an Idea of his Dress, even to the shape of his Buckles and what Rings he wears on his Hands.[3]

The two seemed to drift apart after their time together in Dublin, but John Philip nevertheless stayed at Elizabeth's lodgings when he came to London for his Drury Lane debut.

It was after John Philip's position as an actor at Drury Lane had become secure and it looked likely that he would start getting involved in the management of the theatre as well that he took the pragmatic decision to find a wife. Elizabeth Inchbald apparently did not fit the job description. The actress Priscilla Hopkins was the daughter of William Hopkins, the Drury Lane prompter who had been tasked with writing to the Siddons to give them the unwelcome news that their contract there was not to be renewed. Priscilla's mother had also been a successful actress at Drury Lane. Priscilla had married the actor William Brereton, who was rumoured to have had an unrequited passion for Sarah, and whose benefit night in Ireland had caused Sarah so many problems. Brereton's behaviour had become increasingly erratic and he was eventually sent to a lunatic asylum in Hoxton, where he died in February 1787, leaving Priscilla Hopkins, or Patty or 'Pop' as she was known, a widow.

Pop first came across John Philip in Dublin, when she was part of the company on tour with the Siddons, and he was the leading actor and involved romantically with at least two other women in the company. But now, only eleven months after her husband's death, to her surprise she found herself being chucked under the chin by John Philip, and informed, somewhat pompously, that she would very soon hear a piece of good fortune which would surprise her. She consulted her mother as to what this meant and her mother wisely guessed that John Philip meant to propose, advising her to accept the offer when it came. Her mother was right. Pop's new husband's behaviour on their wedding day proved characteristically eccentric. The two were married on 8 December 1787. When one of the female guests asked John Philip where he planned to hold the celebratory dinner, he replied he did not know. So the guest invited them to her house for an early meal, as the bride was performing at Drury Lane that night. Pop arrived alone but there was no sign of John Philip. Several of the guests wondered if he had forgotten about the celebration altogether. He did, however, finally appear, but soon afterwards his new bride was forced to leave for her evening's performance. Instead of accompanying her, John Philip stayed with his hosts and played with their children. Only once Pop had finished work did he collect her from the theatre and take her to their new marital home in Bedford Square.

Just a few months later, John Philip was made acting manager of Drury Lane Theatre by Richard Brinsley Sheridan. Tom King had resigned from the post that summer and Sarah had written in great excitement to her friend Sir Charles Hotham in September that her brother was to be made the deputy manager. Instead, John Philip took over the management itself the following month, publishing a piece in the press to reassure his detractors that he had not taken the post 'under *humiliating restrictions*', as had been reported, and that 'the power entrusted to me is perfectly satisfactory to my own feelings.'[4] This was the moment 31-year-old John Philip had been waiting for. He immediately introduced some of his own ideas into his productions at Drury Lane. His new production of *Henry VIII*, for instance, had his sister Sarah as Queen Katharine, and boasted new scenery, colourful costumes for all the actors and a splendid procession.

As time went on, in order to cope with the strain of his demanding working life, John Philip resorted to alcohol and, later, to opium. About seven years after his marriage to Pop, there was also a scandal concerning his behaviour towards a member of his company, the 21-year-old Austrian actress and dancer, Maria Theresa de Camp. She had been brought to England at 6 years old to appear on stage at the Opera House; she had learned English and continued working predominantly in musical theatre until she was recruited to appear for John Philip's prestigious company at Drury Lane. She was in rehearsal when John Philip, who was said to be very drunk, came into her dressing room without her consent and assaulted her. Her loud screams brought people to her rescue, but not before the crime had been committed. John Philip was forced to put a piece in the papers apologising for 'the very improper and unjustifiable behaviour' towards her:

> which I do further declare her conduct and character had in no instance authorised; but on the contrary, I do know and believe both to be irreproachable.[5]

There is no record of his sister Sarah's reaction to the news. She was appearing at Drury Lane that season, though not in the production for which Maria Theresa was rehearsing. Her own daughters were not much younger than the Austrian actress. As Hester Piozzi wrote to a friend on the subject, John Philip's public apology felt 'like that of a penitent Hackney coachman under the threatened Lash of a sharp prosecution.'[6] Hester believed that London society saw the incident as something to jest about, rather than as the crime it truly was. She was right. Today John Philip would have been dismissed. Instead, he carried on regardless.

John Philip's career was hampered by his relationship with his boss, the mercurial Richard Brinsley Sheridan. He tried resigning as Sheridan's manager in 1796 but then became embroiled yet again. Eventually, when relations with Sheridan failed to improve, he negotiated to take over the management of the rival Covent Garden Theatre. Inevitably, his sister joined him there. The various adventures at Covent Garden brought the two siblings closer again. But John Philip's health gradually deteriorated through overwork. While Sarah retired officially in 1812, John Philip continued until 1817 when he gave his final performance as Coriolanus.

The gout-ridden John Philip and his wife Pop then retired to Lausanne in Switzerland, where Sarah visited them in 1821 with her daughter Cecilia. John Philip had been forced to sell part of his fine library to the Duke of Devonshire to meet his living costs, but his sister and niece found their relatives living in a comfortable villa overlooking the lake. There, they went on an outing to Berne in the rain, ate chamois and mounted a glacier with two men cutting steps in the ice for them with hatchets. John Philip died two years later, eight years before his sister. His widow returned to England, first to live near Watford and then in Warwickshire, close to Guy's Cliffe, where she was buried in the Greatheeds' family vault.

Sarah also had a professional relationship with her next oldest brother, Stephen Kemble. Stephen was much less intense than John Philip, physically larger, rotund in shape, perfect to play the part of Falstaff. He was famous for acting the role in later life without needing to wear padding. In the autumn of 1783 both Sarah's oldest two brothers, John Philip and Stephen, made their debuts on the London stage – John Philip at Drury Lane, as Hamlet and Stephen at Covent Garden, as Othello. A rumour went around that the rival managements had struggled to recruit the 'great' Kemble and Covent Garden had by mistake hired the biggest, Stephen, rather than the best, John Philip. Stephen's older brother and sister proudly went to support Stephen and watch him perform at the famous Covent Garden Theatre. The *Morning Herald* reported the tears in Sarah's eyes at seeing Stephen's rendition of Othello. A couple of months later, in November 1783, Stephen married the talented actress Elizabeth Satchell, who was in the company.

Yet Stephen and Elizabeth Kemble seemed to struggle financially, unlike Stephen's two older siblings, though the family did what they could to support them. In 1788 Roger Kemble appeared at the Haymarket Theatre at a benefit for his daughter-in-law, Elizabeth, who by now had given birth to the couple's only daughter and would have their only son the following year. Stephen and Elizabeth grew close to Sarah's oldest son, Henry, and a short play written by Henry, *Modern Breakfast; or All Asleep at Noon*, was performed at the Haymarket for his uncle's benefit. The couple settled into performing for George Colman at the Haymarket, rather than appearing at either of the more prestigious, royal patent London theatres, Drury Lane and Covent Garden.

When Colman ran into financial difficulties, Stephen and his family relocated to the Theatre Royal, Edinburgh, and Stephen took over the management there. However, he soon found himself in a legal dispute over the finances and was quickly on the verge of bankruptcy. His famous elder sister came to his rescue, arriving to perform for him in June 1792, at the peak of her fame. She was pleased to write to a friend that she had made £800 for herself and £1,600 for Stephen's theatre on that trip (£103,600 and £207,300 respectively today). Hester Piozzi was less impressed by the support Sarah gave her brother, explaining that:

> Charming Siddons is somewhere in the North, setting up the individuals of her family, like Ninepins, for Fortune to bowl at, and knock down again. *She* meanwhile secures glorious immortality.[7]

When he could no longer make a living at the Theatre Royal, Edinburgh, Stephen worked as a freelance manager for a variety of theatres, mainly in the north of England and Scotland. He retired to Durham where he died, aged 64, nine years before his famous sister, an affable, likeable man but without the theatrical talent of either Sarah or John Philip.

Sarah's youngest brother, Charles Kemble, was twenty years her junior, a year younger than her own son Henry and the same age as her daughter, Sally. As a young man he was a member of the social circle which surrounded Sally and her sister Maria. Like his older brother, Charles went to Douai to study for the priesthood. He then started a career in the post office but soon realised, along with everyone else in the family, that his vocation was in the theatre. By the age of 17 he was playing Orlando in *As You Like It* in Sheffield. Sociable and easy-going, Charles did not have his sister's facility for tragedy, and was thought generally better as a comic actor. He often played romantic leads and the actor William Macready noted that he was a first-rate actor in second-rate parts. He first appeared in London aged 18, in April 1794, when his older brother John Philip opened the rebuilt Drury Lane Theatre. Charles played Malcolm in his brother's production of *Macbeth*, with John Philip in the title role and the pregnant Sarah as Lady Macbeth. Sarah's unofficial biographer, James Boaden, was critical of Charles' performance, explaining that he was:

> ardent and anxious to obtain applause – he sometimes became too boisterous in his action and too noisy in his speech – his voice was frequently not under government and pained the ear.[8]

There were rumours that John Philip did not encourage his brothers to act alongside him in case they rivalled his own acting skills, but Sarah admitted she preferred acting in *Venice Preserved* with Charles to appearing in the play with John Philip.

When Sarah's oldest daughter, Sally, died while Sarah had been away touring in Ireland, it was Charles who met his sister on the road as she returned from Shrewsbury, where she heard the terrible news, and took her to see their widowed mother, who was living at Sadlers Wells in London. He and Sarah were back on stage together at Covent Garden a few months later. The following year, in 1805, Charles married none other than the Austrian actress Maria Theresa de Camp, whom his older brother had assaulted ten years earlier. She was a year older than Charles and already pregnant. It is hard for us to compute that Maria Theresa could have married the brother of her attacker, but these were different times and the theatrical world they moved in was a small one.

The couple settled into a professional life acting together at Covent Garden, with John Philip as their manager. The theatre burned down, but they again appeared when it reopened, despite criticism in the press about the Kembles' nepotism and the high fees the various siblings commanded. Charles and his wife also lived next door to Sarah's country house, Westbourne Farm, for a time. As a couple, they clearly got on well with Charles's famous older siblings. Sarah retired formally in 1812 but returned for her youngest brother's benefit in 1813 and again in 1815, always keen to help raise money for him, despite adverse comments in the press about her now being too old to play the roles in which she was cast.

In 1819 John Philip's financial partner, Thomas Harris, died, and, in an act of generosity, John Philip made Harris's share over to Charles Kemble. The gesture was a supportive one, but it turned out to be problematic. Increasingly deaf, Charles did his best managing Covent Garden, but by now the great days of his brother and sister's glory had gone. Sarah asked that he carry her coffin when she died. Charles's eldest daughter Fanny became a well-known actress. Charles retired after Sarah's death and became an Examiner of Plays, travelling with his daughter Fanny to America to see her perform there. He died over twenty years after his older sister.

Sarah's professional relationships with her sisters were not as straightforward as those with her brothers. Although she was generally careful to keep their various disputes private, she did confide in her friend, the poet Samuel Rogers: 'Alas, after I became celebrated none of my sisters ever loved me as they did before.'[9] Sibling rivalry was clearly strong. It cannot have been easy for Sarah's younger sisters to see her, achieving stratospheric fame and success while they in turn remained jobbing actresses. True to form, Sarah often tried to persuade the management of whichever theatre she was working at that her sisters should be employed there, but her lobbying was not always successful.

The second eldest Kemble daughter, Frances, or Fanny, was four years younger than her famous older sister. As soon as Sarah was settled in John Palmer's company in Bath, she put pressure on him to hire Fanny. She was soon acting there alongside her sister. When the Siddons moved to London for Sarah's triumphant 1782 season, Fanny followed them. In January 1783 she played Alicia to her sister's Jane in Nicholas Rowe's *Jane Shore* and in March, Leonora to her Zara in William Congreve's *The Mourning Bride*. Both parts are the supportive secondary female role without the emotional range of the leads, taken by Sarah. This must have been galling enough for Fanny, who was said to resemble her sister, but worse she received mixed reviews and even had the audience call out some of her lines in anticipation of her saying them. As Sophia Weston noted:

> It is feared…[Sarah] will hurt herself by introducing a sister who is not at all approved.[10]

At the same time, Sarah ensured that her next youngest sister, Elizabeth, was also employed at Drury Lane. Elizabeth made her debut at the theatre playing Portia in *The Merchant of Venice* during the same season. As James Boaden described it, Elizabeth 'was not brought forward in the arrangements of the theatre' and only repeated Portia once again there. When John Philip then joined the company, it must have felt that the Kembles were taking over Drury Lane. That second season, Elizabeth Kemble played Rosalind in *As You Like It*, Alicia in *Jane Shore* and another of the female roles, Almeria, in *The Mourning Bride*. But something must have gone wrong between the sisters, since neither Fanny nor Elizabeth accompanied Sarah to Ireland for her second tour there.

Perhaps the problem was compounded by what was happening to yet another sister, Julia Anne (known as Anne), at the time. For Sarah, whose instinct was always to control the message and to maintain a veneer of respectability, Anne's eccentric behaviour was a constant concern. Nine years younger than Sarah, Anne had been born disabled and was only ever to walk with a limp. She married a Mr C Curtis (his Christian name is not recorded) when she was 19 years old, only to discover that he was already married. Just as Sarah was dealing with her own reputational damage following her two seasons in Ireland, Anne put an advert in the London newspapers, begging for financial help. She could, she stressed, pay for food for herself by doing needlework or by making artificial flowers, but she needed more money. She had clearly fallen on hard times. Worse, though, was the next paragraph. She was, the advert explained, the sister of Sarah Siddons and John Philip Kemble 'whom she has repeatedly solicited for relief, which they have flatly refused her.'[11] It was thanks to them, explained the advert, that she had been compelled to turn to the public to give her the support she so badly needed. A selection of addresses, including one just opposite Drury Lane Theatre, were given as places to leave money for her. Not only was she on the breadline, but she was prepared to make public the fact that her successful, wealthy siblings – her celebrity actress sister and her brother, who would soon become the manager of the very theatre she had included as a place to leave charitable donations – had done nothing to help her.

Next, Anne became involved with a Dr James Graham, who had set up his infamous Temple of Hymen, at Schomberg House in Pall Mall, the same building where Sarah would soon visit Gainsborough's studio to have her portrait painted. Graham was a showman who gave lectures to large crowds of admirers, claiming to be a pioneer in sex therapy. Graham's Temple of Hymen featured a Celestial Bed, adorned with flowers and turtle doves, which emitted aphrodisiac gases from a secret reservoir. Couples were placed in a tilting inner frame, supposedly to be positioned at the right angle to conceive, and organ pipes gave 'celestial sounds' which increased with the ardour of the bed's occupants. Graham regularly lectured his audiences on the importance of giving birth, explaining in graphic detail how to conceive, and arguing that sex should be seen as a patriotic act.

In 1783, just as the three older Kemble sisters were all performing in the company at Drury Lane, Anne also started giving lectures about chastity and female sexuality at the Temple of Hymen, entitled 'On the Influence of Women on Society'.[12] The literature announcing the lectures made it clear that Anne had:

> every appearance of possessing all the virtues of the sex, as well as talents and genius, which if not eclipsed by misfortune, would transmit her name with splendour to posterity.[13]

In other words, she was just as talented as her older sisters, but this had been 'eclipsed by misfortune'. She also published a volume of her own poetry, dedicated to Sarah's patron, the controversial Duchess of Devonshire. In one of the poems, she claimed that too much was expected of her, as Sarah's sister. A little sisterly jealousy was something Sarah was accustomed to endure, but this took things to a whole new level.

James Graham's enterprise soon failed, and he was forced to sell everything he owned and flee to Edinburgh. Again, Anne risked penury. This time she attempted to kill herself by swallowing poison in the precincts of Westminster Abbey. She was quickly rescued and reports in the press doubted whether she had really wanted to end her own life, but, as always, the situation reflected badly on her older sister, 'The Mighty Mrs Siddons', as she was referred to by her detractors in the press.[14] There is even some hint at a journalist trying to blackmail Sarah. Anne then started earning her living as a 'model' in a notorious London Bagnio or brothel under Covent Garden piazza. Prostitution was very far from Sarah's model of respectability. One of Anne's clients attempted to scare her by holding a pistol to his mouth and firing it several times. Anne herself was scornful, claiming he only dared to do this because the pistol was not loaded. So he then put the gun right by her face, pulled the trigger and lodged the contents through the socket of her right eye, blinding her in this eye in the process. The newspaper reporting the story described Anne as 'a woman of *uncommon intellect* and a *proud and strong mind*'. Her problems, it made clear, were not to do with her own personality but 'by the *avarice* of her *nearest relatives*'.[15] The following day Anne sought to put the story right. Perhaps her famous brother and sister had put pressure on her. She placed an advertisement in *The Morning Herald* stating that 'my relations never shut their hearts against me and are now alleviating my misfortunes by the *tenderest attentions*.'[16].

For a time, Anne's life seemed to improve. In 1792 she married William Hatton in Marylebone, at a church often used for Kemble family ceremonies. There is no record as to whether her oldest sister attended. Perhaps Sarah felt it wisest to stay away. Anne and William Hatton then set off for a new life in America, where Anne wrote the libretto for a hugely successful opera, *Tammany: The Indian Chief*, which was performed at the John Street Theatre, New York.

William Hogarth's engraving: *Strolling Actresses Dressing in a Barn*. British Museum. (© *Wikimedia Commons*)

William Siddons, Sarah's husband, by John Opie. National Gallery. (© *Wikimedia Commons*)

The young Sarah: George Romney's *Portrait d'une Femme*, previously attributed to Thomas Lawrence. Musée Cognacq-Jay. (© *Wikimedia Commons*)

Sarah's aristocratic friend, Henrietta Boyle, by William O'Hoare. National Trust. (© *Wikimedia Commons*)

Elizabeth Inchbald, friend to both Sarah and John Philip. *Mrs Joseph Inchbald* by Thomas Lawrence. (© *Wikimedia Commons*)

The Royal Crescent, Bath by Sir Thomas Malton, pictured around 1780, when the Siddons were living in the city. (© *Wikimedia Commons*)

Sarah's friend, Reverend Thomas Sedgwick Whalley: engraving from a portrait by Sir Joshua Reynolds. (© *Wikimedia Commons*)

Thomas Rowlandson's cartoon of Sarah, her brother John Philip and the actor John Henderson rehearsing in the Green Room. (© *Wikimedia Commons*)

Sir Joshua Reynolds' portrait of Sarah as *The Tragic Muse*. The Huntington Library, USA, and Dulwich Picture Gallery, London. (© *Wikimedia Commons. Photographer: Rennett Stowe*)

Thomas Gainsborough's portrait of Sarah. The National Gallery. (© *Wikimedia Commons*)

William Hamilton's drawing of Sarah as Euphrasia in *The Grecian Daughter*. Rijksmuseum. (© *Wikimedia Commons*)

John Bell's engraving of Sarah in the same role. (© *Wikimedia Commons*)

The Rival Queens of Covent Garden and Drury Lane Theatres (1782). Sarah is depicted bare-breasted, fighting with rival actress Mary Anne Yates. British Museum. (© *Wikimedia Commons*)

Henry Pierce Bone's 1797 painting, *The Sleepwalking Scene in Macbeth*, also known as Mrs Siddons as Lady Macbeth. Yale Center for British Art. (© *Wikimedia Commons*)

Henry Fuseli's *Lady Macbeth Seizing the Daggers.* Tate Britain. (© *Wikimedia Commons*)

Richard Westall's engraving of an older Lady Macbeth walking in her sleep. Metropolitan Museum of Art. (© *Wikimedia Commons*)

Thomas Rowlandson's 1804 print, *Melpomene in the Dumps, or Child's Play defended by Theatrical Monarchs*. Metropolitan Museum of Art. (© *Wikimedia Commons*)

James Gillray's cartoon of Sarah as a money-grabbing Melpomene. British Museum. (© *Wikimedia Commons*)

Thomas Lawrence's drawing of Sarah as Sigismunda, flanked by her youngest daughter Cecilia (top left), her oldest daughter Sally (bottom left), her second son George (top right) and her brother Charles (bottom right). British Museum. (© *Wikimedia Commons*)

Sarah's youngest brother Charles Kemble, by Henry Perronet Briggs. National Portrait Gallery. (© *Wikimedia Commons*)

George Harlow's *The Court for the Trial of Queen Katharine*, with Sarah at the centre playing the queen, surrounded by Kembles in other roles. Sir Joshua Reynolds had started a fashion for depicting British history. (© *Wikimedia Commons*)

Josiah Wedgwood immortalised Sarah in a medallion, dated 1784, which her supporters could buy. Wedgwood Museum, Stoke-on-Trent. (© *Wikimedia Commons*)

The Orators' Journey portraying Sarah as Lady Macbeth, riding to perdition with politicians either side of her. British Cartoon Prints Collection. (© *Wikimedia Commons*)

Sir Thomas Lawrence by Richard Evans. National Portrait Gallery. (© *Wikimedia Commons*)

Sarah's eldest daughter, Sally Siddons: an engraving after a drawing by her one-time fiancé, Thomas Lawrence. British Museum. (© *Wikimedia Commons*)

Sarah's second eldest daughter, Maria Siddons, in a mezzotint print by George Clint. Yale Center for British Art. (© *Wikimedia Commons*)

An engraving of Sarah's brother, John Philip Kemble, playing Rolla in Sheridan's successful production of *Pizarro*. University of Illinois, Urbana-Champaign University Library. (© *Wikimedia Commons*)

Hester Thrale Piozzi with her eldest daughter, by Sir Joshua Reynolds. Beaverbrook Art Gallery, Canada. (© *Wikimedia Commons*)

Sarah's dream house at Westbourne Green, near Paddington. British Library. (© *Wikimedia Commons*)

Sarah's niece, Fanny Kemble: lithograph from a painting by Sir Thomas Lawrence. (© *Wikimedia Commons*)

This time her marriage proved to be a lasting one. The couple returned seven years later and settled in Swansea, running a bathing house and lodgings.

One letter from Sarah to her sister Anne exists. Their mother, Sally Kemble, had recently died and it is this which prompted Sarah to write. The tone is proud and distant. She addresses Anne as 'My dear Mrs Hatton'.[17] To Anne's credit, she had clearly been involved looking after their mother in her final months. Sarah is scrupulously polite in writing that it gives her pleasure that Anne has been released from the attendant cares and troubles of looking after Sally. She hopes, she writes 'that the remainder of your life will run on smoothly, peaceably and respectably.' As always, for Sarah, respectability represents something to be hugely prized. It was their parents who had drummed these values into the extended family, after all. The clear subtext is that to date Anne's life had been very far from respectable.

Sarah informs Anne that her sister will, in time, receive a small inheritance from their mother's will. But she is at pains to point out that this is down to their brother John Philip, who has petitioned their parents on Anne's behalf. As Sarah puts it, gloves off:

> I have spared no pains to conciliate my brother on your behalf and the shocking contrast of impropriety and insolence contained in your letters... is not lost upon any of us.[18]

As far as Sarah is concerned, her sister's pleas for money have just been plain rude. It is highly unusual for Sarah to be so forthright in her correspondence with anyone. Her rage spills onto the page. So angry is she that she is prepared to commit herself in writing, knowing that Anne may well leak her letter to the press. At a later point she relented and herself paid Anne an annual stipend of £20, which she made sure to specify in her own will would continue after her death (at £1,727 today, it was not enough, surely, for Anne to live on).

Once Anne's husband William died, Anne opened a dancing school in Kidwelly and spent more time concentrating on her writing. Today her novels are enjoying a renaissance. Under the pseudonym of Ann of Swansea, she wrote fast-paced plots with colourful Gothic themes, strong women characters and perceptive social insights. She carefully steered away from creating any famous actress characters who were high-handed towards their sisters. Whereas Sarah had little time to promote her Welsh identity, apart from one quick visit to an ancestor's grave, for Anne making her home in Wales turned out to be a far better solution than life in London's maelstrom, in her famous sister's shadow.

The lives of Fanny and Elizabeth Kemble, Sarah's two other sisters, followed a more traditional route, and one which caused Sarah less heartache. Fanny had an unsuitable, ill-tempered suitor, a George Steevens, but then, in 1786, she married Francis Twiss, a Shakespearean scholar, who was said to have had a huge crush on Sarah. Their eldest son, Horace Twiss, grew up to become Sarah's favourite nephew and a Conservative MP. He wrote the farewell speech she gave at her retirement. At one point Sarah left her children with the Twisses in Norfolk, while she and William went on yet another tour in Ireland. The Twisses remained close confidantes of the Siddons. Francis Twiss published a Shakespearean index in 1805, dedicated to John Philip. The couple opened a girls' school in Bath in 1807. Fanny died nine years before Sarah, and her husband six years after his wife.

Elizabeth Kemble was the better actress of the two younger sisters who acted professionally alongside Sarah. Thomas Campbell once remarked, in a back-handed compliment, that Elizabeth was 'just what Mrs Siddons would have been if she had swallowed a bottle of champagne.'[19] In 1785, a few years after Sarah had huge success with her new interpretation of Lady Macbeth, Elizabeth married a jobbing actor, who had also worked as a dentist, a Charles Edward Whitlock. The wedding took place in Lancaster. Elizabeth was clearly no longer part of the Drury Lane company. Eight years later the couple emigrated to the United States and Elizabeth made a name for herself in tragedy there. A contemporary even described her as being, for a time, the leading tragic actress in America. Better, doubtless, to forge her own career out of the shadow of her multitalented older sister. Elizabeth was in the States at the same time as her sister Anne, although there is no record as to whether she saw the opera for which Anne had written the libretto. It is tempting to imagine the two sisters meeting up in New York, bonding over their sibling rivalry with Sarah.

The Whitlocks returned in 1805 after ten years abroad, when Sarah described Elizabeth, as 'A noble, glorious creature, very wild and eccentric.'[20] Other observers described Elizabeth as succumbing to the Kemble tendency to run to fat but having a remarkably affable personality. The Whitlocks soon settled in Newcastle and acted there. Sarah told her friend James Ballantyne that she had known nothing of Elizabeth, since Elizabeth was a child. Clearly her sister's performing with her at Drury Lane in the early days were best forgotten as far as Sarah was concerned. One final sister, Jane, had even less of a relationship with Sarah, being twenty-two years younger than her. She married, moved to Edinburgh and brought up six children.

Sarah might have been the Queen of Tragedy, reigning supreme on the London stage, but she nevertheless remained the eldest sister of a dynasty of actors and actresses, all of whom were forging their own careers in the same world and at the same time as her. Her eldest brother John Philip's working life was in every way as illustrious as his older sister's. He managed the theatres where she worked and performed alongside her. Professionally, the two were joined at the hip. Sarah's two other brothers, Stephen and Charles, also had good acting careers and were to be seen on stage with her, playing supportive roles. It was not so simple with her sisters. She and Fanny had a good relationship, although it was accepted that Sarah was the more talented sister. For Elizabeth, her next sister, it was more nuanced. Sarah seemed to airbrush Elizabeth's early performances at Drury Lane out of the picture, as if they never existed. Elizabeth had to resort to emigrating to the United States in order to make a name for herself away from her older sister's shadow. The most problematic relationship was with Anne, disabled from birth, and further injured as an adult, who was endlessly short of money and forever threatening to drag Sarah into the scandals which never seemed to leave her. Sarah's patience with Anne ran thin, although she did eventually pay her sister an annual stipend. The strong sibling rivalry that all the Kembles must have experienced as children is clear to see in their interactions as adults. For Sarah, the presence of her siblings in her professional life was something she simply accepted. It brought with it both advantages and disadvantages. There would never be any escape for her from it.

Chapter 13

Working Life in the Theatre

*'it depends on Mr Sheridan, who is uncertainty personified.
I have got no money from him yet'*[1]

As a lead actress in one of the only two licensed London theatres, Sarah's days there followed a set pattern which lasted all her working life. The London season ran from September through to about June. However, Brinsley Sheridan was notoriously unreliable when it came to paying his London company. As a result, Sarah often had little option but to go on tour between the seasons at Drury Lane. The tours proved to be highly lucrative, but, despite the huge sums she earned, there were always money worries. The London theatre managements, like Sarah herself, were always anxious about bringing in as much revenue as they could. As a result, during Sarah's working life, both Drury Lane and Covent Garden were remodelled and enlarged to accommodate more seats and therefore to bring in more receipts. But the vast new auditoria demanded a very different acting style, which did not necessarily play to Sarah's strengths.

Sarah's working days and nights were structured for her. Rehearsals began at 10 am and if she were late or absent, she risked being heavily fined. Although the actors rehearsed in the same room, they often worked separately in different corners, going through their own lines and actions, or practising sword work or dance steps. Actors worked from 'sides' with their own words written out for them. They would only see the play itself right towards the end of the rehearsal period. Hannah Pritchard, the previous actress to have made the part of Lady Macbeth her own, was said never to have read the whole play. Sarah was unusual in the depth of research she undertook to get a part exactly right. For Lady Macbeth (as previously mentioned in Chapter 6), she went to see some sleepwalkers for herself and even visited an asylum. Inevitably, the rehearsal system encouraged actors to develop their own roles in competition with their fellow performers, rather than working as a supportive whole, as theatre companies do today.

If Sarah were performing that night, she would be required to be on stage at 7 pm. Usually, the evening's entertainment would consist of a performance of the main play, in which Sarah took the lead female role, and which almost certainly ran to five acts, followed by a shorter afterpiece, usually made up of two acts. In the intervals the audience were entertained by songs and dances. Sarah's many fans would often come specifically to see her. When she first appeared as Constance in William Shakespeare's *King John*, in 1783, the character only appeared in a few particularly dramatic scenes, during the first half of the play. Once Sarah had left the stage, the auditorium noticeably emptied. Her audience had no interest in seeing how the play concluded without her.

The London theatres operated as repertory companies with a group of actors hired for the season, who were required to perform in whichever productions the management decided to put on. The system was biased towards revivals, so that rehearsal time could be kept to a minimum. Actors had their roles assigned to them and became known over the years for playing a certain part again and again. Sarah's repertoire was very specific, as we have seen, confined largely to the popular tragic heroines of the time. As she aged, she expanded it to play older parts such as Queen Katharine in *Henry VIII*, Constance in *King John*, and Hermione in *The Winter's Tale* (see Appendix 2). Sarah was unusual in this nod towards the ageing process. Audiences were accustomed to seeing actors and actresses grow old in the same parts without questioning that a 40-year-old was playing Juliet. The practice was totally accepted, just as audiences ignored the fact that actresses were often heavily pregnant.

Certain roles became associated in audiences' minds with certain actors. To cast someone new was to challenge the status quo. In November 1784, for instance, Sarah was cast as Margaret of Anjou in Dr Franklin's *The Earl of Warwick* even though Mary Ann Yates, one of her rivals during her disastrous first Drury Lane season, was felt to have 'owned' the role. An actor or actress taking on someone else's role made it look as if they were usurping that person's position. Sarah was also criticised for appearing too frequently on stage. She should, said one commentator, 'never perform more than once a week, or twelve times in a season.'[2] But she needed to earn, and to do so she performed as often as she could.

There was no health and safety in the London theatres as we would recognise in working practice today. Playing Desdemona opposite her brother John Philip, Sarah was forced to lie for long stretches at a time on a damp bed, and as a result she developed rheumatic fever. She would be troubled by pains in her limbs for the rest of her life. Thomas Campbell, Sarah's official biographer, called this 'criminal negligence', but another biographer, writing about forty years later, disagreed, arguing that these were risks actors were expected to take.[3] Later in Sarah's career, she was playing Hermione in *The Winter's Tale* when her costume caught fire and she was nearly burned alive. In true heroic form, she made great play of helping the man who had rescued her by lobbying to obtain a pardon for his son, who had been condemned by the courts to a lashing.

From June to September every year, London actors toured the various theatres outside the capital. Sarah's lifetime saw a huge expansion in these theatres, as they gradually freed themselves from the draconian laws which had existed when she was a child. Audiences outside London knew Sarah already from the engravings of her portraits and from reading reviews of her performances. They would flock in huge numbers to see her play the roles with which she was associated. During her first tour of Ireland, in 1783, for instance, fresh from her huge success in London, Sarah repeated the same roles she had played back at Drury Lane. The Irish audiences had no wish to see her in anything new, and besides there would not have been time to rehearse anything different.

The following year, Sarah went on tour to Edinburgh. Her Victorian biographer, Percy Fitzgerald, gave a helpful breakdown of her takings there. She played for nine nights, and made £467 (£60,780 today), but this was augmented partly by gifts from aristocratic gentlemen fans, partly by what she made from her own benefit night, and partly by various other presents, to reach an impressive grand total of £967 (£125,900 today). These kind of takings for a mere ten evenings' work, put Sarah's money worries into perspective – they were not entirely rational. The management kept £347 of her fees as their expenses (£45,160 today), but the general feeling was that they had taken too little a cut. It was usual for star actors to give a further generous amount to the regional theatres where they performed, but nothing was forthcoming from the Siddons. Their reputation for meanness was already establishing itself. Inevitably, resentment grew towards the couple from the provincial actors working alongside Sarah. These actors' salaries were paid by the management of the theatres and the less the management made, the less they received.

The regional theatres were often uncomfortable places to work, and the travel between them exhausting. In 1785, pregnant with her son George, Sarah played in Manchester, Leeds, Liverpool, Edinburgh, Glasgow and Belfast. Someone in Glasgow declared 'she was a fallen angel!'[4] But a rival actress, Perdita Robinson, wrote that her success was due to 'the folly of whim, novelty and fashion'.[5] Perhaps both were right. Sarah was known for her stoicism. She never feigned illness, and if her ill health meant that she had to call off on an individual evening, she always made sure to begin again as soon as possible. Sometimes she would arrive at a venue unclear even which play she was to perform that night. Her costumes frequently got lost on the way.

As soon as the play was over every evening, servants arrived to queue through the night for their masters. Once the box office opened in the morning, seats for the next performance could be secured. Audiences in the regions were less predictable than those in London. One night Sarah was in Leeds playing the sleepwalking scene in *Macbeth* when a boy appeared on stage with a glass of beer for her. She kept motioning him away, but he refused to leave the stage until the whole house had collapsed in gales of laughter. Another time, also in Leeds, Sarah's character drank poison on stage, when a heckler called out 'Soop it oop, lass!' and again the audience fell about, and even Sarah (who was known for always remaining in character) saw the funny side of things.[6]

At the end of July 1786, Sarah went to Tate Wilkinson's theatre in York, where she had learned her trade as a young actress, as part of her summer tour. Wilkinson gives a detailed account of this time with him in his memoirs. She was a huge success with the audience in York. Every single box at the theatre was sold out six months in advance. Wilkinson described the time as 'the Siddonian year'.[7] Mobs followed Sarah everywhere. On the evening of 3 August, when she played Belvidera in York, the receipts for that night alone amounted to £192 9s 6d (£26,490 today), the greatest sum ever taken in Britain up to that point for an evening in the theatre outside London. Overall, for her seventeen nights on tour with Wilkinson, Sarah made £1,100 (£151,400 today), but Wilkinson himself was left with only £128 (£17,620 today), hardly worth the effort on his part.

Wilkinson's tour went to Hull, then back to York for three nights only, where the roar from the crowd was so loud not a single word of the plays could be heard. Next the company went to Leeds. There, Tate received angry letters from the theatre in Wakefield, complaining that they had been neglected, so Sarah and Wilkinson extended their schedule to fit in an extra night in Wakefield before Sarah headed on to Liverpool. 'Good God!' as Tate wrote, 'what real fatigue.'[8] While Sarah did well from the box office receipts, as always, Tate only made £4 from the night in Wakefield, (£550.60 today) despite his costs amounting to £62 14s 11d (£8,637 today). For Sarah, performing in these smaller venues, where the adoring audience could see her close up, was a wonderful experience. She told friends that she was happier and more confident here than she ever was on the London stage.

Three years later, in 1789, Sarah again went on an extensive summer tour. She visited York, Leeds, Wakefield and Sheffield in the north. Tate Wilkinson wrote of her time there:

> I heard Mrs Siddons say, that acting Isabella out of London was double the fatigue; ...[but] there the applause on many of the striking passages... invigorated her whole system.[9]

She then toured the south, via Liverpool and Birmingham, taking in Plymouth, Truro, Weymouth (where she played Lady Townley in Colley Cibber's *The Provoked Husband* for the king and queen) and then Exeter. At the end of the tour, Sarah wrote to her friend Elizabeth Harcourt, 'I shall have done with tragedy for a long, long time.'[10] Her health was suffering. In 1795, for the first time, William went to Bath to seek a cure for his rheumatism and Sarah toured alone, ignoring her own poor health. She wrote to her friend Thomas Sedgwick Whalley in August that she had travelled over 900 miles that summer.

Even when her daughter Maria was dying, in 1798, Sarah still went on a short tour to keep the money flowing in. By now she must have become so accustomed to touring every summer that she could not contemplate simply staying by Maria's bedside. Luckily, she was there at the end. The following year, despite her own ill health, Sarah embarked on yet another punishing tour of Bath, Bristol, Newcastle, Edinburgh, Glasgow, Lancaster, Pontefract, York, Leeds, Wakefield, Doncaster, Sheffield and Hull, accompanied by her other grown-up daughter, Sally, whose own soon-to-be fatal lung disease was worsening. Meanwhile William stayed behind and negotiated hard with Brinsley Sheridan for the right fee for his wife to appear again at Drury Lane.

It was always about money. This was despite the fact Sarah made more money from her appearances than anyone else previously recorded on the English stage. The recurring pattern emerged whereby Sarah would exhaust herself performing, all the time dreaming of a quiet country cottage to which she could retire. As early in her career as December 1785, when she was only 30 years old, she wrote to her friends the Whalleys:

> I have three winters' servitude, and then, with the blessing of God, I hope to sit down tolerably easy, for you know I am not ambitious in my desires.[11]

The following year she confided that she now had the £10,000 she needed in order to think about retirement (£1,348,000 today). And yet she continued. As late as 1807 she was still writing to her friend Charlotte Fitzhugh that she just needed to add £300 a year to her present income (£25,400 today), and then she would be perfectly well provided for.

By 1788, Sarah's brother John Philip had become the manager at Drury Lane. But the owner, Richard Brinsley Sheridan, remained as unforthcoming as ever when it came to paying his company of actors. The following year, suffering from the after-effects of yet another miscarriage, Sarah withdrew her services from Drury Lane in protest at not having been paid, and instead undertook a lengthy provincial tour. She described to a friend what it was like trying to get Sheridan to pay her what he owed. On one occasion she went to Sheridan's house with that specific purpose and emerged looking radiant. When asked how it had gone, she admitted that she felt she had succeeded. The two of them had had a long talk, she explained, during which Sheridan revealed to her the extent of his financial difficulties. He had promised faithfully to pay everything he owed her the following month, provided she advance him £50 now (£6,540 today). And she did so.

When Sarah finally withdrew her services, Sheridan, who preferred comedy to tragedy, reputedly boasted that Drury Lane would get by without their Queen of Tragedy, and that he would schedule comedies instead. But, in December 1790, halfway through her brother John Philip's third season, Sarah returned to Drury Lane. Sheridan had finally realised he did indeed require her services and had settled his arrears with her. William described his wife's benefit performance as 'a golden letter day'.[12] *The London Chronicle* reported that the applause celebrating her return lasted an entire five minutes. There was frenzied shouting too from the audience. Yet several newspapers noted that Sarah looked unwell.

The following summer, in June 1791, Drury Lane was closed for it to be demolished and a much larger theatre built in its place. Sheridan wanted a bigger space, to make more money. The company were to move to the Opera House in the Haymarket, also known as the King's Theatre, for two years. Occasionally, when the King's Theatre was booked for operas and oratorios, the company performed at the more intimate Little Haymarket Theatre, which was more suited to Sarah's natural style.

The architect Henry Holland was commissioned to design the new Drury Lane Theatre. Sarah, still unwell, enjoyed her summer staying with friends and drinking the waters at Harrogate. In January 1792, though, she was back in London, somewhat diffident about having to perform there once more. The Opera House was much larger than the old Drury Lane, and this did not suit Sarah's empathetic, emotional style of acting. Yet she knew this was the future. The new, enlarged Drury Lane would cause the same problems, unless she learned to adapt. Her unofficial biographer, James Boaden, described her as becoming increasingly 'grand and imposing' on stage.[13]

Sarah had been taken by Greek and Roman statues, and her new style sought to emulate their strength. She walked more regally, acting from the shoulder, as Boaden described it, using her arms to great effect. Her costume and hair, too, were deliberately influenced by the classical. The love of the Classical Age was all-pervading at the time. Even women's fashion – high-waisted, white muslin dresses – was part of the aesthetics of neoclassicism. The aim was that women should look like living statues. Sarah increasingly played to this. Portraits painted of her began to emphasise her statuesque figure rather than giving details of her actual expression, as if she were a statue rather than a person. The sculptor Thomas Campbell (no relation of her biographer) made a relief of Sarah dressed as a Roman matron, and his posthumous statue of Sarah in Westminster Abbey again showed her looking like a classical heroine. After all, her tragic roles were classical in influence and timeless, just like his representation of her.

On 12 March 1794 the new Drury Lane Theatre opened its doors for the first time with a concert of sacred music. The interior was disproportionately vast. Its total new capacity was for an audience numbering 3,611, some in four tiers of boxes, some in the pit, some in the two-shilling gallery, and some in the upper gallery. A full house would bring in £826 6s per night (£101,000 today) for Sheridan's management. Nothing the like of it had ever been seen before. So much had been spent on the interior that the exterior was unfinished and would remain that way.

On Easter Monday John Philip staged a spectacular new production of *Macbeth* with himself as the hero and his famous sister as Lady Macbeth, as their first appearance in the new auditorium. Sarah was six months pregnant with her youngest child. At the start of the evening a brand-new iron fire curtain rose to reveal a lake made of real water with its own waterfall. The actress Elizabeth Farren spoke the prologue, defying the element of fire ever to dare to destroy this new theatre. No longer would audiences go to the theatre primarily to support their favourite actor or actress. After all, the performers were now distant figures in the huge auditorium. Instead, design and stagecraft were to be all. The new theatre was, as Sarah described it to a fellow actor 'a wilderness of a place'.[14] She would perform there nineteen times that season. Her friend Hester Piozzi confessed her own fears that Sarah's reputation as being grasping when it came to financial remuneration would only worsen as a result.

Sarah, whose youngest daughter, Cecilia, was born in July, was forced to meet with Sheridan just a few days after giving birth, to discuss the unpaid salary he owed her. She wrote to a friend:

> I wish they could…leave me the comfort and pleasure of remaining in my own convenient house and taking care of my baby.[15]

The following year Sarah told Samuel Rogers that she got into her carriage to return from performing in the theatre one night, when Sheridan jumped in after her. Sarah immediately made it clear that she expected him to behave with propriety and not assault her. If he made a move, she said, she would wind down the window and shout out to the servant. He refrained from touching her, but as soon as they reached her house in Great Marlborough Street he bolted out of the door, anxious to escape unseen. To work for someone this erratic and threatening undoubtedly took its toll.

Meanwhile the company at Drury Lane had become embroiled in one of the great theatrical scandals of the century over the production of a play called *Vortigern*, purporting to be by William Shakespeare, but in fact the work of a father and son, both named William Henry Ireland. In February 1795 the father had put on an exhibition of new papers he claimed to have discovered and to have been the work of Shakespeare. Even James Boaden was initially taken in and wrote how excited he was at the discovery. At the same time the son set about writing an apparently entirely original, previously undiscovered Shakespearean tragedy, *Vortigern*. That September Sheridan signed a contract agreeing to stage a production of *Vortigern* at Drury Lane. By the beginning of the following year, he was beginning to have his doubts about the authenticity of the piece. Boaden also changed his mind and made his views public. Both Sarah and John Philip were sceptical. But Sheridan, ever the showman, decided to press ahead. He felt sure the play would be a commercial success, regardless of its true authorship.

Sarah deftly managed to get herself out of the production. Her weak health, she wrote, meant that she could not rehearse, let alone perform. This was not something which had ever stopped her in the past. But John Philip was forced to appear in the play, although he refused to have it billed in the programme as being the work of William Shakespeare. Sarah's comedy nemesis, Dora Jordan, was more gullible, and happy to be cast opposite John Philip. The audience became increasingly sceptical as the play continued. By the third act, laughter at the action was so loud that John Philip had to appeal for silence. Yet William Henry Ireland, the forger, was convinced John Philip had deliberately sabotaged the production by miscasting it and playing it for laughs. This was only confirmed for him when the fire curtain came down directly onto one member of the cast, who was playing a dead body at the time. When the audience heard the play was to be given a second performance, they rose in uproar and the management changed its mind. Sarah had had a lucky escape.

Nevertheless, as the year progressed, her situation with the Drury Lane management only worsened. In May she wrote to a friend from Newport Pagnell, on her way to yet another gruelling tour. She might be appearing at Drury Lane as usual, but:

who can tell? for it depends on Mr Sheridan, who is uncertainty personified. *I have got no money from him yet;* and all my last benefit, a very great one, was swept into his treasury.[16]

William tried in vain to resolve the issue. That autumn John Philip decided he could tolerate Sheridan no longer and resigned as manager, agreeing to stay on in the company as the lead actor. Richard Wroughton took on the role of manager, but it soon became evident he did not have John Philip's flair. As Wroughton was a friend of Dora Jordan's, it was assumed that the programme that year would favour comedies over tragedies. But the leading ladies in the company,

Sarah herself, together with Dora and Elizabeth Farren, all refused to appear unless they were paid. Sheridan, though, knew how to get round Sarah. If he begged hard enough, turning up at her house in his carriage and pledging his honour, she would agree. By November she was writing to a friend:

> Our theatre is going on, to the astonishment of everybody. Very few of the actors are paid, and all are vowing to withdraw themselves: yet still we go on.[17]

In a production of Nicholas Rowe's *Tamerlane*, Sarah was required to faint during the action but, in doing so, she hit her head badly. It was evident as she lay on stage, her limbs exposed to the audience since her costume had fallen away, that something was wrong. The accident felt like a metaphor for everything that was unstable backstage. Elizabeth Farren finally retired, to marry her long-term lover, the Earl of Derby, and Sarah's farewell speech, written by Hester Piozzi, complimented her a little too heartily on being able to give up life as an actress. Despite the increased receipts at the enlarged Drury Lane, Sheridan was still neglecting to pay his actors. By now Sarah was owed £2,000 in unpaid wages (£209,200 today). It was, as she wrote to a friend:

> swallowed up in that drowning gulf, from whom no plea or right or justice can save its victims.[18]

Sheridan's expensive lifestyle as a politician was always more interesting to him than his ventures in the theatre. But he knew that he needed to keep the money rolling in at Drury Lane. He translated a German melodrama by August von Kotzebue called *The Stranger* and cast Sarah in the female lead. When it was staged at Drury Lane in March 1798, the play immediately became a controversial success. Sarah took the part of Adelaide Haller, whose marriage had come to an end because of her extramarital affair, and who has been forced to abandon her husband and children and move elsewhere. John Philip played her husband. The plot follows the gradual reconciliation of husband and wife. Very unusually for the time, Mrs Haller is not judged for her actions. The original English translator, Benjamin Thompson, had written a version where Mrs Haller was entirely innocent of adultery, but Sheridan went back to the more controversial German idea, and his commercial instinct proved to be correct.

The play was billed as a comedy because no-one dies at the end. Instead, Sarah's character is tearfully reunited with her children and the implication is that the Hallers will be reconciled. In four months, Sarah played the role twenty-six times. In their poem *Rejected Addresses*, Horace and James Smith sent up the blank verse in which the play was written:

> And chop and change ribs à-la mode Germanorum
> And high diddle ho-diddle, pop tweedle dee.[19]

As William Makepeace Thackeray put it, the whole play was 'balderdash'. Yet at its core there was 'that reality of love, children and forgiveness of wrong which ... sets the whole world sympathising.'[20] Sarah had her own marital woes at the time she played the role and would return home markedly saddened every evening she performed it.

The year after her daughter Maria's death, Sarah took part in a second triumph for Sheridan at Drury Lane. He had again taken a play by August von Kotzebue and made it his own. This time *Pizarro* followed the Spanish conquest of Peru, and Sarah was cast as a camp follower, Elvira, Pizarro's mistress. Sheridan knew that with Sarah in the cast, he would fill the cavernous Drury Lane, so he negotiated hard with William for her services. With fears growing at a likely invasion by revolutionary France, the play chimed with its audience.

Sarah and Sheridan argued throughout rehearsals over the tone she should take in her role. True to form, Sarah believed Elvira should be honourable and noble, whereas Sheridan saw her as a much broader, fallen woman. John Philip, who was playing Pizarro, stood back over this dispute and refused to take sides, merely noting that his sister had 'made a heroine out of a soldier's troll.'[21] The disorganised Sheridan grated the nerves of his cast by only giving them the last act to learn on the day of the first performance itself. That night an Amazonian Sarah appeared wearing a plumed helmet. She stole the show. Yet again, Sheridan was forced to concede.

The following season John Philip was reinstated as manager at Drury Lane. His hope was that he and Sarah could buy into the title there and become part owners, but this plan came to nothing. Instead, the money problems simply continued as before. A letter from John Philip to his junior urges him to hurry £50 round to the Siddons house immediately, to avoid the Saturday performance of *King John* being jeopardised (£4,052 today). The show did not take place, so presumably the money was not forthcoming. Finally, at the end of the 1802 season at Drury Lane, with Sheridan's creditors closing in, brother and sister took the joint decision to defect to the rival licensed London theatre, Covent Garden.

John Philip was able to buy out one of the shareholders at Covent Garden and take a sixth share in the ownership. The negotiation took some time, though. He went abroad with his wife Pop, leaving the financial wrangling in the capable hands of his old friend, Elizabeth Inchbald. The manager of Covent Garden,

Thomas Harris, was a very different personality from Sheridan, honourable and punctilious. Sarah left for a year-long tour of Ireland. On 27 September 1803, she appeared for the first time at Covent Garden, inevitably playing the old favourite, Isabella, in *The Fatal Marriage*. The Kembles were now installed at Covent Garden in force. John Philip had debuted as Hamlet three days earlier, and their younger brother, Charles Kemble, Sarah's son Henry Siddons, and Henry's wife Harriet were also in the company.

During the following season at Covent Garden, although she played the opening night, Sarah would only appear twice. This was in part due to the new phenomenon of Master Betty, or 'young Roscius', a 13-year-old boy who took London by storm and appeared in all the lead male roles. He was hugely well paid – with a better nightly fee than Sarah had ever received – and had his portrait painted by the best artists. The company members at Covent Garden were compelled to act with him, but both John Philip and Sarah managed to excuse themselves. As Sarah wrote, 'he is a very clever, pretty boy, but nothing more.'[22] Sarah's health continued to be poor, and her domestic life was difficult at the time, plus she was by now financially secure (even if she never felt it), so she could afford to sit out the craze and return to the theatre at her leisure.

In the autumn of 1806 Sarah again started appearing at Covent Garden. That season she performed thirty-four times. In James Boaden's words, Sarah and John Philip were 'acting with undisputed supremacy'.[23] On 8 September 1808 Sarah opened the London season at Covent Garden once more, playing Lady Macbeth. But less than a fortnight later the theatre at Covent Garden was burned to the ground. Some thirty people lost their lives that night, trying to save the famous building. Sarah wrote to her friend James Ballantyne that at 2 am all had seemed as normal, but by 6 am the entire structure had been swallowed up by the fire. Sarah was relieved that her brothers had not been injured – they had learned of the fire too late. John Philip had lost his entire library of theatrical manuscripts. The loan he had taken to buy his share of the freehold of Covent Garden had not yet been paid off. Handel's organ was also lost, as were manuscripts by both Handel and Arne, together with Sarah's large collection of stage costumes and jewellery, including the lace veil which had previously belonged to Marie Antoinette.

Offers of support came immediately, which Sarah found immensely touching. The Duke of Northumberland put up a loan of £10,000 (£829,700 today) towards the fund for rebuilding the theatre, and then, when the first stone was laid, declared that his loan should now be viewed as a gift. Even before the fire the management had intended to refurbish Covent Garden, just as Sheridan had done to Drury Lane. They had also been insured, so their losses were manageable. The whole company moved to the Opera House and then to the

Haymarket Theatre while rebuilding work started at Covent Garden. Sarah threw herself into the effort. At times of crisis, her loyalty towards family always increased. While she and John Philip had drifted apart in the past few years, they now became very close once more. She performed for him forty times over this season. Elizabeth Inchbald, normally such a supporter of the Kemble family, was critical of what she felt to be the over-exaggerated victimhood they adopted after the fire. Doctors waived their fees for the whole family and people inquired anxiously about 'dear Siddons'. Perhaps Elizabeth was right. But the catastrophe brought the family together again.

By 30 December, only three months after the fire, the first stone for the New Covent Garden Theatre was laid by the Prince of Wales. Sarah was concerned that John Philip jeopardised his health by rising from his sickbed to attend. She herself wore a magnificent hat, with plumes of black feathers, which was ruined in the torrential rain that fell that day. The new theatre was said to have cost £150,000 to construct (£12,450,000 today). And so, the management decided to increase the ticket prices. Seats in the open boxes, which had cost six shillings (£24.89 today), were now priced at seven shillings (£27.02 today), while those in the pit went from three shillings and sixpence (£14.52 today) to four shillings (£16.59 today). The entire third tier of the main gallery now became a row of twenty-eight private boxes, each rented out at £300 per year (£24,890), like football season tickets. The new gallery was so steeply raked that when the performers were upstage, the audience could only see their legs.

On 1 September 1809 the New Covent Garden Theatre staged as its opening production the usual choice of Shakespeare's *Macbeth*, with John Philip in the title role and Sarah as Lady Macbeth. The national anthem was sung, and John Philip addressed the audience with a poem, but immediately the play itself began, the audience started yelling at him about the price of the tickets he was charging. Unnerved, Sarah also then appeared on stage. Despite the shouting, brother and sister continued performing, but nothing could be heard of the action at all, except for the odd momentary lull when Sarah's distinct tones filled the silence for a second or so before the noise started up again. *The Covent Garden Journal* described it as 'Perhaps the finest dumb show ever witnessed.'[24] At the end of the evening, two magistrates came onto the stage and read out a statement condemning the riots. The audience found their exits blocked by huge crowds, filling up all the lobbies and passageways as the police started making arrests.

The 'Old Price Riots' as they became known, lasted for sixty-six nights in all, over a period of three months. Throughout, Sarah and John Philip were personally targeted. Their costumes in *Macbeth* were seen as unnecessarily expensive. The press claimed (probably unfairly) that what they wore on the opening night had cost £500 (£38,600 today) and *The Times* wrote that the

Lord Chief Justice sat every day at Westminster Hall for half Sarah's salary. In December Sarah wrote to Charlotte Fitzhugh that for several weeks John Philip and his wife Pop had slept with ladders at their bedroom windows just in case the mob attacked their home and they had to make an escape. One evening a huge crowd did indeed march on their house. When John Philip refused to appear, they broke some of the windows and threw mud at the walls. Nevertheless, every night John Philip went on stage at Covent Garden. On the third night he made the mistake of asking the mob what they wanted, which only increased their anger. It was better, he soon learned, not to rise to them.

In contrast, Sarah stayed away. She was not 'management' after all. She wrote to her daughter-in-law Harriet that the riots were a 'barbarous outrage to decency and reason, which is a national disgrace ... where it will end heaven knows.'[25] The ongoing threats to John Philip and Pop caused her to worry herself into a state of illness. She even vowed to stop performing altogether: 'nothing shall induce me to place myself again in so painful & degrading a situation.'[26] But the series of crises continued to bind the Kembles. John Philip finally managed to negotiate with the rioters, concede over the price of the boxes and bring things to a close. A placard with the words 'We are satisfied' was hoisted. Inevitably, Sarah showed her support by continuing.

Things were never quite the same for Sarah's working life after the Old Price Riots. As a 55-year-old, her power on stage was fading. Various commentators noted that her voice had begun to fail. She could not stop her weight increasing, post-menopause. Sir Walter Scott, seeing her perform on tour in Edinburgh, wrote to the playwright Joanna Baillie: 'I was quite shocked to see her, for the two last years have made a dreadful inroad both on voice and person.'[27] Her close friend, the artist Thomas Lawrence, told Joseph Farington that he felt she ought to retire. And behind the scenes her personal life continued to give her heartache. As Sarah's domestic dramas reached a long, slow climax, they would inevitably take their toll on her life as a professional.

Chapter 14
Maria

'Give a thousand loves to my beloved Maria, and tell her her mother's heart is always with her.'[1]

Sarah's two eldest daughters, Sally and Maria, were always treated as a duo by their parents, family and friends. Sarah's first daughter, Sally, had been born in 1774, just before Sarah's disastrous debut London season. Maria was born in 1779, in altogether happier circumstances, when her parents were established in Bath. Both Sally and Maria appeared on stage with their mother when she gave her 'Three Reasons' speech, explaining why she felt the need to leave Bath and try her hand again in London. Once the family was established there, the two sisters were educated together, first by governesses and then at a finishing school in Calais. Sarah's success meant that she was very much the modern working mother, beset by guilt about missing time spent with her two beautiful daughters. As young women, their lives were very different from the one Sarah herself had led at their age. Thanks to their mother's success, they were like Jane Austen heroines. There was no expectation that they earn their own living. Instead, they enjoyed being part of a lively social circle and spent their time having fun and waiting for marriage. But, bound together as they were, they both found themselves falling in love with the same man.

Thomas Lawrence was born in 1769, so he was six years older than Sally and ten years older than Maria, but only fourteen years younger than their mother. If his relationships with the three different Siddons women were graded in terms of complexity, that with Sarah would doubtless have come out highest. Sarah had first met Lawrence, before either of her daughters had been born, when his father was the innkeeper at The Black Bear Inn in Devizes. Lawrence's father would boast of his son's drawing skills to anyone who stopped there and get the young boy to draw their portrait. Sarah was much taken by him.

In 1779, Lawrence had moved to Bath after his father was declared bankrupt. As a 10-year-old, Lawrence became the sole breadwinner for his family, painting beautiful pastel portraits of the people he met, including Sarah and her mother Sally Kemble. Here in Bath, his friendship with the entire Siddons clan became established. He knew Sally and Maria as young children and watched them grow up. In Lawrence's pastel of Sarah from this time, she wears a black velvet hat and a white muslin cavalier tie. It is charmingly intimate. If you did not know the history, you might think Sarah was a beautiful young aristocrat, waiting for the right suitor, rather than a working actress, already married with three children, and that Lawrence was an established portrait painter, rather than a teenager on the make.

The Siddons moved to London in 1782 and five years later the 18-year-old Lawrence followed them there. He installed himself in Greek Street with his parents and set up a studio in nearby Jermyn Street, seeking advice from the eminent Sir Joshua Reynolds on how to earn his living as a London portrait painter. He renewed his acquaintance with Sarah, now the foremost actress on the London stage, and with her two young daughters. As time went by, Sally could see Lawrence's feelings towards her increasing from friendship into something deeper, and she began to reciprocate. Like her mother and grandmother before her, she was getting involved with her prospective life partner while she was still very young. By the time Lawrence was 27 and Sally Siddons, 21 (remarkably late for a Kemble/Siddons female), it became clear that the two were in love and that Lawrence was hoping for marriage.

Lawrence and his sister Lucy were part of a tight social circle around the two Siddons sisters. They spent their time at balls and soirées. They visited Ranelagh Pleasure Gardens, and an astronomical exhibition called the *Eidouranion*, which showed off a vast machine that provided views of celestial phenomena. Another time they went to see a pair of George Stubbs paintings of a kangaroo and a dingo. Their lives were full of charming, leisurely outings, very different from their mother's, performing as she was on the London stage most nights.

The sisters wore loose-flowing, high-waisted gowns, with sashes and flesh-coloured stockings, to look like Greek statues. Rather than powdered wigs, hair was now displayed in its natural colour, often cropped short or worn swept up, as if pinned in an impromptu moment rather than dressed for hours. The older generation tended to dislike these new fashions, which were influenced by French ideas – a country where violent revolution was taking place. For Lawrence, who was always highly attuned to the visuals of his would-be sitters, the effect on him of these two young women and their other friends was electric.

Lawrence drew both sisters and painted an oil of Sally, so we can get a sense of what they looked like. Thomas Campbell, Sarah's official biographer, wrote that her oldest daughter 'was not strictly beautiful, but her countenance was like her mother's, with brilliant eyes, and a remarkable mixture of frankness and sweetness in her physiognomy.'[2] By contrast, her sister Maria was startlingly beautiful. She was said to be a greater beauty than her mother, or rather to have given a sense of what Sarah would have looked like, if she had not been so weighed down by responsibilities all her life. Sarah's good friend, Hester

Piozzi, preferred Sally as being the kinder of the two, and claimed that Sally was 'prettier than Maria, because her face looks cleaner.'³ Both sisters clearly had great charm and would have expected to attract the interest of a range of male suitors. Lawrence looked like a candidate with a future. By now he had been elected to the Royal Academy, and when Sir Joshua Reynolds died in 1792, he had become Painter in Ordinary to King George III aged only 23.

Sarah's niece, Fanny Kemble, whose father, Charles, was part of the sisters' social circle, later claimed that Lawrence made a formal proposal to Sally in around 1794. It seems more likely that Sarah had some sense of what was happening between the painter and her oldest daughter, and tacitly accepted it, while withholding her approval. She was probably happy for the romance to continue but seems not to have been prepared to entertain the thought of a formal engagement.

Sally's health was already beginning to give her family cause for concern. She had suffered from asthma all her life and the London air caused it to worsen. In autumn 1796, she was overtaken by illness; her asthma worsened dramatically. Sarah's fears for her daughter's life were confirmed. With Sally confined to her sickbed, Lawrence began to spend more time with the 17-year-old Maria. Throughout the whole of the following year, Lawrence and Maria's friendship developed into something altogether more destabilising. It took the form of a flirtatious courtship, conducted via a series of secret notes and clandestine meetings at his studio. Lawrence began to realise that he was far more attracted to Maria than he had ever been to the invalid Sally.

Maria described to her friend, Sally Bird, one such occasion when she returned home late having seen Lawrence. She went straight to her room and then 'came down about the middle of dinner, and my Father asked me where I had been! I told a *story*, and there was an end of it.'⁴ Lawrence's sister, Lucy, was also part of the plot. Maria wrote to her:

> I am very sorry I shall not see your brother before he goes. Tell *Mr Tom* he shall hear from me tomorrow morning because my mother don't like to bear a letter.⁵

Sarah could see that Lawrence was both falling in love with Maria and at the same time out of love with Sally. Sarah herself was a frequent visitor to Lawrence's studio at the time, as he was painting yet another portrait of her which was to be exhibited at the Royal Academy that autumn. Lawrence perhaps confessed to her during one of their portrait sessions at his studio. In addition, both Lawrence's parents died this year, which can only have added to the intensity of his feelings. Already Lawrence was falling into the role of the troubled, misunderstood romantic hero. His relationships with all three Siddons women were passionate, ambiguous, complicated. Which of them attracted him most? He was probably as confused as we are.

At the same time, although he was a success professionally, Lawrence's money troubles seemed to be worsening. His financial circumstances remain hazy to this day. It is hard to understand why he always seemed so short of money throughout his life, despite achieving great worldly success. He was an avid collector of paintings, and perhaps this explains it. Whatever the reason, Lawrence's finances were as confusing as his emotional life.

For her part, Sally, laid low by asthma, seemed to have accepted what was happening and to have professed herself resigned to it. Without the fevered attentions of Lawrence, she began to recover her strength. Maria, by contrast, was beginning to sicken. All the clandestine meetings with Lawrence in cold venues were affecting her health. She contracted tuberculosis, or consumption, a disease which was not uncommon in London at the time, but one with no reliable cure and from which very few ever recovered. Her parents feared that the intensity of Maria's fevered relationship with Lawrence was only making her worse. An elopement or a secret marriage would bring scandal, something which Sarah was always hyper-anxious to avoid. Maria was William Siddons' favourite child. So, when she took it upon herself to speak to her father about her love for Lawrence and the hope that the two of them might marry, William found himself agreeing to a formal engagement.

William reportedly met Lawrence in a cordial manner, accepting him as a future son-in-law, and pronouncing himself relieved that any subterfuge was at an end. As William wrote to Lawrence, characteristically blind to the fevered subtext: 'I think Maria has as fair a prospect of happiness as any mortal can desire.'[6] From now on, Lawrence could visit the Siddons' home in Great Marlborough Street every evening. Financial matters were discussed. William agreed that he would help relieve Lawrence's current money worries, as was the custom of the time. As a married woman, Maria would receive an allowance from her father. Nothing would have been said, of course, of the fact that it was Maria's mother who was responsible for earning all the money they discussed.

There were two clouds hanging over them all. Firstly, while Sally appeared to have stood down with good grace, it is hard to imagine that she can have been completely reconciled to her younger sister planning to sail off into the sunset with the person she had hoped to marry. It was characteristic of Sally to be unassuming in this way, and gives a sense of the strong, demanding presence in her life which Maria must have always been. Secondly, Maria's health was deteriorating rapidly. The initial plan seemed to have been to keep this news from Lawrence. As Sally urged her friend Sally Bird in a letter dated 5 January 1998:

Do not for Heaven's sake breathe a syllable of this [news of Maria's illness] which may reach Mr Lawrence's ears, for I suppose if he could imagine her so seriously ill, he would be almost distracted, now especially, when every desire of his heart is, without opposition, so near being accomplished.[7]

The potential dangers involved in not telling someone that the person they are in love with is seriously, and almost certainly terminally ill, did not seem to concern Sally or anyone else in the Siddons family.

For the first three months of 1798, the newly engaged Maria was locked up in a stuffy sick room. The air was expressly never changed as this was the latest medical treatment for tuberculosis. Hester Piozzi visited and questioned the stale air and the process of bleeding Maria every evening. Occasionally, Maria was allowed down to the drawing room, but the doctor insisted that a very careful eye be kept on her temperature there. The truth could no longer be hidden from Lawrence. Maria became increasingly depressed, particularly when she saw her mother and older sister setting off to see a new comedy at the theatre, while she was confined to bed. Sally, always exceptionally kind, became her sister's ministering angel, never sparing herself to meet Maria's needs.

The next twist in the plot was one that made the real-life drama seem even more like one of the tragedies in which Sarah starred on stage every evening. In February 1798 Lawrence switched his affections for a second time. He had, he realised, made a terrible mistake in becoming engaged to Maria. It was Sally after all with whom he was in love, not Maria. Although he continued to visit his fiancée, she soon noticed that his feelings towards her had altered. Lawrence became violently emotional, moody and restless at this latest reversal. Again, he confessed all of this to Sarah.

Sarah might quite understandably have shown Lawrence the door. Whatever his intentions, his involvement in the lives of her daughters was at the very least detrimental to their health. Instead, she kept this latest shocking news to herself, not breathing a word of it to William. Lawrence had scared her. Always fearful of scandal, she could see immediately that this rejection of one daughter for another was potentially dynamite to anyone wishing to damage the reputation of her family. Moreover, she feared what Lawrence might do to himself if this latest relationship were stopped. He appears to have threatened suicide, and it seems as if she noted his violent behaviour and accepted this threat as a real one.

Sally had enough about her to realise that it would be wrong to exalt in this change in Lawrence's affections and to encourage him to go public. After all, the condition of Maria's health was far too serious to risk it by upsetting her. In March, she wrote to Sally Bird, admitting that Lawrence had found he had been mistaken and that 'in short, we see him no more.'[8] All three Siddons women knew they needed to keep cheerful for the sake of Maria's health, despite the strange situation in which they found themselves.

Sally started to accept social invitations again. She wrote secret letters to Lawrence and to his sister Lucy, asking Lucy if her brother 'was not thunderstruck at this determination.'[9] It was clear to Sally that Lawrence and Maria had not been suited to each other, but, on the other hand, if he had truly been in love with her sister, he would not have fixated on 'those deficiencies in her character which now he has discovered.'[10]

Plans were made for Sarah to tour Scotland and to take Sally with her. The Scottish air would be too cold for Maria so it was decided she should stay with Penelope Pennington in the elegant Bristol suburb of Clifton. Penelope was an old friend of Sarah's from Bath whom she had first known as Sophia Weston; now married to William Pennington, the Master of Ceremonies at Clifton's hot springs, she had adopted the name of Penelope as well as taking on her husband's surname. Everyone believed that the air and the hot springs in Clifton would do Maria good. Worn down by her severe symptoms, Maria herself confessed to her friend Sally Bird that she did not think she would live much longer.

In April, Maria seemed to rally. She went out in the carriage three times and even walked a bit in the open air. She admitted in a letter that she was full of doubts, fears and perplexities. And who could blame her? She felt an obligation to remain cheerful but was distressed by everything. Not only was she struggling with a potentially fatal illness, but she had also heard nothing from Lawrence. She wrote to Sally Bird, wondering where he was. But everyone around her was complicit in keeping the truth from her about the man she loved. No-one dared tell Maria that her sister Sally was in correspondence with him and was hoping to become his wife. Confused as to what was going on, Maria became angry and emotional. To make things worse, her passionate feelings only exacerbated her physical state.

Maria's illness had thrown Sarah's planned tour of Scotland into confusion, and it came to nothing. She wrote to her old friend Tate Wilkinson in York to suggest that Tate's daughter, Patty, come to live with them as a companion. Patty arrived later that year and continued as a fixture with the family right up until Sarah's death, some thirty years later.

Next the whole Siddons family decided to accompany Maria to Clifton. They installed themselves in Penelope Pennington's house at 6 Prince's Buildings in early June. The new plan was that Sarah and William would stay in Clifton for a month. After that, if Maria continued to improve, Sarah would start touring again as usual over the summer months. Maria took the spa waters and rode out on a couple of occasions, but everyone feared how she would fare once the summer had passed, and the weather worsened. Sally left her sister's side to attend a ball but felt guilty about enjoying herself at such a time.

Sarah's tour started as planned in early July. William and Sally accompanied her, while Maria stayed behind with the kind Penelope Pennington. The Siddons' youngest daughter, Cecilia, was sent to a boarding school nearby, so as not to disturb Maria. For a month Sarah, William and Sally were in nearby Cheltenham, before moving on to Gloucester, Worcester, Hereford, Birmingham and Brighton. Sarah hated being away from Maria and worried about her endlessly. She wrote to Penelope Pennington, asking her to 'tell me about her pulse, her perspirations, her cough, everything!'[11] Sarah's anxious enquiries beg the question why she allowed herself to be dragged away from her daughter's sickbed at this time. The answer must surely have been that she was so accustomed to earning money to keep the family afloat that she did not feel she could say no. For her part, Penelope Pennington was far more perceptive. She could see that Maria only had a short time to live.

In August, Sally also fell ill, unable to throw off her asthma. By now, Sarah seemed to have accepted Maria's situation: 'I do not flatter myself that she will be long continued to me. *The Will of God be done* but I hope, I hope she will not *suffer much!*'[12] This prompted Sarah to reflect on how her other daughter would fare as Lawrence's wife, if she were constantly unwell. Illness in a wife, she mused to her friend, often tired a man. Even her own marriage had been compromised by her ill health. She must stop writing, she wrote, and prepare to play the role of Mrs Beverley in Edward Moore's *The Gamester*, which was scheduled for that evening. She was, as she expressed it, 'well-tuned for scenes of woe.'[13] It sometimes felt a relief from having to put on a cheerful, brave face at home, to appear on stage and go through the emotional highs and lows required of her, even if her audience did not entirely understand the context. Sarah wrote to Penelope, admitting that she had continued to keep William in the dark over Lawrence's change of heart and his renewed pursuit of Sally, and ascribing Lawrence's tumultuous feelings to his guilt over his treatment of Maria. She told Penelope that she also remained keen to keep Maria in the dark over the turn of events – letting her know the truth could only worsen her physical state.

Back in Clifton, Penelope started reading a novel to Maria written by Frances Sheridan, Brinsley's mother, *The Memories of Miss Sidney Biddulph*. Maria became distressed at hearing part of the story where it was revealed that the hero was in love with two sisters simultaneously. Although she did not say so, Penelope had surely chosen the novel for this very reason. Maria broke down. She confessed her fears to her hostess. Lawrence, she was sure, had taken up his pursuit of Sally again. Her sister must at all costs be prevented from giving in to him for a second time. Loyal friend that she was, Penelope immediately wrote to Sarah giving an account of all this.

Sarah's reply was unusually rational and detached. Sally, she felt sure, she wrote, was weaning herself off her feelings for Lawrence. As their mother, her instinct was that she should not seek to influence her daughter's decisions 'in this *most IMPORTANT object of their lives*, it has always been my system that they must *decide* for themselves. I will *advise*. I may *entreat*,' but she could do no more.[14] She sounds like a mother of adult 'children' today, reminding herself that they are grown-ups now and she cannot and must not influence them. She admitted that she had never approved of Maria's engagement to Lawrence and remained convinced that Maria would have found marriage to him extremely difficult.

By now Lawrence was in Birmingham, ostensibly visiting his sister Lucy, but in truth intent on seeking out Sally. Sarah was determined to get her eldest daughter out of the way, so it was decided that Sally should be sent back to Clifton to help look after her sister. Before leaving, Sally told her mother she had decided to put an end to Lawrence's expectations. Sarah was delighted at this news. As soon as she had despatched Sally to Clifton, she told Lawrence this latest development herself. The interview with him, she admitted to Penelope, had been exhausting.

Lawrence, the thwarted lover, also headed for Clifton. He stayed in a hotel under the assumed name of Mr Jennings, desperate to get some time with Sally and hell bent on persuading her to change her mind. In a bold move, he contacted Penelope Pennington: 'I stand in the most afflicting situation possible!'[15] Could Penelope give Sally a letter from him? He understood, he explained, that Maria's situation was dangerous, but 'All of my future happiness is at stake in your power.'[16] The middle-aged Penelope, perhaps not particularly fulfilled in her own romantic life, soon became putty in Lawrence's hands. She agreed to meet him, on neutral territory, and urged him to remain rational and composed. But she soon gave him a conditional promise of a rendezvous with Sally herself and agreed to keep him constantly updated.

Lawrence rushed back to Birmingham and managed to secure two separate interviews with Sarah, who was still performing there. He out-acted her, bursting into her dressing room, begging for her help and screaming of his pain. As Sarah subsequently wrote to Penelope: 'I shudder to think on the effect this wretched madman's frenzy has had on you.'[17] Sarah often performed in plays which featured the madness of romantic love, but here she was experiencing it first-hand. She made it clear that she would not agree to Lawrence's wish to see Sally again and rekindle their relationship. He could hope for nothing from her, she said, except good wishes for his future success and happiness. Despite having recently written to Penelope about how she never got involved in her daughters' love lives, she was straining every sinew to keep apart Lawrence – who, for all his emotion, was clearly in love with Sally – and Sally herself, who seemed to have been content to have it decided for her that she should not follow her heart and see her former lover. As for William, he was still living in ignorance of the entire situation. As far as he was concerned, Lawrence was engaged to Maria.

Lawrence headed to London. He wrote to Penelope confessing that his biggest concern was that Maria would influence Sally against him – a confession that proved prophetic. He reassured his kind-hearted, middle-aged correspondent that he was not mad, and diplomatically praised Sarah for her approach. He even admitted to Penelope that he was jealous of any other possible suitor for Sally. Penelope replied promptly. They were all in a terrible situation, she wrote, but Lawrence must stay calm and composed, waiting patiently for a better future. For a moment Penelope seemed to have persuaded Sally that she might indeed be able to resume her relationship with Lawrence, but then Sally changed her mind. While her sister was still alive, she resolved not to see him.

For all her entreaties to Lawrence to remain calm, Penelope was becoming increasingly anxious and discombobulated. She made sure to take copies of all her letters to Lawrence and forwarded on to Sarah any which Lawrence wrote to her. For a second time, Lawrence threatened suicide. He also sent Penelope a drawing he had made of Maria, saying it came 'from feelings of high esteem for the original'.[18] Penelope could see it was intended as a peace offering to Maria, but she wrote back that she did not intend to let Maria see it. She attached her own note to one of her letters to him: 'This torment of a man again importuned me to prevail on Sally to receive his letters and renew their correspondence.'[19]

In Clifton it was Sally's turn to feel unwell. Like some dangerous infection, Lawrence seemed to cause both sisters to sicken whenever they came too close to him. Sally was confined to her room and given laudanum, or so Penelope reported to Lawrence. He wrote back describing how once, when they were all in London, he had stolen into Sally's room and witnessed her under the influence of the drug. The confession feels strangely predatory. Why was he even in the invalid Sally's room at that time? If he knew she were this ill, why did he put such emotional strain on her? In an unguarded moment, Lawrence admitted to Penelope that he had shown some of the letters he had received from Sally to a friend. Penelope was furious at this indiscretion.

While Sally lay ill, Maria was also worsening. Penelope was finding herself overwhelmed by the task of coping with two invalids, at the same time as managing the relationship with Lawrence. Sarah was due back in Clifton on 24 September. Penelope both longed for and simultaneously dreaded her friend's return. Increasingly anxious at Maria's state, she urgently summoned both Maria's parents. Sarah and William left Drury Lane after a performance of *Jane Shore* three days earlier than planned, on 21 September, and drove through the night, to arrive in Clifton early the following evening. They were shocked to see their 19-year-old daughter looking so haggard. All her old prettiness had deserted her. They quickly moved her in a sedan chair to a lodging house across the square and made sure she was given laudanum. Sarah and Sally sat by her bedside and Sally read to her continuously. Penelope did her best to keep Lawrence up to speed on the health of both sisters, and Lawrence showered her with letters in response, demanding to know every detail. By 2 October, the London papers were already reporting Maria's death.

In a moment when they were alone, Maria asked Penelope about the truth of the situation between Sally and Lawrence. Given Maria was close to death, Penelope levelled with her. Maria then spoke to her sister while the two of them were alone, insisting that Sally promise never to marry Lawrence. Even as she lay dying, she still had the power to manipulate her older sister emotionally. For her part, Sally's initial response was to avoid giving any kind of agreement to this loaded demand, so different from her own approach when the situation had been reversed a couple of years before. When Sarah came into the room, Maria repeated the request in front of both Sally and Sarah. Worse, she told Sarah that Sally had agreed to her plan. She insisted Sarah, Sally and Penelope hold hands with her and that they all bear witness to Sally's promise. Penelope then wrote to Lawrence that as far as Sally was concerned 'the impression is sacred, is indelible – that it cancels all former bonds and engagements.'[20]

After this drama, Maria's ending was relatively peaceful. She reportedly bid farewell to everyone and gave her thanks to the entire household. She admitted to her father that she wished to be released. Sarah read prayers to her. Maria entreated her mother to get hold of all the letters she had ever written to Lawrence, and Sarah agreed. Maria looked, Penelope wrote to Lawrence, like an older version of her mother. Not a trace of youth remained. She died at 2 am on Sunday 7 October. Her funeral took place at St Andrew's Church, Clifton. Her gravestone bore an epitaph taken from Edward Young's poem *Night Thoughts* about how she sparkled, died and went to heaven. Hester Piozzi wrote to Penelope that William was particularly distraught. For once, Sarah seemed to have been the more resigned and restrained of the two. She wrote to a friend that she had long expected the news of her second daughter's death.

But Maria's exit did not bring the drama with Lawrence to a close. It only changed the dynamic. Maria had extracted a deathbed promise from her dutiful older sister. Sally was not suffering from tuberculosis, like her sister, but the asthma which had dogged her all her life continued to threaten her. Meanwhile, the impassioned Lawrence stalked all the main players. He declared himself desperately in love with Sally. His deadly passion, recently aimed at Maria, was now directed towards her. He had established a line of communication with Penelope and was determined to keep this open, regardless of the consequences. And his complex, part-personal, part-professional relationship with the celebrated mother of both Sally and Maria continued.

Chapter 15
Sally

'One is gone forever, the second *is as dead to me*, and the third no longer takes the delight in me she once did…'¹

Rather than Maria's death providing a full stop to the tension surrounding her daughters' relationships with Lawrence, for Sarah it was only a pause in proceedings. Lawrence was still passionately pursuing Sally, who, beset by ill health, had been backed into making a deathbed promise to Maria that she would never marry him. Penelope Pennington was still deeply entangled in the whole maelstrom of emotions surrounding Lawrence and the two Siddons daughters. By contrast the girls' father, William Siddons, had been kept in the dark. As far as William was concerned, Lawrence had been engaged to the now-deceased Maria, his involvement with Sally something very much in the past. Amid this, Sarah had her own personal and professional relationship with Lawrence, which only made the situation even more complex.

After Maria's funeral, Sarah travelled back to London. She and Penelope continued their intense correspondence. Sarah professed herself extremely wary that William might discover their letters. Part of Sarah's determination to keep William in ignorance must surely have been the fear that he would forbid them all from ever having anything more to do with Lawrence. This begs the question as to what Sarah's own subconscious wishes were as far as Lawrence was concerned. For many years the two of them had been intimately involved, as he painted her portrait again and again. At some level she was not being honest with herself about her own feelings towards him.

On 13 October, less than a week after Maria's death, Lawrence wrote a passionate letter to Penelope about his pursuit of Sally. Penelope subsequently called his letter 'diabolical'.² It merits being quoted in full:

It is only my Hand that shakes, not my Mind.

I have played deeply for her, and you think she will escape me. I'll tell you a Secret. *It is possible she may. Mark the End.*

You have all played your parts admirably!!

If the scene you have so accurately described is mentioned by you to *one Human Being*, I will pursue your name with execration.³

Lawrence the romantic hero had become Lawrence the sexual predator and Lawrence the controlling bully. His prey (Sally) might, he admitted, escape his clutches. Penelope (his supposed friend) would be pursued and destroyed if she went against his wishes. Everyone involved must be intimidated into silence. What they were all going through, he acknowledged, felt like a fictional drama. Sally, Sarah and Penelope were all acting their very distinctive roles, as if they were taking part in a Siddons tragedy.

Kindly, middle-aged, vulnerable Penelope wrote back bravely that she would not deign to reply to Lawrence's 'unmanly threat'.[4] She would, she made it clear, return all his future letters unopened. She then forwarded what he had written, together with a copy of her reply, to Sarah, querying whether they were right to keep William in the dark. The time had come, Penelope felt, to confess to both William and Sarah's brother John Philip, if only to protect them all, not least young Sally. Penelope was also careful to ask Sarah for the return of the 'diabolical letter' at some future point.[5] Sarah wrote back that she would gladly have confided in John Philip, but his wife Pop was such a gossip that she did not dare risk it. As for William, he was 'unhappily, so cold and repelling, that instead of tender sympathy I should expect harsh words, unkind reproof, and looks that stab with coldness.'[6] The collective strain of many years living together, along with the fallout from Maria's death, was piling huge pressure on Sarah and William's marriage. Meanwhile, Sarah could not put off for much longer her next appearance on the London stage.

The journey to London from Clifton after Maria's funeral had made Sally unwell again, but she recovered after a few days, nursed by her anxious mother. It was Sally, rather than Sarah, who next wrote back to Penelope and who gradually took over the role of corresponding with the well-meaning family friend. Sally had been shown Lawrence's so-called diabolical letter by her mother and had declared he was clearly quite mad. She found himself feeling sorry for his tormented soul. Penelope need not fear for her, she wrote, reassuringly. She was, after all, bound by a sacred promise. She had vowed to Maria, as her sister lay dying, that she would never marry Lawrence. He might be in love with her, but it was a horrifying kind of passion. Her mother, she reckoned, would soon tell her father about what had been going on. 'We cannot, you know,' she admitted, 'quite conquer all our *feelings*, but virtue and reason may regulate our *conduct*.'[7] Sally was perhaps being overly optimistic when confiding in her mother and her mother's middle-aged friend. In truth, she still had very strong feelings for Lawrence, which were not so easily conquered.

Lawrence again tried writing to Penelope but got nowhere and soon gave up. He headed off to Lincolnshire and word reached Sarah that he was beginning to take a romantic interest in a Miss Amelia Locke. She wrote to Penelope:

'Oh! would to heaven she, or any other, might divert his attentions from us!'[8] That would solve all their problems.

At their home in Great Marlborough Street, Sarah and Sally discussed the tactics that Sally should employ when she next met Lawrence. There were family divisions over the affair: Sally's aunt and uncle Francis and Fanny Twiss advised Sally that she should not feel bound by her promise to Maria, since it had been extracted from her under duress. As for Sarah, she could no longer put off taking part in the new autumn season at Covent Garden. She agreed to play the role of Isabella in *Measure for Measure*, specifically because it was more cerebral than her usual emotionally draining tragic roles. As always, personal and professional were intertwined.

Lawrence returned to London, his fiery feelings for Sally unquenched by Amelia Locke. Patty Wilkinson had now arrived at Great Marlborough Street to be a companion to Sally. Lawrence tried his best to get Patty on side, to no avail. What he expressly did not do was to contact Sally direct. Instead, he haunted her. In November, the Siddons saw him at church. Sarah imagined that he must have felt wounded at the fact they ignored him. One day, Sally was looking out of the window of the family home when she caught sight of Lawrence, gazing earnestly upwards. She turned away quickly but was sure he had seen her. She found herself wondering whether he might knock at the front door, but nothing happened.

Lawrence also succeeded in alienating Sally's aunt and uncle, the Twisses, despite their initial support for his cause. When he visited them, his passion appeared so violent, and his determination so utter that Sally was being manipulated into rejecting him, that they felt compelled to tell him they would leave the room unless he changed the subject. 'I am sure,' wrote Sally to her friend, Sally Bird, 'it is for the happiness of us both that all should be at an end.'[9]

Eventually, Sarah decided she must finally come clean with William as to what had been going on. She wrote to Penelope that he met the news:

> With that coldness and reserve which had kept him so long ignorant of it, and that want of an agreeing mind (*my* misfortune, though not his *fault*), that has always checked his tongue and chilled my heart in every occurrence of importance through our lives.[10]

As far as Sarah was concerned, William – as ever – was just not equipped to deal with what she was telling him. His instinct was to let sleeping dogs lie and not mention anything to Sally. But Sarah begged him to talk to his daughter. Sally would find it very strange, she argued, if he did not. He then put forward his view of the situation in no uncertain terms. He loathed the very thought of

Lawrence and would not tolerate any further communication with him. When Lawrence wrote asking for a portrait he had previously painted of Sally so he could copy and return it, William wrote back promptly, refusing his request. In December, perhaps emboldened by her father's attitude, Sally wrote to Lawrence making it clear that she would never marry him. Finally, Lawrence seemed to have accepted the dismissal.

For the next three years, Sally was in limbo. Her social life grew quieter as her health continued to decline. For that reason alone, it was deemed necessary for her to reject any idea of a romance with Lawrence. And yet at some level, she still loved him. In January 1799, when she went to see Sarah perform in a comedy at Covent Garden, Sally was embarrassed at having to pass quite close to Lawrence in the auditorium. Then she travelled with her family to Bath where her mother was performing. There, Sally had a severe attack of asthma and was unable either to attend her mother's benefit night at the Theatre Royal or to go to a local ball. She had loved dancing all her life. She resorted to taking laudanum once again. In March 1799, rumours reached the Siddons that Lawrence was set to marry a Miss Jennings, who lived in Clapham and enjoyed painting. But these proved unfounded. Sally wrote to her friend Sally Bird that she hoped, if he were to marry, he would return all the letters she had written him in the past.

In June, Sally passed so close to Lawrence while walking in Kensington Gardens that she could have touched him. She confessed to her friend that 'Whenever I meet his eyes with that glance that pierces through and through one, it is like an electric stroke to me.'[11] Sarah still feared Lawrence might not be completely over Sally. Yet she could also see the folly of Lawrence's loving someone 'who brings such an affliction for her *portion*.'[12] Looking at it from a twenty-first century viewpoint, the idea that Sarah felt her daughter could not have any kind of romantic relationship with Lawrence just because she was ill seems unnecessarily harsh. It seems as if Sarah was too determined to discount her own daughter, as if Sarah herself, without realising it, was putting herself forward as a rival for Lawrence's affections.

In the early autumn, mother and daughter had yet another conversation about Lawrence. Sarah made it clear that Lawrence now only thought of Sally as a friend. She had requested that he return Sally's letters, which he again promised he would do once he was married. Later in the year Sarah even admitted that she never believed Lawrence had really loved Sally. Hardly the most sympathetic line to take, given Sally's confusion. At one point Sally wrote that she was glad she was 'out of the scrape' with Lawrence but at another she admitted to being plagued by 'tormenting regrets'.[13] There was a further health scare that year when her family feared she would die, but she rallied.

Meanwhile Sarah simply continued her professional life, sublimating her sorrows, or rather turning them to her advantage. Many years later, when she had been retired for nearly twenty years, Sarah told the Irish poet, Tom Moore, that:

> she often got credit for feeling and force of acting when she was only relieving her heart; and that after suffering for a while she found the stage at night a vent for her private sorrows.[14]

Perhaps this was the closest she ever came to admitting that she used whatever sadness she was experiencing at any given point in her private life to feed into the intensity of her performance on stage that night. As an old woman she could confess that she was often praised for acting when, in fact, she was just expressing her feelings. She was perhaps being falsely modest about her acting ability, but at the same time she was acknowledging that her strategy had always been to meld the personal and the professional.

Sally Bird had acted as a confidante to Sally Siddons throughout. Early in 1800 she came to stay with Lawrence and his sister Lucy in Greek Street. Now, through Sally Bird, Sarah began to resume her own relations with Lawrence. He was eager to come and inspect some pictures at Great Marlborough Street and Sarah was happy for him to do so, provided, she explained, Sally knew nothing of it. In February she wrote to Sally Bird:

> Will you so good as to ask Mr L where I can get some very fine Carmine? I find it the best Rouge, covered with a little hair-powder, but I can get none at all equal to some he gave me about two years ago.[15]

In part, this was business. The ageing Sarah needed to look the best she could. Anxieties about her fading beauty must have played their part. She had been intimately involved with Lawrence professionally, after all, for many years. The engravings made of his portraits helped guarantee her continued success. But at the same time asking Lawrence where to procure make-up and reminding him he had done so only two years earlier for her feels treacherous towards her sad, sickly daughter, who still loved this man. Could Sarah not have continued to keep Lawrence at a distance?

During the next season at Covent Garden, Sally wrote to her friend that she knew Lawrence hardly ever missed seeing Sarah perform there and that he went to her mother's dressing room afterwards without fail. He was often in the box of her gossipy aunt, Pop Kemble. If Sally herself ever saw him at the theatre, he would make a quick, formal bow and withdraw. But crucially her mother never spoke to Sally about any of this. Mother and daughter maintained a dignified silence, and as a result they inevitably began to draw apart. If Sarah had only talked to her, confessed Sally, then she would have been able to tell her mother that she had become convinced Lawrence was now entirely indifferent towards her. She had also heard a rumour that he was romantically involved with yet another third party, Betty Tickell, someone she herself disliked. The question mother and daughter both determinedly ignored was whether Sally was indifferent towards Lawrence in return.

In early 1801, a letter of Sally's to Sally Bird gave the answer: 'As for *my heart, it is a single and constant one*, it never gave itself *but once* away, and I believe it *incapable* of change.'[16] Lawrence was her one and only love, and always would be. The sadness of that confession still lingers reading her letter today. It inevitably depressed Sally's spirits. She had always loved singing, but she admitted her singing days were now over. For her part, Sarah distanced herself from her old friend, Penelope Pennington, declining an invitation to stay with her at Clifton that summer, perhaps not wanting to reopen old wounds over Maria's death, and perhaps because she feared being questioned about her own dealings with Lawrence. She had, she admitted, regained some peace, and the waves of misery she had been feeling were subsiding. Notably, she mentioned neither Sally nor Lawrence.

By December 1801, Sally was able to describe herself having friendly times with Patty Wilkinson and another friend, Dorothy Place, sitting round the fireside in Great Marlborough Street, joking about how they were destined to become old maids. Her mother advised them all to get married, apparently (it must have been easier to say this when Sally was in the company of her friends rather than to speak the truth about Sally's health), and Sarah counselled patience until the war with France was over, when she was confident they would all be inundated with suitors. The atmosphere felt more relaxed, even jovial.

In May 1802, Sarah set off on a lucrative tour of Ireland, which was due to last a year, taking Patty Wilkinson with her for company. She found herself overcome by a powerful sense of foreboding before she left. When the moment came to say goodbye to her friend Ann Greatheed – Bertie's wife – she became hysterical, convinced that a great misfortune would take place before the two of them met again. She was right. As so often, the story of her life resembled the plot of one of her stage tragedies. She left Sally and the 8-year-old Cecilia in the care of William and asked Hester Piozzi to keep an eye on them both as well. Sally's health seemed to have improved, and she was finally leading a more normal life, attending social events including her brother Henry's wedding to Harriet Murray. Perhaps this was easier when she was out of her mother's orbit.

In February 1803, Sally wrote to her mother in Ireland, reassuring her that she was well. But on 10 March, William wrote to Patty Wilkinson, rather than to his wife, admitting that Sally had suddenly become very unwell again, but asking her not to distress Sarah by telling her about it. Patty could not keep this news to herself and confessed to Sarah after Sarah's final performance in Dublin. Sarah immediately realised that this was potentially extremely serious. The two tried to book themselves onto a ship bound for England, but the weather was particularly stormy. No boats were sailing. A further letter arrived from William, reassuring them that Sally was better and telling Sarah to go on to her engagement in Cork. In hindsight this looks unforgivably callous on the part of William, insisting his wife continue to earn money for them all rather than return to the bedside of her dying daughter, but there had been these health scares before. Perhaps William really did think Sally would make a quick recovery.

Sarah wrote to her friend, Charlotte Fitzhugh, from Cork on 21 March. She was about to perform that night and was wracked with anxiety, both over her daughter's health and over her inability to make it home. The stormy weather continued and, as a result, Sarah had received no letters from England. Without word from Great Marlborough Street, she decided to terminate her engagement. The manager of the Cork Theatre was disappointed but understood and released her from her contract. Sarah and Patty set off for Dublin, as this would be a safer place to sail from than directly from Cork. Again, though, the winds were too strong. Charlotte Fitzhugh had written a letter to Cork – where she believed Sarah to be – but it did not reach her. Instead, Sarah wrote Charlotte a frantic letter from Dublin on 2 April, accusing her of deliberately keeping silent: 'Oh God! what a home to return to, after all I have been doing! and what a prospect to the end of my days!'[17] Eventually, Sarah and Patty managed to secure for themselves passage on board ship from Dublin to Holyhead.

From there, Sarah and Patty took a series of post-chaises to return to London as quickly as possible. They were waiting for a change of horses in Shrewsbury when a letter arrived from William. It had been written ten days earlier on 24 March. William made it clear that there was no hope. Sally would not last the night. He did not want Sarah to endanger her own health, he wrote, by travelling back home too fast. As Sarah was thinking over the contents of this letter, Patty was called out of the room to receive the news from a messenger that Sally had indeed died. Two hours after William had written his letter, Sally's life had come to an end in the arms of her friend, Dorothy Place, thanks to emphysema brought on by crippling asthmatic attacks. When Patty re-entered the room in the inn in Shrewsbury, Sarah knew from the look on her face what had happened. Patty wrote in her diary that Sarah 'sank into speechless despondency' and retired to bed, 'cold and torpid as a stone'.[18]

Sarah, the fiercely proud mother, had now lost two grown-up daughters to diseases of the lung. Both times, she had felt compelled to go on money-earning tours while a daughter lay dying. This time must have felt far worse. After all, she had been away for nearly a year. Crucially, she had not been by her daughter's side at the end. And in her heart, she also knew that the complex web of relationships with Lawrence had driven Sally and herself apart. She had put her own semi-professional friendship with Lawrence ahead of the hurt which that behaviour inevitably caused Sally. She had sidelined her own daughter. Worse, events had conspired to mean that she had not been able to ask Sally's forgiveness on her deathbed, or at the very least to talk it through with her. In addition, William, her husband, and Sally's father, had actively encouraged her to continue on tour, rather than returning to their dying daughter's bedside. Would she ever be able to find it in her heart to forgive him?

Sarah and Patty travelled on to Oxford, where they received a supportive letter from John Philip. He understood the severity of events. Significantly, Sarah did not return home to William at Great Marlborough Street. Instead, she was met a few miles outside London by her younger brother, Charles, who was, after all, the same age as Sally. Together they went to see their mother, who was living at Sadlers Wells. Their father, Roger Kemble, had also died while Sarah was away in Ireland, but in very different circumstances from Sally. It was suggested that Sarah's distress might be helped by her visiting the spa town of Cheltenham and taking the waters there. So, in May, she went to Birch Farm, an idyllic rural property just outside Cheltenham, accompanied by Patty Wilkinson and her only surviving daughter Cecilia, aged 9. They were joined there by Charles Moore, a young barrister who had always been in love with Sally, and Dorothy Place, who had been with her when she died. Charles Moore would go on to keep a bust of Sally among his personal possessions for the rest of his life. In July, John Philip and Charles Moore embarked with Sarah on a recreational tour of the Wye Valley.

It is easy to understand the sadness Sarah felt at the loss of her oldest daughter, Sally. Throughout her short adult life, Sally Siddons had blamelessly negotiated her way through the psychodrama that was the idiosyncratic triangle of relations between herself, Lawrence and her sister, Maria. Forever hovering in the background, with strong views on it all and without the emotional detachment she claimed, was the powerful presence of her mother. Sarah always protested her adoring love of her two eldest daughters, but her behaviour towards them had been compromised, both by her own relationship with Lawrence but also by the demands of being a famous actress, a household name, fearful of scandal, who needed to earn to support the family. But Sarah had another secret which she never shared with either daughter: a secret so highly charged that it threatened to destroy the respectability Sarah had always prioritised; a secret which would play its own part in the next chapter of her life.

Chapter 16

The Galindo Affair

'I was not blinded on the subject, I never believed it more than a ridiculous passion, chiefly arising from liking to have the attention a man.'[1]

The events surrounding Sarah's unhappy tour of Ireland in 1802 to 1803, her discovering too late that her daughter Sally was fatally ill and her failure to return in time to be with Sally at her death – all of this is tragic enough. Yet at the same time a whole further offstage drama was unfolding in Sarah's personal life. When she arrived in Dublin in June 1802, Sarah agreed to play the part of Hamlet, a breeches role, as it was called, and a certain Philomen Galindo was hired as her fencing teacher. Soon Sarah and the married Philomen had become inseparable. Although for many years Sarah had carefully created a public persona defined by respectability and virtue, she was now prepared to risk it all for a potentially scandalous relationship with a married man.

It was Patty Wilkinson, who was accompanying Sarah on the tour of Ireland, who initially befriended both Philomen Galindo and his wife Catherine and encouraged the friendship between them all. The Galindos were both actors in the Dublin company, alongside Sarah. Patty was probably relieved to find a lively couple closer to her own age than the middle-aged actress she was accompanying, and she doubtless found she could use the new friendship to distract Sarah from her anxieties about the family back in England. Sarah 'complained of langour' at this time, wrote Catherine in the account she published nine years later about what went on between Sarah and her husband, Philomen.[2] We know that Sarah had dreaded coming on tour, rightly intuiting the worst in terms of her daughter Sally's health.

Catherine Galindo was a jobbing actress, and her life was reminiscent of the strolling players with whom Sarah had spent her youth. Catherine's father had inherited property but mismanaged his estate and had been forced to sell up, giving each of his daughters a small annuity. Catherine went to live with her maternal uncle, but her father soon reappeared in her life, having run through what money he still had, demanding she help him. Realising she needed to earn her own living to support both herself and her father, Catherine decided to try life as a professional actress. She performed for three years in England, then two years in Edinburgh, before coming to Dublin. During her first winter season in Ireland, she met Philomen Galindo.

Where Philomen himself was born is a mystery. The origin of his surname is Spanish. He spoke with an accent, which was probably therefore Spanish. Eleven years earlier, in 1790, he had been imprisoned in Newgate Prison for debt. Catherine would describe Philomen, rather unkindly, as young enough to be Sarah's son. The implication is that he was younger than both Catherine and Sarah. Sarah may well have come across Philomen a few years before, when she was performing in Bath and he was running a fencing academy in Bristol, while married to his first wife, Frances Delaroche. We do not know what happened to Frances – perhaps she died – nor to the children of that marriage.

When they met in Dublin, Catherine and Philomen fell passionately in love and decided to marry, albeit possibly bigamously. Unsurprisingly Catherine's family opposed the match. By marrying Philomen, she stood to lose any potential inheritance from her solvent uncle. The couple's wedding took place in 1801, regardless, and they started their married life together in Dublin. Catherine was probably already pregnant, since their first child was born that year. In her words, 'A strong and perhaps fatal attachment united us.'[3] According to Catherine's later account of events, for their first year of married life they were happy together.

From the outset of Sarah's relationship with the Galindos, there were warning signs. Catherine suggested to Sarah that, while she was in Ireland, she borrow the Galindos' curricle, a light, open, two-wheeled chaise, which provided a more pleasant drive than the usual closed carriage. When Philomen drove Sarah out in the curricle for her first airing, she immediately professed herself delighted with it. From then on, Philomen and Sarah would travel together in the sporty curricle, while Catherine and Patty, along with the Galindos' young son, John, lumbered on ahead in the closed carriage. The famous middle-aged actress, finding herself alone with this good-looking, exotic, younger man was able to express her own thoughts and feelings in a way she had checked herself from doing with any other man, and perhaps also with any other woman, for many years.

When Sarah then announced she had decided she would like to play Hamlet, Catherine suspected that the blossoming relationship with Philomen was the famous actress's main motivation. Philomen was to teach Sarah fencing for the role – and he would take the part of Laertes. That may well have been one reason for the decision, but it must surely also have been an attempt by Sarah more generally to regain some kind of sexual power for herself. The ageing process had restricted her to playing almost exclusively matronly roles. Here was a chance to appear on stage as a handsome young man. During all her years as a successful actress in London, Sarah had never played the role of Hamlet. Her last performance had been when she was in her twenties, as a young actress on the circuit, with her whole professional life before her. Here in Dublin, flattered by Philomen's attentions, the 47-year-old Sarah saw the opportunity of extending her repertoire and cross-dressing once more before it was too late.

Sarah was soon making it clear that she needed to be alone with Philomen during rehearsals so she could concentrate on his fencing lessons. She could not learn, she said, while anyone else looked on. When the production opened, it proved a great success, despite some criticism in the press that Sarah had put on weight and that her voice 'has acquired too masculine a tone.'[4] One anonymous journalist even praised the fencing sequences and described Philomen as 'a master of the art'.[5] Sarah wrote to her friend Charlotte Fitzhugh on 2 August that her reception in Dublin had exceeded her highest expectations and that the takings had been good too. Her professional success in a city where she had often experienced problems in the past must have felt gratifying, given her domestic worries.

When the company moved on to Limerick and Cork in early 1803, Sarah seemed to Catherine to be spending more and more time with Philomen, either driving in the curricle or rehearsing with him at the theatre. Catherine began to feel sorely neglected. She was also worried about money, particularly as she was not being called upon to perform. In Cork, Sarah gave a reading of *Hamlet* at a benefit specifically for Catherine, but Catherine complained that she herself did not receive a shilling from the evening. Sarah had raised 50 shillings (£237.50 today) but repairing the curricle and sorting the horses as well as all the other additional expenses the Galindos had incurred to keep Philomen by Sarah's side, had cost the couple at least 60 shillings (£285 today). It was decided that Sarah and Philomen would go on to Belfast and Dublin, while Catherine stayed behind with her young son to take a job in Kilkenny. It was unsurprising that Catherine by now begrudged the celebrated older actress the time she was spending with her husband.

Once they were all reunited in Dublin for the winter season, Catherine wrote in her later account of events that she now scarcely saw Philomen. He would often not return home until 3 am. She tried to remonstrate with him and appealed to Patty and even to Sarah about the situation. Philomen might be good company, she explained, but he ought not to abandon his home and family. Sarah was apparently vexed at this but did nothing to rectify things. At one point Sarah fell ill and Catherine decided to accompany her husband to visit the patient. The next day, Catherine received a note from Patty explaining that it was too tiring for Sarah to have two bedside visitors but asking that Philomen continue to come and visit Sarah alone. Catherine was extremely offended.

Sarah's son George came to stay a fortnight with her in the early spring before leaving to start his new life in India. Perhaps Philomen kept out of the way during the visit. Catherine made no mention of George in her account, nor did George seem to report that anything was amiss when he returned to London. William wrote to Sarah at this point, reassuring her that Sally's health was good and encouraging her to continue earning money in Ireland to send back home. In time, Sarah must have felt this letter was unforgivably callous, leading as it did to her failure to make it to Sally's deathbed. But the flirtation with Philomen made the situation, and the memories of that time, more complex. Was it just William's letter that was to blame? Or was Sarah distracted by her flirtation?

For her part, Catherine felt that there was no reason for Sarah to stay on in Dublin. She did not understand Sarah's financial imperative. To Catherine's consternation, Sarah agreed to an engagement in Cork, but then confessed that she feared travelling alone through the Irish countryside and requested that Philomen go with her. There, her anxieties about her daughter's health finally overcame her, and she did finally decide she should hurry home, eventually arriving back in England, despite the gales which delayed her. In Catherine's later account of events, she was excoriating about Sarah's actions. She condemned the famous actress as a poor mother – the ultimate indignity for Sarah, who had always prided herself on being a maternal role model. Catherine wrote:

> Good Heaven! What ought to detain a mother from the death bed of her expiring child? but other bonds held *you*, other gratifications and attachments were stronger than maternal affection.[6]

She had a point. It must have cut Sarah to the quick to read these words in print for all to see.

Once Sarah heard the news that Sally had indeed died without her being there, she went to stay near Cheltenham. From here, in May 1803, she wrote a series of fond letters to both the Galindos, full of emotion, about how she was beginning to recover her spirits after the tragedy of Sally's death. These Catherine included in her pamphlet, which would be published six years later. Sarah was spending time outdoors, she wrote, reading by a haystack, rambling in the fields, and musing in the orchard, with no-one to pass judgement on her. She clearly had no sense of Catherine's disapproval. She had finally begun to sleep better again, she explained. She did not divulge to the Galindos that she had been prescribed laudanum by her doctor. This was doubtless helping her to recover her equanimity. Her letters to the couple had the same easy, friendly, trusting tone she used when writing to the Whalleys or to Hester Piozzi. Her hope, she wrote, was that one day they would all three live together on a farm such as this.

Some letters were written to both the Galindos and others specifically to Philomen or to Catherine. Her writing to both in equally friendly terms implies that she felt no guilt at this stage about what had transpired between herself and Philomen. To him, she wrote: 'I have been very low myself all this day, and have often wished for the friend who knew so well how to keep me "up, up, up".'[7] To Catherine she wrote that 'Mr G's *oddity* would have done me a great deal of good, and I wanted to be made to stare, to wonder and to laugh.'[8] It was Philomen's optimism and his 'oddity' – perhaps his foreign accent and his humour – which she found appealing and she was now missing. She sent a handkerchief with one of the letters, to remind Philomen of the time he spent teaching her to fence. When he was slow to write back to her, she was sympathetic. She too found writing letters a burden, she admitted. She assured him of her sincere friendship.

In October she wrote to Philomen from London, in the least guarded of all the letters to him which still exist today. Her relationship with William was deteriorating. She confessed to Philomen: 'I have suffered too much from a husband's unkindness, not to detest the man who treats a creature ill that depends on her husband for all her comforts.'[9] The immediate quarrel between William and herself seemed to be over for now, but 'at all events this I am resolved upon, the *next* storm SHALL BE THE LAST.'[10] This kind of confession about the intimate details of her marriage had the potential to be incendiary, were it to fall into the wrong hands. And yet again, Sarah seemed wilfully blind to the interpretation the Galindos might put on her words. Sarah urged Philomen to tell Catherine all about what had happened, and to be gentle to Catherine in divulging the contents of her letter. She loved and missed them both, she wrote.

Catherine had given birth to the couple's daughter in July. The new baby was named Sarah and her famous namesake was co-opted as her godmother. Sarah wrote to Catherine, enquiring after little Sarah. She had, she wrote, received a letter from Philomen the previous day, but it had told her nothing 'other than that he is as much my *slave as ever.*'[11] Perhaps Sarah's insensitivity towards what Catherine must be feeling was to do with the theatrical world Sarah was accustomed to inhabiting. For her, men declaring they were her slaves was probably a figure of speech which was common among her fellow performers. The difference, of course, was that Catherine believed that her husband really was Sarah's slave, and that Sarah was in turn bonded to Philomen.

Rumbling below the surface in all these interactions was the painful fact that the Galindos were desperately short of money – while Sarah was extremely wealthy. Inevitably they put pressure on her to see if she could help them. As a fond friend, she felt she should do her bit. 'Oh! how would it lighten the burden of my sorrows, to get you out of the power of that tyrant Jones,' she wrote.[12] Sarah saw herself as heroically rescuing her two friends from the Dublin theatre manager, Frederic Jones, with whom she herself had not had an easy relationship. Catherine, though, had never seen Frederic Jones as a tyrant. Once again, she questioned Sarah's motivation. At one point Sarah even considered employing Philomen as her manager, but she soon gave up on this idea. Perhaps William took umbrage at the thought of losing the role he had held, even if in name only, for many years.

Sarah and her brother John Philip were beginning their new professional life at Covent Garden Theatre that season, having finally split from Sheridan at Drury Lane. So the situation was particularly delicate. Regardless, Sarah made overtures to the managing proprietor at Covent Garden, Thomas Harris, to ask if he would employ the Galindos in his company of actors. She secured the promise of some work for Catherine there, although on terms which Catherine herself felt were poor. Regardless, Philomen insisted his wife write to Sarah thanking her for her support and accepting the contract.

When he found out about it, John Philip was horrified to find that Sarah was lobbying Harris on behalf of 'persons whom it was a disgrace for her to *know*'.[13] He was very clear in his view of the Galindos. Both had fairly murky histories, but, in addition, John Philip did not rate Catherine as an actress. He had performed in the same company as her in the past and had seen for himself the quality of her work. She was simply not good enough to appear in the new Covent Garden company. He ordered Harris to retract the offer.

John Philip was never particularly good at confrontation. He could not face giving his sister the news that he had prevented her scheme. So he asked his old friend Elizabeth Inchbald to do so on his behalf. She did indeed do his dirty work for him, but then felt she was made to take the blame for the fallout. She placed responsibility for the ugly mess firmly at the door of the two Kemble siblings. Sarah, she made it clear, had allowed herself to be duped by the Galindos.

Next, in an uncharacteristically forthright move which showed how seriously he took the threat, John Philip set off to Dublin to disabuse Catherine of any notion of work in London. Philomen had already travelled to England by now, ready to start work at Covent Garden. Once John Philip arrived in Dublin, he made it clear to Catherine that he did not believe she had the skills to succeed on the London stage. She felt he was intolerably rude to her – the argument had taken place in public – and this only exacerbated her feelings of anger and jealousy towards Sarah and her high-handed brother. But it was by now crystal clear that the Galindos would not be appearing on the London stage that season.

Nevertheless, Catherine decided to follow her husband to England, bringing her young family with her. She wrote to Patty Wilkinson, complaining of her treatment by John Philip. Patty advised her to remain in Ireland, but it was too late. The family had given up their accommodation and their bags were all packed. They would remain in London for the next few years. Philomen joined the Local London Volunteers, a sort of voluntary Home Guard, set up to protect the capital city against a possible French invasion. John Philip and Charles Kemble did the same. For Philomen, this might give him some veneer of respectability, but it would not pay the bills.

Once in England, Catherine noticed a change in Sarah's manner towards her. Where previously Sarah had been over-friendly, now she became cool, distant and at times even haughty. Whereas Sarah continued to confide in Philomen, now she had stopped encouraging him to share these intimacies with his wife. Perhaps, after John Philip's trip to Ireland, Sarah had told herself that it was Catherine who was the problem. Sarah was still experiencing all the sadness and anger that form part of the grieving process following the death of her daughter Sally. Her own marriage was deteriorating, buckling under the strain of recent events. Her family may have disapproved of her relationship with Philomen, but she was unable to wean herself off him just for the moment.

In the spring of 1804, the Siddons rented a cottage in Hampstead where Sarah was beset by ill health. According to Catherine, Philomen was a constant visitor. He was invited to spend every night on the sofa in Sarah's study. The implication of a sexual relationship was just below the surface, though Catherine did not feel the need to spell it out. Her account was written with all the faux-innocence and innuendo of pamphlets of the time. Catherine was eventually invited to visit the Hampstead cottage as well, perhaps to save face, and was also asked to stay the night. She slept alone, while Philomen bedded down on Sarah's sofa, and their little son, Johnny, begged to be allowed to join his father there. Catherine did not speculate as to what William Siddons thought of all this, except to make the point that Sarah and William formally separated that autumn.

The following year, now she was a single woman, Sarah bought her longed-for country house at Westbourne, near Paddington. Philomen was a frequent visitor, dining with Sarah, and again often staying the night. This new purchase was hidden from Catherine for about a month, much to her annoyance, but she was eventually invited there. She must have feared that the house had been purchased specifically as a love-nest. To defuse the situation during her visit, Catherine made a remark about how glad she was that Sarah was now well enough to perform again. At this, according to Catherine's later account, Sarah apparently flew into a violent rage:

and in your passion, which astonished me, you used these words,
"I suppose Mr G you keep nothing a secret that concerns me from Mrs G."[14]

Where in the past Sarah had encouraged the Galindos to share her confidences, now she wanted to shut Catherine out. At this, Catherine left the room and resolved never to visit Westbourne again. Reading Catherine's account today, her painful jealousy and anger are still palpable. There are some minor factual inaccuracies, but there is no reason to doubt that most of the events she described really did take place. One interpretation to put on Sarah's behaviour is that she was unhappy, confused and lonely, and needed Philomen's friendship. Another is that she and Philomen really were having a sexual relationship. As a poison dart, Catherine added that two maids decided to give in their notice at Westbourne, so scandalised were they by Sarah's indecent conduct.

Did Sarah and Philomen have an affair? Clearly Catherine thought so. My instinct is that Sarah was attracted by Philomen and became reliant on his company, and that while it was not entirely chaste, Sarah held back from a full-blown sexual relationship. She simply had too much to lose. She had seen what had happened to her friend Hester Piozzi, who had fallen in love with her daughters' younger Italian tutor and married him. Hester's relationship with her daughters never recovered, and her social status suffered irreparably. And Gabriel Piozzi had been unmarried. Sarah would not have wanted this for herself. Philomen was a married man and divorce would have been unthinkable. If William had already been dead rather than the Siddons deciding to separate, perhaps things might have been different. In December 1806, Catherine gave birth to their third and final child, a son whom they called Philomen. This time, Sarah was not asked to be godmother.

In her pamphlet outlining what had gone on between them all (which was not to be published until 1809), Catherine described a meeting between herself and Sarah in Birmingham. The dates are unclear, but this probably took place in 1806. By chance Catherine was lodging at the same place as Sarah and Patty Wilkinson, who surprised Catherine by being remarkably friendly towards her. Clearly Patty and Sarah had decided the best policy was to kill with kindness. Sarah pressed Catherine to spend the evening with the two of them. She apologised to Catherine for what had gone on and moved her to tears. The Galindos' marriage was going wrong, and the implication was that it was this which was making Catherine unhappy, rather than anything Sarah had done. Catherine's parting words were that, when next they met, however much pain it cost her, she would explain everything to them both. At this, Sarah took her hand and promised 'if you ever should believe me any other than your sincere friend, you will wrong me much.'[15]

In 1807 relations between Sarah and the Galindos took a further turn for the worse. Inevitably, the fallout was caused by money. The actor/manager William Macready was involved in setting up a new theatrical venture in Manchester and needed £3,500 investment (about £300,000 today). Perhaps Sarah saw this as an opportunity to give the Galindos a new life, far away from London. Perhaps she had tired of her friendship with Philomen. Whatever her motives, she loaned Philomen at his request the sum of £1,000 (about £85,000 today) so he could invest with Macready. Although the Siddons were separated by now, William Siddons still controlled and indeed owned all the couple's money. Sarah did not mention the loan to William. She probably felt it would be too awkward to explain, and besides William was now living as an invalid in Bath, and she was by herself in London. She made it clear to Philomen that it must be kept a secret, and that the underlying contract securing it had to be with Patty Wilkinson, not with her.

No sooner had the agreement been drawn up than Sarah began to fret about how slowly the Galindos were repaying her loan. Sarah was someone who always worried about money, as we know, and she had begun to fixate on whether she really could achieve her dream of retirement and life at Westbourne Farm. Catherine claimed that Sarah wrote them a high-handed letter, demanding the return of the loan and forbidding Catherine from ever seeing her again. Philomen tried to arrange for Sarah to appear at the theatre in Manchester, which would have improved box office revenue there, but Sarah refused. By now she would not even open any of the letters he sent her. In Manchester, letters arrived from William Siddons to Macready, asking that Sarah be released from her engagement to perform at another of his theatres. From Catherine's point of view, 'I did not then know, nor could I guess, the cause of all this sudden and violent conduct.'[16] Presumably William had got wind of the financial transaction with the Galindos.

Later in the year Catherine went to London, deliberately to tell Sarah what she thought of her. She accosted Sarah on her way to church. Catherine would not detain her long, she promised. She simply wanted to explain that she 'was now perfectly informed as to the nature of your attachment to Mr G for these many years.'[17] Philomen had finally admitted the truth to his wife. Sarah, turning pale and starting to tremble, denied everything, but Catherine stood her ground. They both knew it was true. How could Sarah have treated her so cruelly when Catherine had trusted her and thought highly of her? At this Sarah wondered aloud why Catherine had held her in such esteem: 'Did you believe me superior to the weaknesses of humanity?'[18] Catherine was doubtless a partial witness, but, according to her account, Sarah appeared to be admitting her own guilt.

In February 1809 Catherine finally published her incendiary account of what had gone on, in an open letter addressed to Sarah. Catherine was surely motivated to publish, not only out of bitterness and anger but also out of her need for money. Her wealthy uncle had died and unsurprisingly had left her nothing in his will. The Manchester investment had disappeared into thin air. Catherine wrote that by now she and Philomen had been separated for eighteen months, implying that Philomen had turned violent against her. Three court records from the Irish Court of Chancery the same year give the lie to this separation. Philomen was the defendant, accused of owing money to a third party, and Catherine was also named. Whatever happened between the Galindos, it was clearly messy.

Patty Wilkinson seemed to give Catherine some help in getting her pamphlet against Sarah published. Patty would continue as Sarah's companion for many years. And yet she actively supported Catherine over this issue. She had been involved throughout, and indeed had been the person to encourage the friendship with the Galindos back in Dublin. She was the same age as Catherine and must have sympathised with her many problems. Patty's endorsement calls into question the idea that everything Catherine wrote in her account was pure fiction. Patty clearly believed her.

The publication of Catherine's pamphlet could have been fatally damaging to Sarah, had it happened earlier in Sarah's professional life. 'This diabolical business,' as she described it to the Whalleys, might have sunk her if it had emerged when she was less established.[19] By now she was widowed, soon to retire and caught up in the public campaign to reopen the New Covent Garden Theatre, although reliant, as always, on her own celebrity status. 'This time, unlike the way she handled the past Irish scandals, she decided not to appear on stage and argue her case in person. Silence was the better option, she decided. Horace Twiss, her favourite nephew, and later a respectable Tory MP, urged her to take the Galindos to court, but Sarah told him she preferred to let the whole affair lie. The Galindos had three children, she explained, and she did not wish to inflict further damage on their lives by condemning their parents to prison. Sarah knew from her own experience how close to the breadline the family were. Besides, the Galindos had already cost her far too much money. She would do anything to avoid a further encounter with the harridan Catherine. Luckily all her friends: 'are decidedly of the opinion that it is unnecessary, as it would be HUMILIATING, HARASSING and EXPENSIVE.'[20] What she did not admit to Horace was that many of Catherine's accusations were true. Had the case gone to court, she might not necessarily have won.

As for the Galindos, their hand-to-mouth life continued. They probably did separate for good. In 1823, Philomen spent time in Marshalsea prison, having failed to pay a debt of £17 15 shillings and 10 pence (£1,715 today). There is no mention of Catherine in the court papers. Catherine died in Dublin six years later in 1829 and Philomen died in London in 1840. Two of the Galindo children settled in the Manchester area and their youngest son became a Church of England priest. Their oldest son emigrated to the United States. At some level the Galindos must have reminded Sarah what her own life might have been, had her talent not rescued the Siddons from a life of penury. When Catherine wrote in her pamphlet to Sarah that she had 'wreak[ed] your whole revenge upon me and my innocent children,' the words sank deep.[21]

Overall, Sarah had a lucky escape. Previous biographers have dismissed Catherine's pamphlet as mere tittle-tattle. Yet her allegations have the ring of truth. There is no doubt that Sarah grew dangerously close to Philomen, just at the time that her daughter Sally died and her marriage was finally coming to an end. This kind of scandalous publication by a wronged wife would have sunk many a younger actress, with a less established reputation. Luckily, by now Sarah was a permanent fixture in the British consciousness. She had become a national treasure – matronly, strong in her Christian beliefs, someone who had endured much suffering, yet who was surrounded by a loving family. Her own writings demonstrate that this was how she saw herself. Not as someone who indulged in a middle-aged affair with a younger, married man. And this self-image was strong enough to withstand the ravings of a single, wronged wife, with no reputation of her own, 'whom everyone supposes to be quite mad, too.'[22]

Chapter 17

Marriage's End

'How everybody does hate that perverse Fellow! and how he does hate his beautiful and enchanting Wife.'[1]

Right from the start the Siddons' marriage had its problems. Sarah's parents opposed the match and several of their fears would prove correct. They could see that William was not a sufficiently strong actor to make a good living. He was good-hearted, but he lacked his wife's vivacious spark. He had always been a handsome man and the Siddons remained a good-looking couple, presenting a united face to the world, but their friends tended, justifiably, to speculate about the state of their relationship. Hester Piozzi was particularly forthright. Others probably had the same thoughts, even if they did not commit them to paper. For twenty-five years the marriage rumbled on, punctuated by the births of their various children – but a series of events brought William and Sarah to crisis point.

Money had always been a problematic subject. We have seen how William gave up earning very early in the marriage, leaving his wife to bring in all their income and to do the lion's share of the domestic duties as well. Initially the Siddons simply craved financial security, but as time progressed, and her success became established and their children grew up, the demands for Sarah to bring in ever more money only increased. Their lifestyle needed to be maintained. As Sarah wrote to her friend Charlotte Fitzhugh on 14 July 1801: 'I must go on *making*, to secure the few comforts that I have been able to attain for myself and my family. It is providential for us all that I can do so much.'[2] The pressure is evident. In 1801 William made one of several ill-advised investments – this time, in the new theatre at Sadlers Wells – without consulting Sarah. Perhaps it was no coincidence that his parents-in-law were living at Sadlers Wells at the time. They had never rated him and yet here was his chance to prove himself. Instead, he lost every single penny of the £3,000 he had invested (£243,100 today) – nearly a third of Sarah's earnings for that year.

Not only did Sarah earn while William did not, but she was also beautiful and famous, while he was simply Mr Siddons. He had to learn to stand by dutifully, while she got all the praise. Sarah mixed with royalty and the aristocracy; William stayed at home. Sarah's beauty was captured in portrait after portrait;

only one likeness of William survives. Even today a marriage can come under intolerable strain when one partner is hugely more celebrated than the other. For the Siddons, at a time when this situation was highly unusual, it cannot have been easy.

Sarah was also the archetypal working mother. She burned with maternal passion for her children and was riddled with guilt whenever she was away from them. She was always determined to prove herself domestically. When the family went on their holiday in Yorkshire, long before she was famous but when it was already becoming obvious that she would be the breadwinner, her friend Elizabeth Inchbald describes Sarah as spending her time doing the washing and ironing every afternoon. Not for her the concept of 'me time'. Physical separation from her family only made Sarah ache to do more. Again and again in her letters, she described the pain of having to be parted from her children, fretting about how they were doing without her. William, on the other hand, was a presence at home – but not always a particularly sensitive one. He was happier tending his vegetable garden at the house in Nuneham Courtenay and discussing his investments, rather than engaging emotionally with his children.

Perhaps it was inevitable that William would look elsewhere for physical affection to build up his self-esteem. Sarah knew of the existence of at least one mistress. There were probably more. Male infidelity was nothing unusual at the time. Sheridan was constantly unfaithful to both his wives, for instance. But the Siddons' creed was based on the supreme virtue of married life. We do not know whether Sarah confronted William. There was no real danger that his being unfaithful to her would cause a scandal in the press, as hers to him would have done, but it still represented a betrayal. Worse, he gave her venereal disease. Initially she thought that the illness she began to suffer was simply to do with her nerves. But by 1792 she knew the truth.

As they grew older, both the Siddons suffered from increasing bouts of ill health. William had acute arthritic pain in one foot and sciatica in the other. By 1795 he was going everywhere on crutches. Hester even speculated that his problems were so severe that Sarah might be widowed, and that Hester would be able to match-make her friend with a wealthy lawyer they both knew. Sarah had also begun to suffer from rheumatoid arthritis. The painful blisters around her mouth, which friends and family saw her picking at endlessly, were pronounced as being erysipelas. My own suspicion is that they were the progression of syphilis, but that this incendiary fact needed to be kept secret. Hester also speculated that her friend had scrofula (tuberculosis of the neck). Sarah often felt sick. She frequently fainted. Her letters to her friends are full of confidences that she was feeling low. Her depression is understandable. Her responsibilities were formidable. William was, by now, emotionally distant. As a young woman Sarah tended to lose weight when she was unhappy, and her friends and family worried about how thin she was becoming. As she aged, she would put on weight instead. Neither was satisfactory, given that she needed to continue to appear on stage to please her adoring audiences.

The greatest strain on the Siddons marriage, however, was undoubtedly the fate of the family they had created together. Several of their children died young. This was not unusual at the time but must still have been painful. The Siddons' oldest son Henry was not a success professionally. Did Sarah ever speculate that he was like his father? Their second son George, who, as a child gave them so much joy, decided to make a living for himself far away from the family home in India. But far worse were the deaths of their daughters Maria in 1798 and then Sally in 1803. The gossipy Hester wrote to some friends in 1801, three years after Maria's death, about Sarah:

nothing does her any good…or produces any but a momentary Relief… anxiety of mind increases it almost to Distraction, but …she has Martyred herself with unavailing Remedies, and will try no more.[3]

Hester went on to report that Sarah had become painfully thin and was taking laudanum to ease her suffering. The mutual friends must promise not to tell anyone about this, though, since 'Confession of Illness is to her a Ruin.'[4] As we have seen, Sarah deliberately sought to keep William unaware of the complex web of emotions surrounding Maria on her deathbed. As far as he was concerned, Maria was engaged to Lawrence. Only Sarah knew the truth, that Lawrence had turned his attention to Sally instead. William was not present for the promise Maria extracted as she lay dying from Sally, that her sister would never marry Lawrence. I find myself wondering if William ever questioned why Maria's fiancé was not asked to be at her bedside when she died. Clearly the Siddons household operated in a culture of secrecy.

Worse were the circumstances surrounding Sally's subsequent death. This time, Sarah was not at her daughter's deathbed. William had been so intent on the need for his wife to continue earning that he had played down the situation and encouraged Sarah to stay in Ireland for longer than necessary. Every mother can relate to the suffering Sarah must have gone through as a result. It would have been well-nigh impossible for her not to lay the blame at William's door. On the other hand, and probably largely unspoken, were two mitigating factors. As we have seen, Sarah may have been swayed by her blossoming relationship with Philomen Galindo. At the very least this would have been a distraction. And before that, her decision to renew her close friendship with Thomas Lawrence, even though she knew Sally was still in love with him, caused mother and daughter to grow apart in Sally's final years. If only Sarah had made it to Sally's deathbed, she would have been able to beg forgiveness.

The Siddons' only surviving daughter was the much younger Cecilia, conceived when they were reconciled after Sarah discovered that William had given her syphilis. Cecilia bore an uncanny resemblance to Maria. Sarah confessed that this sometimes made it hard even to look at her. Cecilia's parents were always over-fearful about her health, haunted by her sisters' fate. Sarah explained to her friend Hester that 'she has that cruel tendency in her Constitution that has already cost me so many Sighs and grounds and tears.'[5] Inevitably, Cecilia was indulged. Sarah admitted this to the Galindos and also confessed that she herself had suicidal thoughts at times, fantasising about following Sally and Maria into the afterlife. All the harder, then, to brace herself to go out and perform again at Covent Garden, after all the suffering she had gone through. She had achieved fame and fortune, yet 'I do not think myself at liberty to give myself up to my own selfish gratifications.'[6]

Sarah's letters to the Galindos the summer after Sally's death reveal that the Siddons' marriage came under huge strain at that time. 'I have been sorely harassed with domestic cares', she wrote to Catherine; 'the present cloud is dispersed but how soon it may gather again I fear to think,' she confessed to Philomen.[7] Sarah implies William threatened her physically. Yet ending their long marriage would have enormous consequences. Divorce would be out of the question. Sarah's carefully constructed public image was based on her being the respectable, married actress. By now she had become a national treasure, personifying all that was best in being British. Then there were the feelings of their family to consider. Sarah had always been the virtuous oldest daughter and sister. She disapproved of her sister Anne's scandalous life. Her parents may have been set against her marrying William, but once the deed had been done, they would surely have expected her to continue as his wife. The fact that the patriarch of the Kemble family, Sarah's father Roger, had died while she was away in Ireland may well have played a part in the Siddons' decision to separate. They no longer had to prove to Roger that he had been wrong to oppose their marriage.

Sarah's biographers have tended to play the separation right down. James Boaden, her unofficial biographer, did report that the couple had formally separated, citing 'some inequalities of *temper*' as being the cause.[8] Perhaps Sarah's decision to ask Thomas Campbell to write an authorised biography soon afterwards was partly at least an attempt to refute this. Campbell is clear that 'the report that they were separated from alienation, was absolutely unfounded.'[9] He seeks to gloss the whole thing over, 'their partial separation, if such it could be called, was one of convenience, if not of absolute necessity.'[10] Both suffered from ill health, and this meant that William had to be in Bath, while Sarah worked in London, but they often went to see each other, regardless, after their 'partial separation' he argued.[11] Sarah's various Victorian and twentieth-century biographers have followed suit. Sarah's celebrity instincts to control the message seem to have worked admirably.

The spring of 1804 found William and Sarah spending time together in the cottage they had rented in Hampstead. He persuaded her to have a painful new electrical treatment for rheumatism (as mentioned in Chapter 8). Her surgeon advised her against this quack remedy, saying it would not harm her but equally would do her no good. She went ahead anyway. Did she perhaps reflect, when the pain she experienced turned out to be extreme, that yet again William's instincts were the wrong ones? The two helpless invalids were then laid up together. The problem spread from Sarah's hips to her toes, so she was unable to move her left side and was bedridden for several weeks. Finally, circumstances meant that they had time to talk to each other.

There must have been a lot to say. William had not pulled his weight. He had been insensitive to the needs of his family. He had been unfaithful, and he had even given her a venereal disease. So determined had he been that she kept earning, that he had hidden from her the real condition of Sally's health. He had been the cause of her failure to see Sally at the end. For his part, he would have argued that Sarah showed little interest in him apart from humouring him. Her relationships with Galindo and Lawrence must have troubled him. What were her motives? She had shut him out of her relationships with their daughters. Any spark they once had was long gone. Separation must have seemed the only sensible course. Yet it needed to be handled carefully. There was to be not the slightest whiff of scandal.

A few letters from that period give some insight into what was going on. Sarah wrote to Hester in September 1804 that she was 'quite apathised by disgust and disappointment', notionally by her debilitating illness, but also, as subtext, by her painful talks with William as to the state of their marriage.[12] Inevitably, the fear was that the press might get wind of what was happening. Good-hearted Elizabeth Inchbald, who had got between Sarah and her brother John Philip over the Galindo affair, still wrote to a friend about Sarah:

> By-the-bye, what wicked accusations have been laid against this woman! Poor John Bull loves to set up, but then he loves equally to pull down.[13]

Elizabeth bought into the party line. Anything derogatory said about Sarah or written about her in the press was wholly unjust.

Sarah's own simmering anger at the strain she was under, thanks to William, shows through in another letter to Hester later that autumn, when she was visiting her friend Charlotte Fitzhugh's home and William followed her there:

> Pray did the Newspaper inform you that Mr Siddons had *'done me the honour of a visit to Bannisters.'* I only wish I could have Seen and heard you read this Senseless Paragraph![14]

In October the couple separated formally, having drawn up a financial settlement a few months earlier. William gave Sarah £20,000 (£1.82 million today) and promised to leave the rest of his fortune to her on his death. By investing £20,000, she would bring in £1,000 per year extra income for herself (£93,620 today). Sarah returned to London, while William went to set up home in Bath.

William soon became a familiar figure in the city, walking everywhere on his two sticks. It was decided that their daughter, Cecilia, should attend a school there, run by a Miss Lee. Hester made a note in her diary that Cecy was 'sick and spoiled, fretful and fragile – her mother has put her to Miss Lee for Education, but they are fearful she will not live.'[15] It would have made sense to have Cecy at school near her father, rather than in London with her mother, who was still emotionally entangled with the Galindos and moving out of the family home into temporary lodgings in Prince's Street.

For Sarah the situation must have felt precarious. Rumours about her abounded. The gossip about her relationship with Lawrence never seemed to go away. On 1 December William placed an advertisement in the press on Sarah's behalf, promising a £1,000 reward (£93,620 today) to whoever could uncover where a rumour had originated, which had spread 'the most wicked and injurious slanders' that Sarah was having an adulterous relationship with the painter.[16] Even the Prince of Wales reportedly told his father, George III, always a great admirer of Sarah's, that she had run away with the artist. Lawrence had been working on a new full-length portrait of Sarah, which had been exhibited at the Royal Academy earlier in the year. He painted it by candlelight and Sarah reportedly sat until 2 am at one point, so he could get it finished. Inevitably, gossips saw an opportunity for scandal. Sarah must have had to beg William to place the advertisement for her. There were no takers for William's reward. Yet, if Sarah were having a sexual relationship with anyone at this time, it was surely with Philomen. At the same time a mad young Irish student became convinced that he was in love with her and had to be bound over to keep the peace. For someone who had avoided the scandal of sexual intrigue all her professional life, the situation felt as if it were spiralling out of control.

A letter from Sarah to William dated 16 December 1804, which Sarah made sure was included in Thomas Campbell's authorised biography, bears quoting in full:

> My Dear Sid,
> I am really sorry that my little flash of merriment should have been taken so seriously, for I am sure, however we may differ in trifles, *we can never cease to love each other.* You wish me to say what I expect to have done. I can expect nothing more than you yourself have designed me in your will. Be (as you ought to be) the master of all while God permits; but, in case of your death, only let me be put out of the power of any person living. This is all that I desire; and I think you cannot but be convinced that is reasonable and proper.
> Your ever affectionate and faithful, "SS".[17]

She still ran the risk, on his death, of being in thrall to whomever he decided to leave his fortune. Hence, she was forced to beg that he ensure she would be safely protected. In practice, when William did die, he left specific bequests including property to their two sons, Henry and George, and an allowance for Cecilia, plus money to pay for her education. The rest of his estate he left to 'my wife Sarah Siddons ... [as] sole executrix of my last will'.[18] Rightly so since his entire fortune was due to her exertions.

Hester had always been very much on Sarah's side while the two were married, but once they separated, she became fonder of William and more critical of Sarah. An entry in her diary reads:

> I know not why [William's]...wife turned him out so in his Old Age Poor Fellow! or whether he turned *himself* out; but the World is beginning I see to blame *her* and pity *him;* they had better have gone on together.[19]

William visited Hester at her house in Wales and then returned to Bath. Once Hester spent time alone with William and was no longer Sarah's confidante about the state of her marriage, she saw William in a different light.

A letter of William's to Hester from Bath makes no mention of Sarah at all. Instead, he jokes about his cats and mentions Sarah's sister, Fanny Twiss, and her husband, with whom he is clearly still on very good terms. A second talks of his finding a letter from Sarah on his table, on his return from Wales. She had sent the Piozzis love, apparently, and admitted that she was currently finding writing letters difficult. He had written a long ode about the recent victory at the Battle of Trafalgar, which he was hoping would be read aloud at the Theatre Royal. He sounds reconciled to his new life, while she still comes across as emotionally unsettled.

Relations between the two remained remarkably cordial. William visited Sarah's new house, Westbourne Farm, for six whole weeks the following summer. He even wrote a poem, extolling its delights. Sarah was in better health, he reported to Hester. The pair then spent the summer together at Broadstairs with their son Henry's two little girls, who were recovering from measles. Again, Sarah ensured that Thomas Campbell included in his biography a warm letter of hers to Henry, praising the children, and admitting they seemed to prefer to play games with William and with her ever-present companion, Patty Wilkinson, rather than with Sarah herself. The Siddons had shown they could successfully co-grandparent.

Some eighteen months later, on 11 March 1808, William died suddenly. He was 64, Sarah, 52. She had been staying with him in Bath the previous month and had performed there, but she was working in Edinburgh when she heard the news. She immediately broke off her acting engagement and returned to London for a fortnight. There was much to reflect upon. William had died, Sarah wrote to their friend Elizabeth Harcourt 'as he had prayed to die, without a sigh.'[20] To Hester, Sarah allowed herself to be more open about her own feelings: 'There is something so awful in this sudden dissolution of so long a connection, that I shall feel it longer than I shall speak of it.'[21] She hoped, she wrote, that she would have a death like his, 'forgetting and forgiving all my errors', as, by implication, she felt people were forgetting and forgiving his.[22] Tellingly, again, Sarah was happy for Thomas Campbell to include this letter. It helped her image, certainly, while at the same time reflecting her true feelings.

After such a long marriage it cannot have been easy for William and Sarah, when they finally spent time together in 1804, both invalids in the rented cottage in Hampstead, to come to the realisation that neither of them wanted the status quo to continue. There was much ground that needed to be covered. It was to their credit that they largely managed to emerge without too much anger and bitterness. They continued to see each other and even to holiday together with their grandchildren. William's correspondence after he and Sarah separated shows that he managed to carve out a contented life for himself. Hester, certainly, thought more of him as a single man than she had as a married one. For Sarah, the end of her marriage meant some initial emotional turbulence. But longer term, she could finally fulfil her long-held dream of owning a country property. Now she was able to begin thinking of retiring from the stage and living a quieter life.

Chapter 18

Retirement

'I have no more to say but – Farewell! and God bless you!'[1]

The split from William and his subsequent death left Sarah financially secure, after all her years of working to support the family. Her health was deteriorating and the longing she had for a quieter existence – something which had consumed her for many years – finally looked like an achievable goal. As for her professional life, a fire had destroyed Covent Garden, soon after she and her brother John Philip had taken the momentous decision to leave Sheridan's Drury Lane and make the rival theatre their base. The disaster had meant that Sarah felt she needed to support John Philip and the rest of the family in the plans to rebuild and reopen the building. Inevitably, she appeared alongside John Philip in the production of *Macbeth* which opened New Covent Garden in 1809. Yet, earlier that year, she had drawn up an official agreement with the management there that this season would be billed as her last. Sarah was 54 years old and retirement beckoned.

Despite the billing, Sarah did not retire that season. Nevertheless, she performed far less frequently and those who came to see her on stage increasingly commented on her frailty. Sir Walter Scott wrote to a friend, having seen Sarah play in Edinburgh the following March: 'I was quite shocked to see her, for the last two years have made a dreadful inroad both on her voice and person.'[2] She had put on weight, and this restricted her choice of roles. At one point, playing Isabella in William Shakespeare's *Measure for Measure*, she knelt and found she could not get up again. Two cast members had to hurry forward so they could come to her assistance. Lawrence told their mutual friend Joseph Farington that he thought she ought to retire. He had seen her in Shakespeare's *King John* and her voice had failed at one point. But he had also seen her as Volumnia in Shakespeare's *Coriolanus* and was highly complimentary.

The following spring, in April 1812, the writer Henry Crabb Robinson was in the audience when Sarah played the part of Margaret of Anjou in Dr Franklin's *The Earl of Warwick*. He admitted that 'her advancing age is a real pain to me. As an actor she has left with me the conviction that there never was, and never will be, her equal.'[3] That same summer, only a few weeks before her magnificent retirement evening, he recorded seeing her recite Milton's *Comus*. This time he was not so impressed. The role was for a 16-year-old girl and Sarah looked her age, he noted, dressed in a low-brimmed gipsy hat with dangling feathers, in an unbecoming garment which made her seem all the larger. She looked 'old and I had almost said ugly – her fine features were lost in the distance and her disadvantage of years and bulk [were] made as prominent as possible.'[4]

Having been determined to retire, Sarah nevertheless had mixed feelings about what she was about to do. Knowing this might be her last chance and having not gone on her usual tour or given a single performance throughout the summer of 1811, she took up the challenge of the next Covent Garden season with relish. She appeared on stage fifty-seven times, reprising many of the roles that had made her reputation, in a sort of greatest hits season. She played Mrs Beverley in *The Gamester*, Elvira in *Pizarro*, Euphrasia in *The Grecian Daughter*, Mrs Haller in *The Stranger*, Belvidera in *Venice Preserved* and Isabella in *The Fatal Marriage*, the role which had made her name at Drury Lane all those years ago (see Appendix 2). From her Shakespearean repertoire she performed the roles of Lady Macbeth, Isabella in *Measure for Measure*, Queen Katharine in *Henry VIII*, Constance in *King John*, and Hermione in *The Winter's Tale*.

That season Sarah could command a higher nightly fee than ever before – some fifty guineas per night, according to the secretary of the Covent Garden Theatre (£4,000 today). And she still enjoyed the fruits of her fame. Lord Byron came to see her perform and was bowled over by her power on stage: 'Nothing ever was, or can be, like her,' he pronounced.[5] She decided to take temporary lodgings in Pall Mall that season, rather than commute each night from Westbourne Farm. Thomas Campbell, her official biographer, remembered seeing a long line of carriages parked up along the street. He assumed at first that a member of the royal family must be at St James's but then realised that they all 'belonged to the visitants of the Tragic Queen.'[6]

On 12 June 1812, just a couple of weeks before the date set for her retirement, Sarah confessed her apprehension to her friend Hester Piozzi: 'In this last season of my acting, I feel as if I were mounting the first step of a ladder conducting me to the other world.'[7] She had spent her whole life on stage. The thought of leaving it must have felt like a sort of death. The night was fixed for 29 June 1812 and the production, of course, was to be *Macbeth* with John Philip taking the title role and Sarah playing Lady Macbeth, her most celebrated part. She had asked her nephew, Horace Twiss, her sister Fanny's son, to write the poem she intended to recite for her farewell. The planning went on for several months. In March, Sarah had approved a draft from Horace but asked him to consult with others who could be more objective than her about it. In early June, a Miss Berry wrote in her journal that she had met Sarah at a party and that the famous actress took her into a corner to try out Horace's verses on her.

On the special night, the theatre was full. Audiences for Sarah's previous performances had been met with a written warning that there were no more spaces available for her retirement performance. Each ticket bore a red seal with the word 'Farewell' embossed on it. Thomas Lawrence, her soulmate and perhaps her oldest fan, was in one of the boxes. Joseph Farington, their mutual friend, sat as close to the stage as he could. Richard Brinsley Sheridan, the manager of the rival Drury Lane Theatre, was there in the orchestra with his second wife, all past disputes with Sarah and John Philip put to one side. The poet Samuel Rogers had written Sarah a verse prologue for the occasion. We do not know what Sarah wore, but for previous performances she had tended to favour a Mary Stuart costume of black velvet, with a white ruff and lots of jewellery. It seems likely this was how she looked that night.

The play progressed until the actors reached the end of the Lady Macbeth sleepwalking scene – the scene she had revolutionised by her innovation of going through the motions of washing her hands, as she slept. Sarah uttered Lady Macbeth's final lines in the play: 'What's done cannot be undone – To bed, to bed, to bed!'[8] At this there was a standing ovation. It seemed as if it would never come to an end. Eventually John Philip realised that the audience probably had no wish to see the rest of the play. The curtain was lowered, but the applause continued. He sent one of the cast members to ask the audience what they would like to do. He was met with yet more noise. He took this to mean that they preferred the play to stop there. After about twenty minutes the curtain was raised again to reveal Sarah, dressed all in white and sitting at a table.

Sarah came downstage to gaze out at her audience. Again, the applause was so loud it was impossible for her to make herself heard. After a time, she curtsied and bowed, and the audience duly fell silent. It was exactly 10 pm. She then recited her nephew Horace's poem. She had decided, just as she had when she gave her 'Three Reasons' speech, all those years ago in Bath, to resort to trite, clichéd verse as the best means of conveying her feelings to her public. She spoke of herself in the third person. Horace Twiss's four stanzas, arranged into rhyming couplets, finished with:

> On her, who parting to return no more,
> *Is* now the mourner she but *seemed* before –
> Herself subdued, resigns the melting spell,
> And breathes, with swelling heart, her long, her last Farewell![9]

Her recitation took a full eight minutes to perform.

It did the trick. Again, Sarah was met with tumultuous applause. She withdrew, bowing, to be led off by an attendant. She seemed to be greatly moved by the effect she had had on her fans, but Farington noticed that she did not shed tears. John Philip then came on stage, wiping the tears from his own eyes, to ascertain that the audience really did want the evening to finish there. A note by John Philip on the manuscript of Horace Twiss's poem recorded that the receipts that night totalled £820 (£57,540 today). The actress Dora Jordan, Sarah's comic nemesis, was envious of the result Sarah had achieved. Her own life would take a very different turn. When her lover, the Duke of Clarence, left her and their large family two years later, she would be left virtually penniless and go on to die alone and in poverty. She longed, she wrote at Sarah's retirement, to make her own final stage appearance. The path of impeccable, matronly respectability, which Sarah had always chosen to tread, looked preferable at this point to that of royal mistress.

Yet, the 57-year-old Sarah could not give up her theatrical life quite that easily. She missed the intellectual stimulation of studying for a role and then performing it. She might have dreamed of a life of seclusion at Westbourne Farm, but inevitably she got drawn back into life on the stage. That autumn, she agreed to perform in Newcastle, alongside the 19-year-old William Charles Macready, as his wife – Mrs Beverley – in Edward Moore's *The Gamester* (see Appendix 2). It was Macready's father, William, whose investment in the Manchester theatre the Galindos had joined, after receiving a loan from Sarah. Her husband, William, had cut short a contract at that time for her to play in Newcastle. Perhaps this partly justified in her mind her decision to take to the boards again so soon. Perhaps, also, she felt Newcastle was sufficiently far away from London not to count. Young Macready was tactfully complimentary about Sarah's performance and recorded that she gave him some careers advice. He should study as much as he could, she told him, and not marry until he was 30. He must keep his mind on his art.

Retirement was not easy. Sarah had been accustomed to being lauded wherever she went. It must have been difficult at first to become just another member of society. A particularly poisonous verbal portrait of Sarah in retirement was painted in a letter from the aristocrat Charles Spencer Stanhope to his brother John that autumn. He regretted that he had not seen Sarah at her friend Charlotte Fitzhugh's home in Hampshire, he wrote. He admitted that Sarah was not particularly popular with the Fitzhughs' social circle. Her attitude, apparently, was 'graciosissima pomposissima', as he put it. She 'monopolis[ed the sofa] most infamously with her corpulent latitude', bowing like a queen to those she counted as admirers, which 'cannot but disgust'.[10] When Sarah had performed at the house in the past, Charlotte had apparently behaved like her maid and had been thrown into hysterics during the play, convinced that Sarah had died, when she was in reality only acting.

The retired Sarah made a far more favourable impression on the American writer and diplomat, Washington Irving. Even though she was no longer on the stage, he commented that her manner 'still partakes of the state and gravity of tragedy'.[11] It was difficult for her, Irving felt, to throw aside such a long-acquired habit of solemnity. She was very gracious, he noted, and told them an anecdote with enormous emotion about her admiring the scenery in North Wales. Her face was handsome, He did not notice any wrinkles. But her body had lost its shape, even though she remained a dignified figure.

Sarah's theatrical voice often gave the impression she was putting on airs and graces. A possibly apocryphal story tells of her buying some material and asking the draper, 'Will it wash?' in tones which sounded as if she were declaiming the lines in one of her Drury Lane tragedies.[12] Another reported her inadvertently talking about one of her favourite foods in blank verse.

Thomas Campbell, Sarah's authorised biographer, described her coming to dine at his house. She preferred not having to be paraded in front of strangers, he noted. But once, two Americans turned up unannounced, one of whom was Washington Irving's brother. The Campbells could not get rid of them. When Sarah's carriage approached, Campbell went out to warn her. It was the only time, he wrote, that he ever saw a cloud pass across her brow: 'She received my apology very coldly, and walked into my house with tragic dignity,' to face her public.[13]

Now she was retired, Sarah threw herself into the life she had always dreamed of achieving. She entertained her friends at Westbourne Farm, and later at her house in Regent's Park, delighting in throwing large lunch parties. The year after her retirement, she took her daughter Cecy and her companion Patty Wilkinson on a trip to Paris, her first visit to the city. Once her brother John Philip had also retired, she would visit him in Lausanne. Now she could also spend more time sculpting with her friend Anne Damer at Anne's studios in Strawberry Hill. Yet the memory of her enormous talent as an actress still lingered. Byron, for instance, refused to go and see Sarah's successor as the leading tragedienne at Covent Garden, Elizabeth O'Neill, because he preferred to keep intact his memories of Sarah's *'beau idéal* of acting'.[14]

In February 1813, only eight months after her retirement, Sarah embarked on a new venture. Queen Charlotte contacted her to ask if she would read to the royal family along with a selected audience at Windsor. Sarah was delighted and plans were laid for her to read several passages from the works of Shakespeare. Sarah stayed the night at Frogmore Cottage, where the queen was most anxious to ensure she made herself at home. Sarah's first reading took place at Frogmore the next evening and was a great success with her royal patrons. Queen Charlotte even presented Sarah with a gold chain with a jewelled cross as a thank-you present. The next day Sarah gave a more intimate reading to the queen and several of the princesses, this time choosing John Milton's *Paradise Lost* and Thomas Gray's *Elegy Written in a Country Churchyard*. She was even permitted to sit down while she read, rather than having to stand in the presence of royalty.

This led to another adventure. Sarah decided to do some dramatic readings from Shakespeare and Milton at the Argyll Rooms in central London. A large red screen acted as her backdrop, and a light shining from behind it illuminated her head as if she were wearing a halo. She sat at a raised reading desk, on which lay quarto volumes of the texts. That way, there was no need to commit everything to memory. Sometimes she recited and sometimes she read aloud. She was dressed all in white with her dark hair swept up in the fashionable à la Grecque style. The effect was notably elegant. When she needed to consult her books, she brandished a pair of glasses, which she waved gracefully. Several audience members were reminded of Reynolds' portrait of Sarah as *The Tragic Muse*. Whereas on stage she would only have played one role on any given night, here she could take on all the different parts. Her Macbeth was particularly notable.

The readings were an instant success. The six she gave initially at the Argyll Rooms brought in a profit of £1,300 (£90,240 today). In a wise move, she donated the proceeds of the first of these nights to the widow of a fellow actor, Andrew Cherry, who had been in Tate Wilkinson's company. The effect was that the readings were seen not primarily as a money-making venture, but as a chance for selected members of the public to spend an intimate evening with this great actress. For the pleasure of doing so, they were normally charged half a guinea each (£35 today). Various accounts from members of the audience were unanimous in their praise. Sarah made the texts come alive. The Anglo-Irish novelist, Maria Edgeworth, writing to Thomas Campbell, explained how she felt that 'I had never before fully understood or sufficiently admired Shakespeare, or known the full powers of the human voice and the English language.'[15] The Scottish legal scholar, Professor George Joseph Bell, was particularly complimentary about Sarah's portrayal of Hamlet seeing the ghost. He felt the presence of the spectre more fully than he ever had on stage, he explained. Hester Piozzi was more critical – she and Sarah were growing apart at this point – but she admitted it was 'a very great performance, and … her attitudes and gestures, and figure, are incomparable.'[16]

Sarah gave these readings in many different locations over several years. Both universities of Oxford and Cambridge asked her to read to their academics. Cecilia went with her to Cambridge and wrote to Patty that the trial scene from *The Merchant of Venice* had been a particular success. Sarah even gave a reading at a Mrs Forsyth's boarding house in Broadstairs, that night's proceeds going to the Margate Sea-Bathing Infirmary.

Once Sarah had moved into her house in Regents Park, she often gave private readings there. One evening the painter Benjamin Haydon was among the guests, as was Sarah's old friend, Thomas Lawrence, by now Sir Thomas and President of the Royal Academy. That night, as so often, Sarah read from *Macbeth*. There was a short interval, where tea and refreshments were provided. Before the two had finished eating, a bell sounded, like a church bell calling the faithful to prayer, as Haydon described it, and their hostess began again. Silently, shamefacedly, the audience crept back to their seats, balancing their cups and saucers on their knees. Lawrence, 'the *enfant terrible*' as Haydon described him, 'but lately restored to grace', had a mouth full of toast. Soon his eyes began to water with the strain of keeping quiet.[17] Now and then he would give a sly crunch, looking guilty and overawed, pretending to pay attention to Sarah's powerful voice proclaiming 'Eye of newt and toe of frog' before he took another furtive bite.[18]

In 1813, only a year after her retirement, a concerted attempt was made by Sarah's supporters to persuade her to return to the stage. Books entitled *Recall of Mrs Siddons to the Stage* were placed at the stationers Hookham & Eber's in Old Bond Street and at the London Coffee House in Ludgate Hill. The public were invited to sign, to entreat Sarah to change her mind. One of these books survives and sports 518 signatures, many from well-known figures of the day. Wisely, Sarah resisted. The following year Lord Byron and the Drury Lane Committee tried to persuade her to return for a single season, but again she refused. It suited her far better to appear when she pleased, rather than having to be at the beck and call of any management. In her notebook she copied down Byron's poem *She Walks in Beauty*: 'A mind at peace with all below,/A heart whose love is innocent!'[19] This was her ideal.

That said, Sarah did agree to giving selected benefit performances. In June 1816 she performed on behalf of her brother Charles and his wife, who had run into financial difficulties managing Covent Garden. She also travelled to Edinburgh, after the death of her eldest son, Henry, and gave performances over ten nights to raise money for his widow and children. She was keen to choose roles which suited her age and appearance, holding back on playing Lady Beverley from Edward Moore's *The Gamester*. Perhaps she had learned her lesson from acting alongside the much younger Macready a couple of years earlier. Nevertheless, her son George wrote from India to his cousin, Horace Twiss, wishing his mother would give up acting altogether. Hester, too, wrote to their mutual friend, Thomas Sedgwick Whalley, lamenting the fact Sarah had felt the need to tread the boards again to help her son's family.

At the request of Queen Charlotte, Sarah was persuaded to give a performance at Covent Garden Theatre, as Lady Macbeth, for the specific edification of two of the royal children, Princess Charlotte and Prince Leopold. Princess Charlotte was unwell on the night itself, but the Covent Garden management decided to press on regardless. The essayist William Hazlitt was in the audience and wrote of Sarah: 'The homage she has received is greater than that which is paid to Queens.'[20] Sarah was stage royalty, and worthy of more veneration than that shown to the minor royals in her audience. Yet Hazlitt also admitted that he thought it a mistake she played the role at this late stage of her life. Prince Leopold, it was reported, was bored by her performance. He spent the whole time glued to the text of the play, never looking up at Sarah herself, despite his mother's jogging his elbow and tapping him with her fan.

In September 1814, as a 59-year-old widow, Sarah took her daughter Cecilia and their companion, Patty Wilkinson, on a two-month visit to Paris. Hostilities between the two nations had been suspended, with Napoleon's imprisonment in Elba, and lots of British had flocked to see the city as result, despite the fact the Battle of Waterloo would take place only nine months later. The Duke of Wellington was also in Paris and the two famous people were introduced at a reception. They stood together in the middle of the room in total silence. Neither could think what to say to the other, to get the conversation going. Despite their huge fame, both were shy socially. They were simply overawed by the situation in which they found themselves.

The party also went to the Louvre to see the many treasures Napoleon had plundered from other European capitals. Thomas Campbell described taking Sarah's arm to look at a statue of Pericles. She was quiet for a few minutes before finally remarking:

> What a great idea it gives us of God to think that he has made a human being capable of fashioning so divine a form.[21]

As always, Sarah's simple, practical faith played out in the way she interpreted life and her way of expressing her thoughts was somewhat theatrical. Campbell noted that everyone in the hall seemed to be watching Sarah, even though many did not realise that she was the famous British tragedienne. In his words, 'she made you proud of English beauty, even in the presence of Grecian sculpture.'[22]

In 1817, five years after her own official retirement, when Sarah was aged 62, her brother John Philip also retired from the stage. He chose the role of Coriolanus in Shakespeare's play of the same name for his final London appearance – but a few nights earlier he had played Macbeth for the last time and Sarah had taken the role of Lady Macbeth. At the end of *Macbeth*, he fell into the arms of his younger brother, Charles, who laid him gently to the ground. A banquet for 300 guests was held in John Philip's honour. Thomas

Campbell composed an ode to be recited at the event. A commemorative vase was commissioned, and a silver medal struck, with a profile of John Philip on one side and words praising him as the last of all the Romans on the other. Sarah allowed herself to be uncharacteristically candid when she mentioned to the poet Samuel Rogers that she felt too much was being made of the event. Never known for her feminist views, she nevertheless remarked ruefully to Rogers: 'Well, perhaps in the next world women will be more valued than they are in this.'[23] A rare shaft of sibling rivalry had been allowed to shine through to the outside world.

That same year, Sarah moved back to London from Westbourne Farm to 27 Upper Baker Street. By now her daughter Cecilia was 23 years old and wanted the chance of a better social life. The house looked north onto Regents Park, almost as if it were in the countryside, but at the front it sported gracious sash windows and a railed parapet. The drawing room was panelled in dark oak, with a portrait of John Philip as Hotspur over the mantlepiece, giving what contemporaries felt was an old-fashioned effect. Sarah built on an extra room as a studio for her sculpting. Hester recorded being invited there to a magnificent lunch party, which did not start until 5 pm. The reason why the two friends had grown apart is not entirely clear, but Charlotte Fitzhugh stayed on afterwards as a go-between, and the two Grande Dames shook hands and made it up. Hester died a couple of years later, ten years before Sarah.

Sarah's last performance on stage was on 9 June 1819, when, aged 64, she played Lady Randolph in John Home's *Douglas* at Covent Garden, for her brother Charles's benefit. Charles's money worries had continued. When the actor playing Sarah's son addressed her with the words 'thou excellest all of womankind,' the audience broke into three rounds of spontaneous applause.[24] Charles's daughter, Fanny, who would later herself become an actress, remembered being taken as a child early in the afternoon by her father to see the dense crowd outside, waiting for the theatre doors to open for the big night. And she heard the huge roar from the audience, welcoming 'a solemn female figure in black' when Sarah appeared on stage.[25]

Sarah would live for twelve more years. In the early stages, she was still remarkably energetic. Her daughter Cecy described her climbing a glacier when they went to visit John Philip and his wife Pop, in Switzerland. Aged 67, Sarah published a child-friendly version of the works of John Milton, whose poetry she had loved all her life. Sarah's strong, instinctive Christian faith never left her and all her life she had found Milton's telling of the Christian story extremely powerful. Her role as an elderly celebrity continued. When David Garrick's widow died, Sarah was bequeathed a pair of gloves said to have been owned by William Shakespeare.

Benjamin Haydon recorded in his diary how he had struggled for six years with his painting *Christ Entering into Jerusalem*. The Royal Academy had turned the painting down for their annual exhibition, so Haydon decided to exhibit it by itself in 1820. The opening day, the room was full of the great and the good, all come to see the painting for themselves. No-one dared to criticise the unusual depiction of Christ or pass verdict on the painting itself. At 5 pm Sarah walked in and there was a respectful silence. Eventually, Sarah was asked if she liked the painting. She paused, dramatically. Haydon felt his reputation hanging in the balance. Slowly, deliberately, Sarah gave her opinion: 'It is completely successful.'[26] Haydon breathed a sigh of relief.

Two years later, at a party given by Lord Lansdowne, George IV introduced the French ambassador to a severe old lady dressed in crepe with a black veil across her white hair. She seemed, he noted, as if she were the queen. 'I am Mrs Siddons,' she told him.[27] In 1827, when Sarah was 72 years old, Sir George Smart remembered how they had both been dining at a mutual friend's house, when some wags asked Sarah how old she was. They had placed bets and wanted to hear who was right. She was 78, she replied. When they had gone away, Sir George asked why she had told them she was older than she really was. When an old lady reached a certain age, explained Sarah, it was always better to add about ten years, so that people could comment on how superb you looked. But she did age, nevertheless. Three years before she died, the barrister Joseph Jekyll reported to a friend that he had 'Sat two hours with my old friend Mrs Siddons, a majestic ruin.'[28]

Sarah did not find it easy to give up the theatrical life she had always lived. She was only 56 years old when she officially retired and would live nearly twenty more years. Her health played a part in this decision to bring a halt to her professional life, as did her comparative financial security following William's death. She had long dreamed of a life of quiet retirement in the country. And yet, after a suitably memorable final performance at Covent Garden, she was soon lured back to tread the boards again, albeit on her own terms. It cannot have been easy to turn down requests, particularly for benefits to help her extended family. Performing was in her bones. Life must have felt strange without it. And besides, she enjoyed her position as the famous elderly actress who was also a national treasure. A good compromise was reached with the evenings of Shakespeare and Milton readings to selected audiences, which she devised and which proved to be a great success. Here she could still delight her audiences and bask in their applause. Overall, Sarah's final years were relatively peaceful. The pressures to earn to support her husband and children had evaporated. Gone were the troubles with the Galindos or the emotional painful deaths of her two daughters. She had had many years as a wife, but single life suited her very well. In retirement, she achieved a quiet dignity.

Epilogue

'with demonstrations of the strongest grief'.[1]

Sarah died on 8 June 1831, in her seventy-sixth year. She had been retired for nearly twenty years. And yet her funeral was attended by over 5,000 people. She was buried with due pomp and circumstance, as befits one of the greatest performers to have ever trod the boards, and someone who was rightly regarded as a national treasure. Her final years had been relatively quiet. Her niece Fanny Kemble, her much younger brother's eldest daughter, who was herself an actress, wrote a description of how Sarah now appeared supremely indifferent to everything around her, almost as if she were already dead. This sounds like dementia. Fanny attributed this lack of interaction to the fact her aunt had led her life in an 'overstimulating atmosphere of emotion, excitement and admiration', as if Sarah had operated in a constant fever of heightened stimulation, and that this had resulted in her losing her cognitive ability.[2] We would query this today. A full-on life no more leads to dementia than a very quiet one. But Fanny's words do give an interesting insight into how Sarah's way of life had been viewed by her immediate family; too many feelings swirling around, too many fans poring over her every mood. Sarah might try to cut a dignified figure, but to her family she was always intense and over-emotional.

Sarah's relationship with Thomas Lawrence continued, one key element in this passionate existence, albeit the two saw less and less of each other as the years progressed. In 1824, when Sarah was 69 and Lawrence was the 54-year-old President of the Royal Academy, Lawrence went out of his way to praise a portrait of Sarah to his students. This was *The Tragic Muse*, the famous painting by a former president, Sir Joshua Reynolds. When Sarah heard of this, she wrote to Lawrence. Where normally her letter-writing style is relatively straightforward, the phrasing here is so convoluted it is difficult to discern exactly what she meant. She found it hard, she wrote, to find words 'for the various and thronging ideas that fill my mind' at the thought of Lawrence eulogising Reynolds' painting.[3] So far, so straightforward. She then seems to go on to say that she would not exchange his praise for all the fame she had ever acquired, thanks to the many performances of tragedies in which she had been involved. Sarah was prone to hyperbole, but there seems almost a desperation in this admission to a man whose friendship had caused her such heartache over the years. And even she surely did not believe what she was writing. Perhaps she was just missing her old friend.

A couple of years later, Lawrence wrote Sarah a note. James Boaden, who was engaged in his unauthorised biography of Sarah at the time, had asked if he could use an engraving of one of Lawrence's portraits of her in the book. Lawrence was anxious that he choose the right one. Could Sarah help him? This seems a straightforward request, save for the over-elaborate way Lawrence signed off: 'With a thousand respects and a fixed, the very highest, Esteem, that has never known diminution, Ever, Dear Mrs Siddons, Obliged and Devoted Lawrence.'[4] It is as if both parties had their eyes fixed on their reputation beyond the grave. Two years after that, Sarah wrote to Lawrence asking for help on behalf of a mutual friend and this time finished: 'I have no more to say but Farewell! and God bless you! Sarah Siddons.'[5] The same year, she was dining with her brother Charles, Fanny Kemble's father, when she laid a hand on his arm and asked that, when she died, he and Lawrence carry her coffin to her grave. Lawrence was reportedly extremely moved when he heard of this. As fate would have it, though, he died before Sarah, the following year.

As so often with Lawrence, the emotional situation was complex. In Lawrence's later years he developed a huge crush on Sarah's actress niece, Fanny Kemble, who was said to bear an uncanny resemblance to her aunt. Writing about the experience many years later, Fanny noted that she risked becoming the fourth woman in the family 'whose life he would have disturbed and embittered'.[6] The 19-year-old Fanny had ambitions as an actress, and her father was having difficulties balancing the books at Covent Garden where he was manager, so it was decided that she should take on the role of Juliet in William Shakespeare's play. Sarah made sure to go and see her niece's debut on 5 October 1829, and cried with joy at seeing Fanny perform. Her brother Charles set up a box opposite the prompter's where Sarah could sit to watch her niece, undisturbed. She went several times; despite the fact the spot was draughty. For his part, Lawrence sat through performance after performance, sending Fanny obsessively detailed notes on how well or badly she had done each night. He noted every change in the inflection of her voice and in the variety of her gestures, heaping overwhelming praise on the young actress.

On Fanny's birthday, Lawrence sent her an engraving of Joshua Reynolds' *The Tragic Muse*, beautifully framed, with the inscription:

> This portrait by England's greatest painter, of the noblest subject of his pencil, is presented to her niece and worthy successor, by her most faithful and humble friend and servant, Lawrence.[7]

But he then had second thoughts. He hurriedly asked for the picture to be returned, so he could remove the words 'worthy successor'. He realised they risked becoming a hostage to fortune. When the engraving arrived back in his studio, Lawrence and his servant stood looking at it. Suddenly, Lawrence turned to his servant and asked that it be covered up. He could no longer bear it.

Another time, Lawrence was showing a drawing he had made of Fanny to her mother, who said that it reminded her very much of Sarah's dead daughter, Maria Siddons, to whom Lawrence had been engaged. As he replied that he agreed with her, Lawrence's voice choked with emotion. He wrote to another mutual friend that Fanny's eyes and hair put him in mind of the young Sarah. Her voice, too, was both powerful and sweet. And her intelligence reminded him of all the Kembles. Fanny admitted, even though she was forty years younger than Lawrence, that she might have been tempted to start some kind of relationship if he had not died quite suddenly. For his part, three days before his death, he had written to a female friend about how in his mind Fanny was linked to 'Lovechains' and 'skeletons of Roses'.[8]

Lawrence died on 7 January 1830, just seventeen months before Sarah, reportedly of ossification of the heart. To her credit, Fanny immediately sent a note to her cousin Cecilia, with whom she was very friendly. Cecy should prepare her mother for the news, she wrote. She would inevitably be very shocked, Fanny signed off affectionately to her cousin. She understood that Lawrence's real relationship was with Sarah, not with her, even though Lawrence had been preparing to start work on a full-length portrait of her in the role of Juliet, just as he had done for Sarah in the past. When Sarah died, under two years later, Fanny performed the role of Lady Macbeth at Covent Garden the night of her death in her honour. But everyone involved was painfully aware that she would never be the actress her famous aunt had been. Instead, Fanny went on to become a respected writer. She married an American, who owned slave plantations, and wrote movingly about her abolitionist sympathies towards his slaves.

In April 1831, Sarah was struck down by a serious illness. Her 'medical attendant' as her official biographer, Thomas Campbell, described him, was alarmed to see that what was reported as erysipelas had reoccurred on Sarah's ankles.[9] By the end of the month it looked as if she had made a good recovery. On Tuesday 31 May, however, she decided to venture out in her carriage. The weather was colder than she had realised. She contracted a high fever and the inflammation on her legs blew up again. This time she was seen by a Dr Leman, who reportedly made the situation worse by stuffing her full of food, so the gangrene she was now experiencing became increasingly painful. A week later, after having suffered acutely for several days, Sarah entered a coma. She died the following morning, Wednesday 8 June at around 8 am, at her home in

Regents Park. Her niece, Fanny Kemble, later wrote an account of Sarah's death, glossing over any pain. Her aunt had died, wrote Fanny, 'peaceably and without suffering, and in full consciousness'.[10] As so often, the message had been softened to enhance Sarah's image. It is worth noting that her symptoms were those of the fourth and final stage of gummatous syphilis, which can recur many years after the earlier stages, where soft, tumour-like balls of inflammation form and affect the nervous system and the liver.

Sarah's funeral took place a week later on Wednesday 15 June. At 10 am, a procession, which included a carriage containing her brother Charles Kemble and nephew Horace Twiss, who were both executors of her will, together with her son Henry's two boys, left her house in Baker Street and made its way to St Mary's Church in Paddington Green, where there was a new burial ground. Sarah's son George and his family, who were all living in India, were not represented. The family were followed by eleven mourning coaches, all filled with actors from the two big London theatres where she had made her professional life, Drury Lane and Covent Garden. The procession must have been extremely slow and respectful, as the mourners did not enter the church, which was under two miles away, until 11.30 am. At least 5,000 people lined the route, many of whom shed tears. At Sarah's request, her gravestone consisted of a very simple plain slab, with no mention of her fame or even her life as an actress:

> Sacred to the Memory of
> Sarah Siddons
> Who departed this life June 8, 1831, in her 76th year.
> 'Blessed are the dead who die in the Lord.'[11]

An unknown young woman, veiled, reportedly knelt beside the coffin 'with demonstrations of the strongest grief'.[12] Sarah would doubtless have liked this touch.

On the wall of the chancel a marble memorial was erected, and Sarah's son George, who had lived all his adult life in India, was, in time, buried there along with his wife. Nearly twenty years later a statue by the Scottish stonemason Thomas Campbell (not the Thomas Campbell whom Sarah had entrusted with her official memoirs) was erected in Westminster Abbey, beside that of Sarah's brother John Philip Kemble. She had her due place among the great men and women of Britain. This memorial was placed there thanks to the efforts of the actor William Charles Macready, with whom Sarah had performed when he was a young man, and to whom she had given some careers advice. Some fifty years later the famous Victorian stage actor Sir Henry Irving – who had come across Sarah when he was very young – unveiled a further statue of Sarah, in the pose she adopted for Reynolds' portrait *The Tragic Muse*. It stands today in the churchyard of St Mary's, Paddington. Sarah stares languidly out at the traffic roaring by on the A40.

Sarah left £35,000 (£3,381,000 today) in her will to her two surviving children – her son George and her daughter Cecilia – as well as to her son Henry's widow. The sum is large but not enormous, given the amount Sarah had made during her working life. She left some money to her companion, Patty Wilkinson. To her brother Charles she left a portrait of himself, and to her wayward sister Anne, who had always been a source of anxiety for her, she left provision that Anne's £20 annual allowance would continue for the rest of Anne's life (just under £2,000 per year today). To her friend Charlotte Fitzhugh, with whom she had often stayed at the Fitzhughs' Hampshire home, she left a mourning ring. Her other close friends – Hester Piozzi, Elizabeth Inchbald, Sir Thomas Lawrence and Thomas Sedgwick Whalley – had all died before Sarah. She left a mulberry ink stand, said to have been used by William Shakespeare, to George and Cecilia, along with the pair of Shakespeare's gloves Garrick's widow had in turn bequeathed to her. Everything was planned and ordered. Sarah's son George and his wife and family eventually came back to live in England. Sarah's daughter Cecilia married a Scottish solicitor named George Combe two years after her mother's death, and the couple went to live in the South of France. He reputedly insisted a phrenologist check his new wife's head before marrying her. Maybe he feared the damage that might have been caused by her theatrical parentage.

And what of Sarah's legacy? The problem with acting, and indeed with writing a biography about an actor, is that a performance only exists in the moment. No-one after 1819 (the final time she appeared on stage) has ever experienced Sarah Siddons' genius as an actress. And yet Sarah did play a key part in the changing of theatrical style. She focused intently on an emotional truth in characterisation, which is something we value highly to this day. Before her, David Garrick often came out of character to engage with the audience. Sarah never broke that infamous fourth wall. For her, character was all. And she was also revolutionary in her ability to emote. The enormously powerful effect she had on her audiences is clear in their reaction. She stood at the cusp of a societal change from the Age of Reason, where thought was all, to Romanticism, with its concentration on feelings and sensations. Sarah led the way to a performance style which was far less restrained, far more passionate and empathetic. As we have seen, the desire of theatre managers to increase their takings by rebuilding their theatres to accommodate much larger houses meant that, later in her career, this emotional element of Sarah's performances was increasingly difficult for her to achieve, given how far the audience were now seated from her. But, taking her career overall, it was nevertheless a key element in her armoury.

Sarah improved the status of female actors. She used the fact that she was a respectable married woman and a proud mother to her own advantage. Before she became such a success as an actress on the London stage, her fellow female performers had tended to be either former prostitutes or mistresses of wealthy men. Sarah kept her distance emotionally from her contemporary actresses. She only ever grew close to Elizabeth Inchbald, herself a married woman when they met, and who soon gave up acting altogether. She kept her distance from Dora Jordan, the mistress of William, Duke of Clarence, and who was often seen at the time as Queen of Comedy, while Sarah was Queen of Tragedy. Even Sarah's actress sisters failed to thrive performing alongside her, despite her early attempts to include them in the companies where she worked. None of her daughters had acting careers. And yet, thanks to Sarah's success, acting as a profession for women changed fundamentally. It no longer simply implied sexual availability, although it remained financially precarious for all but a very few. But Sarah's influence can be seen in the subsequent hugely successful careers of Ellen Terry and Mrs Patrick Campbell.

Sarah also blazed a trail in the way she controlled her own image. She understood that her celebrity status was something extremely valuable and which gave her great power. She ensured that engravings were made of her many portraits, so she became a famous face not just for the London theatre audience but also throughout Britain. She grasped the fact that reputation was all. She projected herself as someone socially acceptable, virtuous, married, a dedicated mother. As a result, she climbed from a relatively impoverished childhood to a successful adult life, numbering many of the rich and famous among her friends and acquaintances. She capitalised on the fact that she became the darling of the royal family. When stories circulated in the press about her financial meanness in Ireland, she worked hard to argue her own case. Like a modern-day celebrity, she knew that her status with her public might rise or fall at any point, and she feared the loss of her reputation. Yet later in life she was prepared to risk possible reputational damage by befriending Philomen Galindo. When Philomen's wife published incendiary accusations about her, Sarah was confident enough not to refute them. Far better, she judged, now her reputation as the darling of the nation was established, to lay low.

Sarah's success at this game is proven by the fact that her biographers have largely taken at face value the narrative she constructed about her own life. Even though several of them mentioned that William gave her syphilis, for instance, they did not question the contemporary accounts which attributed her poor health and eventual death to the skin disease erysipelas. They have accepted without question the account of events which caused Sarah to be sent to work as a maid at Guy's Cliffe, after her parents sought to end her relationship with William Siddons. They have tended to play down Catherine Galindo's account of Sarah's behaviour with Catherine's husband, and the fact that Sarah and William formally separated soon afterwards. Nor have they thought to analyse why it was so important to Sarah that she was seen as respectable. The last full-length biography of Sarah was published in 1970. Since then, academics have pointed out that Sarah behaved like a modern-day celebrity. This book has sought to expand on these ideas and relate them to Sarah's entire life, giving, it is intended, a much more rounded picture.

Talking of pictures, perhaps Sarah's greatest legacy today is in her portraits, rather than her skills as an actress. Thomas Gainsborough's elegant society portrait hangs in The National Gallery in London. There are two versions of Sir Joshua Reynolds' image of Sarah as The Tragic Muse, lifting a working actress to godlike status, one in the Huntington Art Gallery in America and one in the Dulwich Picture Gallery in London. Sir Thomas Lawrence's many images of Sarah give away the half-kept secret that she was the love of his life, despite his relationships with both her elder daughters and her niece. The portraits emphasise Siddons' beauty and glamour. They only hint at her complex, often tragic life.

Sarah's celebrity status has echoes for us today but so too, I would argue, does her status as a beleaguered working mother. She did not inherit wealth and it soon became evident that she would be the sole breadwinner in her marriage. Even today that is relatively unusual. In Sarah's lifetime it was virtually unheard of. What is not the case today, but was for Sarah, was that despite her earning all the money, everything the couple owned was legally William's and not hers. Sarah felt strongly maternal towards her children, and clearly found being away from them while she was working extremely difficult. Worse, she failed to make it back in time from her tour of Ireland to be at the deathbed of her daughter Sally. The guilt surrounding working motherhood must have been particularly extreme for Sarah at that point, but many of us can relate to her fetishizing the washing and ironing while on a family holiday or writing anxiously to her friend Hester about how her own children were doing without her.

For Sarah, her personal life, her friends and, above all, her family, were probably more important overall than her enormous success as an actress. She was always an incredibly hard worker. When her London seasons failed to pay, she set off on exhaustive summer tours to ensure the bills were covered. As time went on, it became evident that this was detrimental to her health. She never stopped being a working actress – albeit better paid even than Garrick. She never sought to take on any managerial responsibilities, nor to write any plays. And she was also careful to remain resolutely non-political. Her professional life as solely an actress meant that her reputation today, I would argue, is less than she deserves.

For those of us seeking to give historical women their due place in history, Sarah is relatively unrewarding. She nearly always accepted the condition of women at the time without question. I suspect she would have shuddered to be called a feminist. And yet she was someone who was clearly outstanding at what she did. As the reviewer in *The Morning Post* wrote, during Sarah's triumphant season at Drury Lane 'such a constellation of accomplishments were probably never exhibited in the dramatic world.'[13] She proved it was possible to be a successful actress without being objectified as sexually available. She also succeeded in continuing her career as an important, powerful performer as she aged physically, something which even female actors today often find difficult. Her own life bears the telling, not least because the tragic roles she took on professionally so often found their own echoes in her personal life.

Sarah's life still resonates with us now. She understood innately the importance of image and guarded hers fiercely. I find myself thinking that – had she been alive today – she would have loved using Instagram to promote her brand. The story of her rags to riches journey is a powerful one, as are her struggles to achieve a satisfactory work-life balance. She learned the craft of acting at her parents' knees and she made it her own. The definition of what makes a good actor or actress is always something ephemeral. Clearly Sarah had what it takes. She conveyed emotion with such power that her audiences' response to her acting was unprecedented. The chance to see Sarah perform soon became a hot ticket. She knew instinctively the power of live theatre. As a young actress she had taken time to come to the realisation that she did not have a particular facility for comedy and that it was as a tragedienne that she excelled. Then there was no stopping her. For William Hazlitt, famously, she was 'tragedy personified'.[14] Her own life offstage had its fair share of tragedies too. Hazlitt's description still holds firm today.

Appendix I
Characters

Frances Abington – an ex-prostitute, Frances was an actress in Garrick's company when Sarah had her first disastrous London season. She specialised in comic roles. She recognised that Sarah was more talented than her colleagues realised.

Reverend Henry Bate – sent by Garrick to 'scout' Sarah, he recruited her for her disastrous London season with Garrick. A playwright and newspaper proprietor.

Sally Bird – a good friend of Sally and Maria Siddons. Sally Siddons died in her arms, while Sarah was returning from Ireland.

James Boaden – wrote an unauthorised biography of Sarah which was published during her lifetime, as well as biographies of her brother John Philip and her friend Elizabeth Inchbald.

Henrietta Boyle (became Henrietta O'Neill) – a young aristocrat who met Sarah when she was performing in Cheltenham and became her first society friend. Sarah visited Henrietta at her married home in Northern Ireland.

William Brereton – an actor who was said to have fallen in love with Sarah in her prime. He became embroiled in the scandals that surrounded Sarah when she toured Ireland. His wife was Pop (or Patty) Hopkins, who later married Sarah's brother John Philip Kemble. He died in a lunatic asylum.

Fanny Burney – a well-connected novelist who was in attendance when Sarah performed for the royal family. Her attempt at writing a play in which Sarah performed was a failure.

George Gordon, Lord Byron – the famous poet was a great admirer of Sarah's and tried to persuade her to return to the stage after her retirement.

Thomas Campbell – Sarah asked this Scottish poet to write her authorised biography and sent him detailed notes as guidance.

Queen Charlotte – the wife of George III. Like Sarah, Queen Charlotte defined herself as a loving mother. She was a keen patron of Sarah's.

Ann Crawford – an actress of the previous generation, for whom Arthur Murphy had written his play *The Grecian Daughter*. Ann was performing in a rival Dublin theatre when Sarah made her debut in Ireland and did better than Sarah with audiences there.

Richard Daly – the manager of the Smock Alley Theatre, Dublin. He and Sarah did not get along.

Anne Damer – a friend of Sarah's in later life, Anne encouraged Sarah to pursue her interest in sculpture. The two liked to work alongside each other at Anne's home, Strawberry Hill in Twickenham.

Maria Theresa de Camp – an Austrian actress who was sexually assaulted by Sarah's oldest brother John Philip but went on to have a happy marriage with Sarah's youngest brother Charles.

West Digges – an Irish actor. An accident on stage rendered him permanently paralysed. Sarah's involvement in his 'benefit' led to a potentially dangerous scandal.

Mr Evans of Pennant – Sarah's possibly fictional Welsh suitor, a rival to William for her affections.

Joseph Farington – a friend of the Siddons, Farington was a landscape painter and diarist.

Elizabeth Farren – a contemporary of Sarah's, an actress who had a long affair with an aristocrat, the Earl of Derby, whom she eventually married.

Charlotte Fitzhugh – the wife of a Conservative MP, Charlotte became a firm friend of Sarah's in middle age and often hosted her at Bannisters Lodge, her house in Hampshire.

Thomas Gainsborough – the portrait artist who famously painted Sarah as herself rather than in character, as if she were a society hostess. He had problems painting her nose.

Catherine Galindo – an actress whom Sarah met in Ireland and who wrote and had published a pamphlet accusing Sarah of wrecking her marriage.

Philomen Galindo – a fencing master of Spanish descent who grew close to Sarah during the choreography for her stage fights when she appeared as Hamlet in Ireland in middle age. He and Sarah became scandalously close.

David Garrick – the famous actor/manager of Drury Lane Theatre, London, who recruited the young Sarah to join his theatrical company during his final season. It went badly wrong. He died soon afterwards.

King George III – a great admirer of Sarah's, he encouraged her to read Shakespeare to his children.

King George IV – Sarah knew George IV from childhood, and, like his parents, was concerned about his rebellious lifestyle.

Ann Greatheed – the wife of Bertie Greatheed and a good friend to Sarah.

Bertie Greatheed – an aristocrat who knew Sarah when he was a boy. She came to work at Guy's Cliffe in Warwickshire for his mother, Lady Mary. Bertie had ambitions as a playwright in later life, which Sarah had to handle with care.

Lady Mary Greatheed (née Bertie) – Sarah's employer at Guy's Cliffe when the young Sarah took a break from acting to work at the grand house in Warwickshire.

William Hamilton – portrait artist who liked to paint Sarah performing the roles which had made her famous.

George and Elizabeth Harcourt (2nd Earl Harcourt and his wife Lady Elizabeth) – owners of Nuneham Courtenay in Oxfordshire, where they let one of the houses, Rectory Cottage, to the Siddons. Sarah remained a good friend of Elizabeth's for the rest of their lives.

Thomas Harris – the manager of Covent Garden Theatre.

William Hazlitt – the essayist who was a great admirer of Sarah's.

John Henderson – an actor who played opposite Sarah in regional theatre and wrote to the theatrical manager, John Palmer, recommending her for Palmer's theatre in Bath.

Priscilla (also known as Pop or Patty) Hopkins – the actress daughter of the Drury Lane prompt, she first married the actor, William Brereton. On his death her second husband was John Philip Kemble, Sarah's brother. Pop was known as a great gossip.

William Hopkins – the prompt at Drury Lane who had to write the letter to Sarah and William telling them their contract had not been renewed.

Sir Charles Hotham – a friend of both Sarah and William's, he kept up a lively correspondence with them both.

Elizabeth Inchbald – an actress and playwright, Elizabeth became friends with Sarah when they were acting together in regional theatre. Elizabeth fell in love with John Philip, and they were close friends, but he did not marry her.

Dr Samuel Johnson – the writer and lexicographer. Sarah was taken to visit him by Hester Thrale (later Piozzi) when she was successful.

Dora Jordan – the Queen of Comedy when Sarah was Queen of Tragedy, Dora led a more scandalous personal life than Sarah's, as the mistress of the Duke of Clarence.

Charles Kemble – Sarah's youngest brother, himself an actor and, in time, a theatrical manager. Kemble's daughter was the actress, Fanny Kemble.

Elizabeth Kemble – Sarah's younger sister who decided to try her luck professionally in America, to get away from her famous sibling.

Fanny Kemble – Sarah's niece, who also became an actress and performed at Covent Garden in her aunt's memory on the night Sarah died. Fanny was emotionally involved with Sir Thomas Lawrence at the end of his life.

John Philip Kemble – Sarah's oldest brother, John Philip was also an actor. He managed Drury Lane Theatre. Brother and sister moved together to perform at Covent Garden, where John Philip also became the manager. The two were close professionally and personally all their lives.

(Julia) Anne Kemble (later Hatton) – Sarah's most troubled sister, with whom she had a problematic relationship.

Roger Kemble – Sarah's father, himself an actor/manager of a theatrical troupe.

Sally Kemble (née Ward) – Sarah's mother, a powerful personality, to whom the success of her children was attributed.

Stephen Kemble – Sarah's brother, known for his portrayal of Falstaff. Stephen was not as successful as his older brother and sister.

Tom King – an actor. He recommended Sarah to Garrick and managed Drury Lane Theatre.

Sir Thomas Lawrence – the portrait painter and fourth President of the Royal Academy. Lawrence was an infant phenomenon as a painter. He met Sarah as a child, then came across her in Bath and again in London. The two remained close friends – some said more than friends – all their lives. Lawrence was romantically involved with two of Sarah's daughters and her niece.

William Charles Macready – an actor with whom Sarah performed after her retirement, giving him some careers advice. She sought to solve her problems with the Galindos by loaning them money to go into partnership with Macready's father in Manchester.

Mary Monckton – a society hostess, who invited lots of her friends to come to a soirée at her home one evening and stare at Sarah.

Charles Moore – a barrister friend of Sally and Maria Siddons, who was in love with Sally.

Harriet Murray – an actress whose marriage to Sarah's oldest son, Henry Siddons, was a very happy one.

Sir Joshua Reynolds – the famous portrait painter and first President of the Royal Academy, Reynolds painted Sarah most famously in his large canvas *The Tragic Muse*.

George Romney – a portrait painter who used classical influences in his portraits of Sarah.

Penelope Pennington – *see* Sophia Weston

John Palmer – the owner/manager of the Old Orchard Street Theatre, Bath, where Sarah made her name.

Hester Piozzi (known as Hester Thrale during her first marriage) – the writer and thinker, who took Sarah to meet the famous Dr Johnson. The two women became good friends in middle age. Initially Hester sided with Sarah against William when there were problems in the Siddons' marriage, but later she favoured William.

Hannah Pritchard – an actress of the previous generation, whose performance of Lady Macbeth was viewed as definitive before Sarah's.

Anna Seward – a poetess who got to know Sarah in Bath and struggled to get a seat to see Sarah during her triumphant first season.

Richard Brinsley Sheridan – the playwright, theatre manager and politician, Sheridan was responsible for Sarah's triumphant London season in 1782. He owned Drury Lane Theatre and employed her as an actress in his theatrical company for many years. Sheridan was notoriously tight-fisted when it came to paying his employees.

Thomas Sheridan – the father of the well-known Richard Brinsley Sheridan, Thomas Sheridan was also a theatre impresario. He was Irish by birth. He spotted Sarah's talent while she was living in Bath.

Cecilia or Cecy Siddons – Sarah and William's youngest child, Cecy was often indulged by her parents. The death of both her elder sisters meant that Sarah and William were always hyper-anxious about her health.

Elizabeth Anne Siddons – Sarah and William's daughter who was born in Bath but only lived to the age of 6.

George Siddons – Sarah and William's second son. A robust, happy child; as an adult, he went to India to make his living and did not return to live in England during his parents' lifetimes.

Henry Siddons – Sarah and William's oldest son, Henry tried to make a living as an actor but then took over the management of the Edinburgh Theatre Royal. He died of tuberculosis aged 41.

Maria Siddons – Sarah and William's second daughter. She was romantically involved with the painter, Sir Thomas Lawrence, as was her sister Sally. Maria made Sally promise on her deathbed that Sally would never marry Lawrence. She died aged 19 in 1798.

Sally Siddons – Sarah and William's oldest daughter. She was romantically involved with the painter, Sir Thomas Lawrence, but died aged 27 in 1803.

Sarah Siddons – the greatest tragic actress of her generation, Sarah was born to a theatrical family, the Kembles. After a false start at Drury Lane under Garrick's management and some time learning her craft in the provinces, Sarah returned in triumph to the London stage and never looked back professionally from that point onwards.

William Siddons – Sarah's husband. They met as actors, but William soon gave up the profession to become Sarah's manager. The marriage had its problems, not least because William gave Sarah a venereal disease. They eventually separated.

'Gentleman' Smith – an actor who played opposite Sarah during her first disastrous London season and later played Macbeth opposite her famous portrayal of Lady Macbeth.

Frances (known as Fanny) and Francis Twiss – Sarah's sister and brother-in-law. Fanny performed alongside her sister early in her career but was eclipsed by Sarah's talent. She and her husband later opened a school in Bath. They remained close to the Siddons.

Horace Twiss – son of Fanny and Francis, Horace was Sarah's favourite nephew. He became a Conservative MP.

Sophia Weston (also known as Penelope Pennington) – an heiress who first got to know Sarah in Bath. When Sarah's daughter Maria became fatally ill, she was moved to Penelope's house in Clifton, Bristol, where Penelope found herself embroiled in the passionate love triangle which consisted of Maria, her sister Sally and Sir Thomas Lawrence.

Thomas Sedgwick Whalley – a close friend of Sarah's, whom she met during her years in Bath. Whalley was ordained but spent most of his time living a life of leisure at his home in Royal Crescent in Bath and enjoying the arts.

Patty Wilkinson – Tate's daughter, Patty came to be a companion to Sally and more significantly to Sarah when Maria Siddons died. She supported the Galindos against Sarah but despite this stayed living with Sarah until Sarah's death.

Tate Wilkinson – the manager of the Theatre Royal in York, Tate was a strong early supporter of Sarah's talent.

Mary Ann Yates – an actress who was in the Drury Lane company for Sarah's disastrous Garrick season. Yates was nearly thirty years older than Sarah. The rivalry between them continued when Sarah triumphed at Drury Lane a few years later, as a cartoon of the two fighting each other, bare-breasted, attests.

Elizabeth Younge – an actress who was in the Drury Lane company when Sarah made her disastrous debut there under Garrick. Younge was fifteen years older than Sarah. The two later toured Ireland together.

Appendix II
Sarah's Main Stage Roles

Belvidera in Thomas Otway's *Venice Preserved*
The play was written in the seventeenth century, so was about 100 years old when Sarah began performing it. Belvidera is one of the main characters in the play, which is set in the city of Venice. It follows the story of a group of Venetian conspirators, who plot to overthrow the ruling government and establish a republic. Belvidera is the daughter of a nobleman who has fallen from grace and is now living in poverty. Despite her humble circumstances, Belvidera proves herself to be a proud and strong-willed woman who remains fiercely loyal to her husband Jaffier, one of the conspirators.

Throughout the play, Belvidera struggles to reconcile her love for Jaffier with her loyalty to her father and her duty to society. She is torn between her desire to help Jaffier and his fellow conspirators and her fear of the consequences of their actions. When Jaffier betrays his allies and reveals their plot to the government, Belvidera is devastated by his actions and is left to face the consequences alone. Learning of her beloved husband's death, she is driven mad by the news and dies of grief.

Belvidera is above all a symbol of the nobility and strength of the human spirit, even in the face of adversity and tragedy – a classic Siddons heroine. Her love for Jaffier is deep and unwavering, despite his betrayal. She is a model of virtue who loves a flawed hero right up until her own death.

Calista in Nicholas Rowe's *The Fair Penitent*
Rowe wrote his play about fifty years before Sarah was born. The central character in the play, Calista, is portrayed as a complex and multi-dimensional figure. She is a young woman who is married to Altamont but finds herself torn between her duty to her husband and her desire for the charming and seductive Lothario.

Throughout the play, Calista's character develops as she struggles with her own morality and desires. Despite her initial portrayal as virtuous and innocent, she is tempted by Lothario and ultimately – unusually for a Siddons heroine – succumbs to his charms.

As the play progresses, Calista's guilt and shame consume her, and she becomes increasingly desperate for redemption. She ultimately seeks repentance and attempts to make amends for her mistakes. She takes her own life in despair:

'Nothing but blood can make the expiation, / And cleanse the soul from inbred, deep pollution.'

Calista is a tragic figure, whose downfall is the result of her own weakness when it comes to loving the wrong man with an overwhelming passion. Her inability to resist temptation leads to tragic consequences. The audience empathises with her, despite her flaws.

Overall, Calista is a compelling and thought-provoking character, whose story offers insight into the complexities of human nature and the challenges we all face in navigating our own desires and morals. The play ends with an exhortation to the audience to uphold their own marriage vows, something Sarah took seriously in her own life.

Constance in William Shakespeare's *King John*

Constance is a prominent character in the play, the mother of the young Prince Arthur, who is in line to inherit the English throne from the flawed King John. Sarah often played the part later in life when she was herself known as a devoted mother. Constance's role in the play is to highlight the struggles of a virtuous woman in a male-dominated world, and to emphasise the importance of family and loyalty in times of political turmoil.

Throughout the play, Constance is a forceful and passionate figure, who fiercely advocates for her son's right to the throne in a particularly powerful scene. She is unafraid to confront those who stand in her way, including King John himself, and is willing to use any means necessary to secure her son's future.

At the same time, Constance is a tragic, maternal figure, who is constantly haunted by the spectre of her own powerlessness when it comes to deciding her son's fate. She is acutely aware of the ways in which women are marginalised in society.

Through Constance's character, Shakespeare explores themes of family, loyalty and the struggle for power in a world ruled by men. She is a symbol of the ways in which women are often excluded from positions of authority, and a reminder of the importance of fighting for justice and equality, even in the face of seemingly insurmountable obstacles.

Elvira in August von Kotzebue's *Pizarro*

Sheridan took the play, by the German August von Kotzebue, and translated it into English, following his success with another of Kotzebue's plays, *The Stranger*.

Pizarro is set in sixteenth-century Peru, during the Spanish conquest of the Inca empire. The title character, Francisco Pizarro, is the commander of the Spanish forces, and the play centres around his attempts to conquer and colonise the region. It resonated with the English audiences of the time, who were fearful of invasion by revolutionary France. The plot revolves around the conflict between the Spanish conquerors and the indigenous people of Peru, and it explores themes of colonisation and imperialism.

Sarah's role, Elvira, is a camp follower, Pizarro's passionately loving mistress. Sheridan expanded her character from the original. In his version she becomes a tragic figure who is caught between her loyalty to Pizarro and her sympathy for the plight of the native people. Her character adds a layer of complexity to the play and raises questions about the ethics of conquest.

Sarah believed Elvira should be honourable and noble, despite her lowly birth, while Sheridan saw her as a broader character, an irredeemably fallen woman. Sarah appeared on the opening night wearing an Amazonian helmet and triumphed in the role.

Euphrasia in Arthur Murphy's *The Grecian Daughter*
The play was written in 1772, during Sarah's adult life, for the actress Ann Crawford, but Sarah soon adopted it as her own. It tells the story of Euphrasia, a Greek princess who is taken captive by the Roman army and is being held in Sicily. Euphrasia's father, Evander, is imprisoned in a cave, where his daughter visits him. She even uses her own breast milk to succour her father (offstage). Although Evander dies in the play, there is a happy ending for Euphrasia, who lives on to reign with her husband and son.

The play explores themes of loyalty, honour and sacrifice, as Euphrasia struggles to navigate the complex political landscape of ancient Greece and Rome. She is torn between her loyalty to her father and her love for her husband and child.

As the play unfolds, Euphrasia is forced to make a series of difficult choices, including whether to betray her father and support the Roman cause, or to risk everything to save her family and her people. Ultimately, she chooses to stand by her principles and sacrifices herself to save her father and her people – the classic Siddons heroine.

Through the character of Euphrasia, Murphy offers a commentary on the timeless themes of loyalty, honour and sacrifice, and the importance of standing up for what is right, even in the face of overwhelming adversity. Euphrasia is a powerful and inspiring character, whose story serves as a reminder of the enduring strength of the human spirit.

Isabella in Thomas Southerne's *Isabella, Or The Fatal Marriage*
Southerne's play was written at the end of the seventeenth century. It tells the story of Isabella, a young woman, whose husband Biron is presumed dead at sea. Beset by poverty, she throws herself at the mercy of her father-in-law, but

he will only help her by taking her son to live with him, provided she gives up all her parental rights. This she refuses to do. Instead, she has little choice but to accept an offer of marriage from Villeroy, who has always been in love with her. No sooner is the marriage consummated than Biron returns. It emerges that her evil brother-in-law, Carlos, knew Biron was alive all along. As the play progresses, after a series of theatrical misunderstandings, Biron is killed, and Isabella commits suicide in a tragic and devastating ending.

Isabella's character develops and matures through the play as she learns to assert herself. She also becomes more compassionate, reaching out to those around her and offering them support and kindness. Throughout, she is a virtuous, blameless heroine – no wonder Sarah loved to play this part – steadfast in adversity, despite the cruelty she encounters. In rehearsal, Sarah caused her own son Henry, who was cast as Isabella's son, to burst into tears, so convinced was he by her performance. Through the play, Isabella becomes a symbol of resistance against tyranny and oppression. It illustrates the importance of fighting for one's own freedom and dignity, even in the face of overwhelming odds.

Jane Shore in Nicholas Rowe's *Jane Shore*

The play was written about forty years before Sarah's birth. It tells the historical story of the events Shakespeare told in his play *Richard III* but from a different perspective.

When the play opens, the princes are in the tower and Gloucester (later Richard III) is trying to consolidate power. Although Jane Shore is a married woman, she was the mistress of the late Edward IV, Gloucester's brother, when he was king. It is very atypical for Sarah to play someone who has broken her marriage vows: 'Ruin ensues, reproach and endless shame,/And one false step entirely damns her fame,' as she puts it.

Jane mistakenly accepts the help of her friend Alicia and Alicia's lover, Lord Hastings, in petitioning Gloucester on her behalf. But Alicia is a false friend and envious of Jane's virtue. Gloucester wants the throne over Edward IV's two young sons, the princes in the tower. Jane argues their case. She shows compassion towards her late lover's two legitimate children.

As Jane's fortunes decline, she becomes the target of scorn and ridicule from those around her. Alicia rejects her, despite Jane's begging her for some bread to eat. Although Jane is reconciled with her husband, who still loves her and forgives her, she nevertheless dies of starvation: 'Let those, who view this sad example, know/What fate attends the broken marriage vow.'

Jane's story serves as a powerful commentary on the fickle nature of power and the vulnerability of those who become entangled in the politics of the time. She is made to suffer for her past transgressions, while still remaining the virtuous heroine. Audiences apparently entirely believed that Jane, as portrayed by Sarah, was dying of starvation in front of them.

Lady Randolph in John Home's *Douglas*
The play was written around the time of Sarah's birth. Its Scottish author, John Home, returned to Scotland to see Sarah, an English actress, perform it in his homeland.

In the play Sarah's character, Lady Randolph, had been married to Lord Douglas but he was killed in battle, and their only son lost to them. So she agrees to marry Lord Randolph, although he knew she could never love him.

A young man arrives, named Norval, who we learn is in fact Lady Randolph's long-lost son and therefore heir to the Douglas estate. Another nobleman, Glenalvon, has designs on the inheritance and wants to marry Lady Randolph. He discovers the truth but falsely tells Lord Randolph that his wife has taken a lover – the young Norval. This seems to explain why they are so close.

When the truth is revealed, Glenalvon and Norval both die violently, the latter killed by Lord Randolph, tricked into the murder of his stepson by the treacherous Glenalvon. Norval dies in his mother's arms. Lady Randolph cannot cope with the grief that she has lost her only son for a second time and so throws herself off a precipice.

Throughout the play, Lady Randolph is depicted as a complex and multi-faceted character, who struggles with conflicting emotions and desires. Her love for her son and her fury at the fate of their situation serve to reveal her sense of duty and moral principles. The inevitable suicide feels the right ending for this beleaguered Siddons heroine.

Mrs Beverley in Edward Moore's *The Gamester*
Moore wrote *The Gamester* for David Garrick to play the title role, a couple of years before Sarah was born. It remained popular throughout Sarah's working life.

Sarah's part, Mrs Beverley, is the wife of a man who is addicted to gambling and unable to resist the allure of the many gaming tables which were popular at the time.

Throughout the play, Mrs Beverley is portrayed as a strong and steadfast character, who is deeply committed to her husband and their family. Despite the challenges she faces because of Beverley's addiction, she remains loyal to him and attempts to help him overcome his weaknesses.

As the play progresses, Mrs Beverley is forced to confront the harsh realities of Beverley's addiction, and the toll it takes on their family. She struggles with her own feelings of anger and resentment, but ultimately remains committed to her husband, even as he loses everything. Beverley takes poison at the end, in his prison cell, and leaves his wife to a life of poverty, bringing up their family.

Mrs Beverley's story serves as a reminder of the impact that addiction can have on individuals and their families, as well as the strength and resilience required to overcome such challenges. The play would have been especially poignant for George III and his wife, Queen Charlotte, as several of their sons were addicted to gambling.

Mrs Haller in August von Kotzebue's *The Stranger*

Seeking to revive his fortunes at Drury Lane, Sheridan adapted Kotzebue's German melodrama *The Stranger* to great acclaim.

Sarah took the part of Mrs Haller, who has been unfaithful to her husband and is now living in a rural location, he having compelled her to leave their family in disgrace. She is dearly loved by the people among whom she now lives, incognito, as a woman known as Mrs Smith. Several men seem to be in love with her, thanks to her general virtue.

A male stranger has come to live nearby, although Mrs Haller/Mrs Smith has not met him. He is very melancholy, but heroic, saving someone from drowning. Mrs Smith confesses the truth about her past to an aristocratic lady visitor.

We learn that the Stranger is Mrs Haller/Smith's husband, and that he is deeply saddened at his marital past. He is invited to supper at the main house by the aristocratic visitors. He accepts but asks if he can send for his two children. When he comes into the room on the night of the supper party and sees his wife, he exits in shock while she faints.

Mrs Haller knows that she can never be forgiven – her transgression is too great. She asks only that she has an interview with her husband and that she gets to see her children.

In a soliloquy the husband admits he is still in love with his wife. When they meet, she is overwhelmed at hearing him say her name. She gives him a paper so he can divorce her, but he tears it up. He promises to support her financially, presenting her with a casket of jewels, but she gives them back to him. She asks about their children, whom she longs to see. The couple part: 'in a better world we shall meet again.' When the children are finally brought out, the couple embrace them with tears of joy, and the end is left ambiguous. Will they get back together?

The story is a powerful commentary on the themes of redemption and forgiveness, and it serves as a reminder of the power of love and compassion to heal even the deepest wounds.

Queen Katharine in William Shakespeare's *Henry VIII*

The role of Queen Katharine was a favourite of Sarah's as she grew older. Queen Katharine of Aragon is a central character in Shakespeare's play. As the first wife of King Henry VIII, she has a crucial role in the play's exploration of power, loyalty and the consequences of personal ambition.

Throughout the play, Queen Katharine is depicted as a virtuous and loyal queen who remains steadfast in her devotion to her husband, despite his infatuation with Anne Boleyn. She is an embodiment of grace, dignity and strength, and her moral authority commands the respect of all those around her.

As the play unfolds, Queen Katharine becomes embroiled in a bitter dispute with her husband over their marriage, which ultimately leads to her downfall. Despite her unwavering faith and loyalty to the king, she is unable to prevent the annulment of their marriage and is eventually forced to leave the court.

Despite her tragic fate, Queen Katharine remains an inspiring figure in the play. Her courage and determination in the face of adversity serve as a powerful reminder of the strength and resilience of the human spirit, and her unwavering commitment to her moral principles sets an example for all those who witness her struggle. It is easy to see why Sarah liked playing the part.

Zara in William Congreve's *The Mourning Bride*

Congreve wrote the play at the end of the seventeenth century. It is set in Granada, in Spain. Zara, a queen who has been taken captive, is in love with a prisoner named Osmyn, whereas Manuel, the King of Granada, has designs on her. Zara learns that Osmyn is in fact Alphonso, a noble Spaniard in disguise, and that he is in love with Almeria, the princess of Granada, and she with him. Zara has the famous lines: 'Heaven has no rage like love to hatred turned, /Nor hell a fury like a woman scorned.'

Zara persuades Manuel, the king, that her mute slaves should strangle Osmyn/Alphonso, as a means of Manuel's fulfilling his evil plans to maintain hold of the throne, and at the same time of Zara taking her revenge. In a misunderstanding, Zara believes this has happened, when, in reality, it was Manuel who was killed. Furious, Zara stabs her eunuch, Selim, for betraying her and then takes poison to die dramatically alongside him, lamenting that she did not get to kill herself in front of Alphonso, so that he would realise the extent of her love.

Zara is a complex character who struggles with conflicting emotions of passionate love, which are at odds with her desire for honour and duty. Her actions lead to the downfall of many of the other characters in the play. For Sarah, Zara is more exotic than her usual heroines, and more of an outsider to the main action than is normal for Sarah's roles. Zara is proud and determined as a character, and she has a particularly noteworthy, emotional death scene.

Bibliography

Biographical Writing about Sarah Siddons
Anonymous, *The Beauties of Mrs Siddons*, (London, 1786)
Asleson, Robyn, (ed.), Bennett, Shelley, Leonard, Mark, & Shearer, West, *A Passion for Performance: Sarah Siddons and Her Portraitists*, (Getty Publications: USA, 1999)
Bailey, Priscilla, *Sarah Siddons: A great actress*, (Newnes Educational Publishing Co., 1953)
Ballantyne, James, *Characters of Mrs Siddons*, (Edinburgh, 1812)
Bate, Jonathan, 'Shakespeare and the Rival Muses: Siddons versus Jordan', in R. Asleson, (ed.), *Notorious Muse: The Actress in British Art and Culture, 1776–1812*, (Yale University Press, 2003)
Boaden, James, *Memoirs of Mrs Siddons*, 2 vols., (London, 1827)
Boatner-Doane, Charlotte, 'Sarah Siddons and the Romantic Hamlet', in *Nineteenth Century Theatre and Film*, (Manchester, 2017)
Booth, M., (ed.), *Three Tragic Actresses*, (CUP, 1996)
Brahms, Caryl, *Enter a Dragon, Stage Centre: An Embroidered Life of Mrs Siddons*, (London: Hodder, 1979)
Buchanan, Linda, 'Sarah Siddons and her Place in Rhetorical History', *Rhetorica: A Journal of the History of Rhetoric*, (Berkeley, 2007)
Campbell, Thomas, *Life of Mrs Siddons*, 2 vols., (London, 1834)
Copeland, Nancy, '"Simple Art and Simple Nature", Sarah Siddons versus Ann Crawford', *Restoration and Eighteenth-Century Theatre Research*, (University of Chicago, 1987)
Ffrench, Yvonne, *Mrs Siddons, Tragic Actress*, (London, 1954)
Fitzgerald, Percy Hetherington, *The Kembles: An Account of the Kemble family*, 2 vols., (London, 1871)
Haycraft, Molly Costain, *First Lady of the Theatre: Sarah Siddons*, (New York, 1958)
Highfill Jr., Philip H., Burnim, Kalman & Langhans, Edward, *A Biographical Dictionary of Actors, Actresses, Musicians, Dancers, Managers and Other Stage Personnel in London, 1660–1800*, (Carbondale: Southern Illinois University Press, 1987)
Holcroft, Thomas, 'Mrs Siddons and her roles,' in J. Agate, (ed.), *The English Dramatic Critics: An Anthology 1660–1832*, (London, 1932)
Holland, Peter, (ed.), *Garrick, Kemble, Siddons, Kean: Great Shakespeareans: Volume 2*, (London, 2014)
Johnson, Marian, *A Troubled Grandeur: The Story of England's Greatest Actress, Sarah Siddons*, (USA, 1972)

Kelly, Linda, *The Kemble Era – John Philip Kemble, Sarah Siddons and the London Stage*, (London, 1980)
Kennard, Nina, A., *Mrs Siddons*, (London, 1893)
Knapp, Oswald, *An Artist's Love Story: Told in the Letters of Sir Thomas Lawrence, Mrs Siddons and her Daughters*, (London, 1904)
Lennep, William van, (ed.), *The Reminiscences of Sarah Kemble Siddons, 1773–1785*, (USA, 1942)
Mackenzie, Kathleen, *The Great Sarah: The Life of Mrs Siddons (with portraits)*, (London, 1968)
McDonald, Russ, *Look to the Lady: Sarah Siddons, Ellen Terry and Judi Dench on the Shakespearean Stage*, (USA, 2005)
McGillivray, Glen, 'Rant, Cant and Tone: The Voice of the Eighteenth-Century Actor and Sarah Siddons', *Theatre Notebook*, (London, 2017)
McPherson, Heather, *Art and Celebrity in the Age of Reynolds and Siddons*, (USA, 2017)
—— 'Masculinity, Femininity and the Tragic Sublime: Reinventing Lady Macbeth,' *Studies in Eighteenth-Century Culture*, (USA, 2000)
—— 'Picturing Tragedy: Mrs Siddons as the Tragic Muse Revisited,' *Eighteenth Century Studies*, (USA, 2000)
Manvell, Roger, *Sarah Siddons: Portrait of an Actress*, (London, 1970)
Parsons, Clement, *The Incomparable Siddons*, (London, 1909)
Pascoe, Judith, *The Sarah Siddons Audio Files: Romanticism and the Lost Voice*, (Ann Arbor: University of Michigan Press, 2011)
Perry, Gill, Roach, Joseph & West, Shearer, *The First Actresses: Nell Gwyn to Sarah Siddons*, (USA, 2011)
Rogers, Pat, 'Towering Beyond Her Sex: Stature and Sublimity in the Achievement of Sarah Siddons', in Cecilia Macheski and Mary Anne Schofield (eds.), *Curtain Calls: British and American Women in the Theater, 1660–1820* (Athens: Ohio University Press, 1991)
Rosenthal, Laura, 'The Sublime, the Beautiful, "The Siddons"', in J. Munns and P. Richards, (eds.), *The Clothes that Wear Us: Essays on Dressing and Transgressing in Eighteenth-Century Culture*, (University of Delaware Press, 1999)
Royde-Smith, Naomi, *Portrait of Mrs Siddons, a study in four parts*, (London, 1933)
Russell, William, *The Tragic Muse*, (London, 1783)
Shaughnessy, Robert, 'Siddons [née Kemble], Sarah', in *Oxford Dictionary of National Biography*, (Oxford, 2004)
Siddons, Sarah Kemble, *The Beauties of Mrs Siddons*, (London, 1786)
Siddons S. and W., *The Letters of Sarah and William Siddons to Hester Lynch Piozzi in the John Rylands Library*, ed. A. Kalman Burnim, (Manchester, 1969)
Thomas, T.C., *Sarah Siddons*, (The Brecknock Society, no date)
West, Shearer, *The Image of the Actor: Verbal and Visual Representation in the Age of Garrick and Kemble*, (London, 1991)
—— 'Siddons, Celebrity and Regality: Portraiture and the Body of the Ageing Actress,' in Mary Luckhurst and Jane Moody (eds.), *Theatre and Celebrity in Britain, 1660–2000*, (Basingstoke: Palgrave, 2005)

Wilson, Michael S., 'The Incomparable Siddons as Reynolds' Muse: Art and Ideology on the British Stage', in Kate Greenspan and Ann Hurley (eds.), *So Rich a Tapestry: The Sister Arts and Cultural Studies*, (London, 1995)

Woo, Celestine, 'Sarah Siddons as Hamlet: Three Decades, Five Towns, Absent Breeches and Rife Critical Confusion', *ANQ: A Quarterly Journal of Short Articles, Notes and Reviews*, (London, 2007)

Young, Thomas, *The Siddoniad: a characteristical and critical poem*, (Dublin, 1784)

Works by Sarah Siddons' Contemporaries

Boaden, James, *Memoirs of the Life of John Philip Kemble, Esq.*, 2 vols., (London, 1825)

Boswell, James, *Boswell's Life of Johnson*, (ed.) George Birkbeck, (Oxford, 1887)

Burke, Edmund, *Philosophical Enquiry into the Origins of Our Ideas of the Sublime and Beautiful*, (London, 1787)

Burney, Fanny, *Diary and Letters of Madame D'Arblay*, (London, 1842)

―― *The Early Journals*, (London, 1889)

Davies, Thomas, *Dramatic Miscellanies: Consisting of Critical Observations on Several Plays of Shakespeare*, (Dublin, 1784)

Farington, Joseph, *The Farington Diary*, (Hutchinson, 1922–28)

Galindo, Catherine, *Mrs Galindo's Letter to Mrs Siddons*, (London, 1809)

Garrick, David, *The Letters of David Garrick*, (ed.) David M. Little and George M. Kahrl, (OUP, 1963)

Genest, John, *Some Account of the English Stage in 1660 to 1830*, (Bath, 1832)

Hazlitt, William, *Characters of Shakespeare's Plays*, (London, 1817)

―― *Criticism and Dramatic Essays*, (London, 1851)

―― (ed.), *Memoirs of the late Thomas Holcroft*, (London, 1816)

―― 'On play-going and on some of our old actors', in *A View of the English Stage, or a series of dramatic criticisms*, (London, 1818)

―― *The round table: lectures on the English poets*, (London, 1998)

―― *Collected Works*, ed. A.R. Waller and A. Glover, (London, 1903)

Kemble, F.A., *Record of a Girlhood*, 3 vols., (London, 1878)

Lawrence, Thomas, *Sir Thomas Lawrence's Letter-Bag*, (ed.) George Somes Layard, (London, 1906)

Macready, W.C., *Reminiscences*, (London, 1875)

Piozzi, Hester, *The Intimate Letters of Hester Piozzi and Penelope Pennington, 1788–1821*, (ed.) O.G. Knapp, (London, 1914)

―― *Thraliana: The Diary of Mrs Hester Lynch Thrale*, (OUP, 1951)

―― *Piozziana: or Recollections of the late Mrs Piozzi, with Remarks*, (ed.) E. Mangin, (London, 1833)

Pope, William Bissell (ed.), *The Diary of Benjamin Robert Haydon*, (Harvard University Press, 1960)

Rogers, Samuel, *Recollections*, (London, 1856)

Seward, Anna, *The Swan of Lichfield*, (London, 1936)

Stirling, A.M.W., *The Hothams, Being the Chronicles of the Hothams of Scarborough and South Dalton*, 2 vols., (London, 1918)

Taylor, John, *Records of My Life*, (London, 1832)

Whalley, Thomas Sedgwick, *Journals and Correspondence, edited with a Memoir and Illustrative Notes by H. Wickham*, (London, 1863)
Wilkinson, Tate, *The Wandering Patentee, or A History of the Yorkshire Theatres from 1770 to the present time*, 4 vols., (York, 1795)

General Reading
Ackroyd, Peter, *The English Actor: From Medieval to Modern*, (London, 2023)
Barker, Kathleen, *The Theatre Royal, Bristol: The First Seventy Years*, (Bristol, 1969)
Barry, Jonathan, & Brooks, Christopher (eds.), *The Middling Sort of People: Culture, Society and Politics in England, 1550–1800*, (Basingstoke: Macmillan, 1994)
Begiato, Joanne, *Manliness in Britain 1760–1900: Bodies, emotion and material cultures*, (Manchester University Press, 2020)
Bingham, Madeleine, *Sheridan: The Track of a Comet*, (George Allen and Unwin, 1972)
Byrne, Paula, *Perdita: the Life of Mary Robinson*, (Leicester, 2005)
Colley, Linda, *Britons: Forging the Nation, 1707–1837*, (New Haven: Yale University Press, 1992)
Corfield, Penelope, *The Georgians: The Deeds and Misdeeds of Eighteenth Century Britain*, (Yale University Press, 2022)
Davis, Tracy, *The Economics of the British Stage 1800–1914*, (CUP, 2007)
D'Ezio, Marianna, *Hester Lynch Thrace Piozzi: A Taste for Eccentricity*, (Newcastle Upon Tyne, 2010)
Engel, Laura, *Fashioning Celebrity: Eighteenth-century British Actresses and Strategies for Image Making*, (Ohio State University Press, 2011)
Engel, Laura, and McGirr, Elaine, (eds.), *Stage Mothers: Women, Work and the Theatre, 1660–1830*, (Lewisburgh: Bucknell University Press, 2014)
Erickson, Amy Louise, *Women and Property in Early Modern England*, (London & New York: Routledge,, 2020)
Franklin, Michael John, *Hester Lynch Thrale Piozzi*, (Cardiff: University of Wales Press, 2020)
Garlick, Kenneth, *Sir Thomas Lawrence*, (Routledge and Kegan Paul, 1952)
Goldring, Doug, *Regency Portrait Painter: the Life of Sir Thomas Lawrence*, (London, 1951)
Gower, Ronald Sutherland, *Sir Thomas Lawrence*, (London: Goupil, 1900)
Greig, Hannah, *The Beau Monde: Fashionable Society in Georgian London*, (OUP, 2013)
Jenkins, Annabel, *I'll tell you what: a life of Elizabeth Inchbald*, (USA, 2021)
Kelly, Linda, *Richard Brinsley Sheridan: A Life*, (London, 1997)
Kendall, Alan, *David Garrick: A Biography*, (London, 1985)
McCormack, Catherine, *Women, Art and the Power of Looking*, (London, 2021)
Moody, Jane and O'Quin, Daniel, (eds.), *The Cambridge Companion to British Theatre, 1730–1830*, (Cambridge University Press, 2007)
Nussbaum, Felicity, *Rival Queens: Actresses, Performance and the Eighteenth-Century British Theatre*, (University of Pennsylvania Press, 2010)
—— 'Actresses and the Economics of Celebrity, 1700–1800' in (eds.) Luckhurst and Moody, *Theatre and Celebrity*, (USA, 2005)

―― *Torrid Zones: Maternity, Sexuality and Empire in Eighteenth-Century Narratives,* (Baltimore, 1995)
Ottaway, Susannah, R., *The Decline of Life: Old Age in Eighteenth-Century England,* (CUP, 2004)
Porter, Roy, *English Society in the Eighteenth Century,* (London, 1982)
Richards, Sandra, *The Rise of the English Actress,* (USA, 1993)
Ritchie, L., *David Garrick and the Mediation of Celebrity,* (Cambridge, 2019)
Roberts, R.E., *Samuel Rogers and his Circle,* (London: Methuen, 1910)
Rosenfeld, Sybil, *Temples of Thespis: Some Private Theatres and Theatricals in England and Wales, 1700–1830,* (London: The Society of Theatre Research, 1978)
Russell, Gillian, *The Theatres of War: Performance, Politics and Society, 1793–1815,* (Oxford, 1995)
Steedman, C., *Labours Lost: Domestic Servants and the Making of Modern England,* (Cambridge, 2009)
Senkiw, Anna Louise, *Made in the Media: Actresses, Celebrity and the Periodical Press in the Late Eighteenth Century,* (unpublished Phd, Mansfield College, Oxford, 2019)
Staves, Susan, *Married Women's Separate Property in England, 1660–1817,* (Harvard, 1990)
Stern, Tiffany, *Rehearsal from Shakespeare to Sheridan,* (Clarendon Press, 2000)
Stone, Lawrence, *Broken Lives: Separation and Divorce in England, 1660–1857,* (OUP, 1993)
Summerson, John, *Georgian London,* (London, 1978)
Syson, Lydia, *Doctor of Love: Dr James Graham and His Celestial Bed,* (Richmond: Alma, 2008)
Tomalin, Claire, *Mrs Jordan's Profession: The Story of a Great Actress and a Future King,* (London, 2012)
Vickery, Amanda, *The Gentleman's Daughter: Women's Lives in Georgian England,* (London, 2003)
―― *Behind Closed Doors: At Home in Georgian England,* (London, 2009)
Warner, Marina, *Monuments and Maidens: The Allegory of the Female Form,* (London, 1985)
Woo, Celestine, *Romantic Actors and Bardolatry: Performing Shakespeare from Garrick to Kean,* (New York, 2008)
Worrall, David, *Celebrity, Performance, Reception: British Georgian Theatre as Social Assemblage,* (CUP, 2013)

Archives
Bath Record Office
Bristol University, Manvers and Mitcheson Collection
British Library, Addison Manuscripts
British Theatre Association
British Theatre Museum
Cambridge University Library
Folger Shakespeare Library, Washington DC, USA
Hampshire Archives

Harvard Theatre Collection, Houghton Library, Cambridge, Massachusetts, USA
Hull History Centre (Hull University Archive)
Huntington Library, San Marino, California, USA
Garrick Club
Hereford City Library and Museums
The National Archives, Kew
LSE: The Women's Library
Manchester, John Rylands Library
Oxford Bodleian Library, Special Collection
Royal Academy, London, Lawrence Papers
Society of Theatre Research
Staffordshire and Stoke-on-Trent Record Office
Victoria and Albert Museum, London, Enthoven Collection
Wiltshire and Swindon History Centre
West Yorkshire Archives

Newspapers
The British Magazine and Review
The Coventry Mercury
The English Review
The Examiner
The Freeman's Journal
The Ipswich Journal
The Middlesex Journal
The Morning Chronicle
The Morning Herald
The Morning Post and Daily Advertiser
London Magazine
Parker's General Advertiser
Public Advertiser
The Rambler's Magazine
St James's Chronicle
The Whitehall Evening Post

Note: all comparisons between financial figures in Sarah's day and today come from the following website: https://www.measuringworth.com/calculators/ukcompare

Notes

Introduction
1. Lennep, p.6.
2. Parsons, p.23.
3. Fitzgerald, 1.50.
4. Lennep, p.10.
5. Kennard, p.38.
6. Ibid.
7. Manvell, p.32.
8. Highfill, p5.
9. Ibid.
10. Fitzgerald, 1.52.
11. Lennep, p.4.
12. Ibid.
13. Fitzgerald, 1.59.
14. Lennep, p.6.
15. Parsons, p.27.
16. Lennep, p.6.
17. Ibid.
18. Parsons, p.31.
19. Lennep, p.6
20. Ibid.

Chapter 1: Childhood
1. Manvell, p.314.
2. Ibid.
3. Ibid.
4. Highfill, p.1.
5. Parsons, p.9.
6. Kennard, p.13.
7. *The Coventry Mercury*, 22 December 1766.
8. Manvell, p.314.

Chapter 2: Mr Siddons
1. Kennard, p.23.
2. Fitzgerald, 1.22.
3. Boaden, p.28.
4. Campbell, 1.46.

5. Ibid., p.47
6. Ibid.
7. Ibid.
8. Fitzgerald, 1.30.
9. Parsons, p.16.
10. Kennard, p.20.
11. Ibid., p.23.

Chapter 3: Starting Out
1. Garrick, p.1038.
2. Lennep, p.1.
3. Fitzgerald, 1.32.
4. Courtesy of the British Library Board, Addison Manuscripts, No. 25,383.
5. Ibid.
6. Ibid.
7. Ibid.
8. Garrick, p.1026.
9. Ibid.
10. Courtesy of the British Library Board, Addison Manuscripts, No. 25,383.
11. Ibid.
12. Parsons, p.22.
13. Wilkinson, 1.252.

Chapter 4: Bath
1. Lennep, p.8.
2. Ibid., p.7.
3. Ibid., p.8.
4. Ibid.
5. Manvell, p.64.
6. Fitzgerald, 1.91.
7. Ibid.
8. Ibid.
9. Manvell, p.50.
10. Ibid.
11. Engel, p.217.
12. Ffrench, p.76.

Chapter 5: Triumph
1. *The Examiner*, 15 June 1816.
2. Manvell, p.68.
3. Campbell, 1.59.
4. Fitzgerald, 1.105.
5. *The Morning Post*, 10 October 1782.
6. Lennep, p.10.

7. Ibid., p.11.
8. Ibid.
9. Boaden, 1.292.
10. Ibid., 299.
11. Ffrench, p.59.
12. Boaden, 1.299.
13. Lennep, p.11.
14. *The Morning Chronicle*, 11 Oct 1782.
15. Boaden, 1.314.
16. Ibid., 312.
17. Kelly, p.21.
18. *The Whitehall Evening Post*, 12–15 April 1783.
19. Burney, *The Early Journals*, 5, 21, note 94.
20. *The Morning Chronicle*, 5 December 1782.
21. Davies, 3.147.
22. Bath Record Office, B091.5 Acc. 37-740.
23. Fitzgerald, 1.186.
24. Burney, 2.141.
25. Fitzgerald, 1.166.
26. *Parker's General Advertiser*, 24 March 1783.
27. Ibid.

Chapter 6: Lady Macbeth
1. Parsons, p.120.
2. *The Examiner*, 15 June 1816.
3. Boswell, 2, 484-5.
4. Campbell, 2.11.
5. Parsons, p.121.
6. Campbell, 2.17.
7. Shakespeare, *Macbeth*, Act 1, scene 5.
8. Parsons, p.120.
9. Shakespeare, *Macbeth*, Act 5, scene 1.
10. Ibid.
11. Piozzi, *Piozziana*, pp.85–6.
12. Fitzgerald 1.242.
13. Shakespeare, *Macbeth*, Act 5, scene 1.
14. Fitzgerald 1.245.
15. Ffrench, p.110.
16. Ibid.
17. *The Examiner*, 16 June 1816.
18. Ibid.
19. Kennard, p.150.
20. Ffrench, p.119; Johnson, p.144.
21. Bath Record Office, B091.5 Acc: 37-740.
22. Johnson, p.149.

Chapter 7: Ireland
1. Fitzgerald 1.138.
2. Kennard, p.85.
3. Fitzgerald 1.138.
4. Ibid.
5. Fitzgerald 1.145.
6. Ibid.
7. Ibid., p.191.
8. Manvell, p.92.
9. Campbell 1.259.
10. Parsons, p.110.
11. Ibid.
12. Fitzgerald 1.186.
13. Campbell 1.258.
14. Highfill, p.12.
15. Ibid., p.13.
16. Parsons, p.97.
17. Ibid., p.99.
18. LSE: The Women's Library, 9/18/01.
19. Moody, p.228.
20. Parsons, p.102.
21. Ibid., p.103.
22. Lennep, p.29.
23. Highfill, p.13.
24. Boaden 2.104.
25. Ibid., p.110.
26. Ibid.
27. Lennep, p.30.
28. Campbell 1.280.
29. Fitzgerald 1.206.
30. Parsons, p.104.
31. Ibid., p.107.
32. Moody, p.89.

Chapter 8: Behind the Scenes
1. Bath Record Office, B091.5 Acc.37-740.
2. Manvell, p.140.
3. Burnim, p.60.
4. Ibid., p.63.
5. Piozzi, *Thraliana*, 2.850.
6. Ibid.
7. Ibid., 2.808.
8. Ibid., 2.867.
9. Fitzgerald, 2.26.
10. Parsons, p.208.

11. Campbell, 2.358.
12. Ibid., 2.360.
13. Parsons, p.187.
14. Johnson, p.93.
15. Ffrench, p.125.
16. Burnim, p.51.
17. Ibid., p.62.
18. Parsons, p.188.
19. Piozzi, *Thraliana*, 2, 992.
20. Burnim, p.75.
21. Johnson, p.170.
22. Fitzgerald, 1.219.
23. Parsons, p.238.
24. Ibid., p.239.
25. Burnim, p.81.
26. Ibid., p.87.
27. Ibid., p.88.
28. Parsons, p.187.
29. Johnson, p.156.
30. Bath Record Office, 091.56.
31. Ibid., B091.5 Acc. 37:739040.
32. Manvell, p.152.
33. Piozzi, *Thraliana*, 2.769.
34. *The Morning Chronicle*, 22 March 1791.
35. Courtesy of the British Library Board, Addison Manuscripts 73737 (3/40).
36. Parsons, p.243.

Chapter 9: Celebrity
1. Fitzgerald, 1.220.
2. Bath Record Office, B091.5 Acc. 37:740.
3. Ibid.
4. Perry, p.133.
5. Fitzgerald, 1.186.
6. *The Morning Post and Daily Advertiser*, 14 October 1782.
7. *The Rambler's Magazine*, February 1783.
8. Boswell, 2. pp.484–5.
9. Ibid.
10. Boaden, 1.135.
11. Farington, 3.737.
12. Stirling, 2.232.
13. Davies, 3.147.
14. Lennep, p.17.
15. Ibid.
16. *The Morning Post and Daily Advertiser*, 12 March 1785.

17. *Public Advertiser*, 1 May 1783.
18. Farington, 4.1297.
19. Lennep, p.17.
20. Ibid.
21. *St James's Chronicle*, 27 April 1784, and *Public Advertiser*, 28 April 1784.
22. Parsons, p.253.
23. Ibid., p.44.
24. Manvell, p.137.
25. Courtesy of the British Library Board, Film 1686, Letter 11.
26. *The Ipswich Journal*, 5 April 1788.
27. Boaden, 1.301.
28. Ibid.

Chapter 10: Royalty
1. Lennep, p.21.
2. Colley, p.270.
3. Boaden, 1.365.
4. Parsons, p.249.
5. Ibid.
6. Ffrench, p.85.
7. Lennep, p.21.
8. Ibid., p.22.
9. Highfill, p.16.
10. Manvell, p.99.
11. Whalley, 1.445.
12. Ibid., 2.257.
13. Ibid.
14. Piozzi, *Thraliana*, p.916.
15. Boaden, 2.354.
16. Johnson, p.166.
17. Fitzgerald, 2.295.
18. Mackenzie, p.113.
19. Bath Record Office, Notebook B091.5 Acc.37:739040.
20. Piozzi, *Piozziana*, pp.85–6.

Chapter 11: Revolution and Society
1. Boaden, 1.298.
2. Pope, 2.268.
3. Ibid., 1.307.
4. Parsons, p.252.
5. Stirling, 2.221.
6. Fitzgerald, 2.300.
7. Manvell, p.291.
8. Boaden, 2.116.

9. Ibid.
10. Ibid.
11. Ibid. 1.312.

Chapter 12: The Kembles
1. Whalley, 1. 478.
2. Farrington, 4. 1345.
3. Harvard Theatre Collection, MS Letter, 26 June 1781.
4. Boaden, *Kemble*, 1. 407.
5. Fitzgerald, 1.316.
6. Piozzi, *Pennington*, p.120.
7. Ffrench, p.159.
8. Boaden, 2. 312.
9. Ffrench, p.100.
10. Parsons, p.151.
11. Fitzgerald, 2. 99.
12. Ibid., p.100.
13. Ibid., p. 102.
14. Ffrench, p.98.
15. Fitzgerald, 2.105.
16. Ibid., p106.
17. Folger Shakespeare Library, Y.c. 432.6.
18. Ibid.
19. Manvell, p.117.
20. Ffrench, p.221.

Chapter 13: Working Life in the Theatre
1. Fitzgerald, 1.343.
2. Ffrench, p.106.
3. Campbell, 2.62.
4. Fitzgerald, 1.252.
5. Ffrench, p.21.
6. Kennard, p.151.
7. Highfill, p.17.
8. Fitzgerald, 1.262.
9. Wilkinson, 3.102.
10. Fitzgerald, 2.297.
11. Parsons, p.235.
12. Kelly, p.83.
13. Manvell, p182.
14. Ibid.,1.310
15. Campbell, 2.187–8.
16. Fitzgerald, 1.343.
17. Campbell, 2.202.
18. Ibid., 225.

19. Ffrench, p.167.
20. Kelly, p.123.
21. Boaden, *Kemble*, 2. 239.
22. Kennard, p.218.
23. Boaden, 2. 354.
24. Mackenzie, p.136.
25. Folger Shakespeare Library, Y.c.432.14.
26. Ibid.
27. Parsons, p.264.

Chapter 14: Maria
1. Knapp, p.55.
2. Ibid., p8.
3. Ibid., p.9.
4. Ibid., p.13.
5. Ibid., p.15.
6. Ibid., p.17.
7. Ibid., p.16.
8. Ibid., p.26.
9. Ibid., p.31.
10. Ibid., p.32.
11. Ibid., p.52.
12. Ibid., p.57.
13. Ibid., p.59.
14. Ibid., p.66.
15. Ibid., p.77.
16. Ibid., p.78.
17. Ibid., p.81.
18. Ibid., p.102.
19. Ibid., p.107.
20. Ibid., p.133.

Chapter 15: Sally
1. Knapp, p.213.
2. Manvell, p.214.
3. Knapp, p.138.
4. Ibid., p.139.
5. Manvell, p.241.
6. Knapp, p.152.
7. Ibid., p.150.
8. Ibid., p.159.
9. Ibid., p.174.
10. Ibid., p.176.
11. Ibid., p.193.
12. Whalley, 2.100.

13. Knapp, pp.202–3.
14. Fitzgerald, 2.225.
15. Ibid., p.206.
16. Ibid., p.212.
17. Ibid., p.48.
18. Manvell, p.281.

Chapter 16: The Galindo Affair
1. Galindo, p.28.
2. Ibid., p.6.
3. Ibid., p.4.
4. Highfill, p.26.
5. Ibid.
6. Galindo, p.31.
7. Ibid., p.60.
8. Ibid., p.62.
9. Ibid., p.66.
10. Ibid.
11. Ibid., p70.
12. Ibid., p.48.
13. Fitzgerald, 2.42.
14. Galindo, p.18.
15. Ibid., p.23.
16. Ibid., p.21.
17. Ibid., p.24.
18. Ibid.
19. Parsons, p.227.
20. Ibid.
21. Galindo, p.26.
22. Parsons, p.227.

Chapter 17: Marriage's End
1. Piozzi, *Thraliana*, 2.1052.
2. Kennard, p.198.
3. Highfill, p.25.
4. Ibid.
5. Burnim, p.75.
6. Galindo, p.55.
7. Ibid., p.68 and p.66.
8. Boaden, 2.336.
9. Campbell, 2.311.
10. Ibid., 310.
11. Ibid.
12. Burnim, p.75.
13. Fitzgerald, 2.96.

14. Burnim, p.76.
15. Piozzi, *Thraliana*, 2, 992.
16. Farington, 3.26.
17. Campbell, 2.316.
18. The National Archives, Kew, PROB 11/1478/11
19. Campbell, 2.1070.
20. Parsons, p.186.
21. Campbell, 2.321.
22. Kennard, p.223.

Chapter 18: Retirement
1. Lawrence, p.209.
2. Parsons, p.264.
3. Ffrench, p.231.
4. Highfill, p.30.
5. *London Magazine*, January 1820.
6. Campbell, 2.340.
7. Ibid., 234.
8. Shakespeare, *Macbeth*, Act 5, scene 1.
9. Fitzgerald, 2.151.
10. West Yorkshire Archives, Bradford, SpSt/6/1/137.
11. Fitzgerald, 2.228.
12. Ackroyd, p.110.
13. Campbell, 2.264.
14. Ffrench, p.234.
15. Campbell, 2.351.
16. Ffrench, p.235.
17. Ibid., p.236.
18. Shakespeare, *Macbeth*, Act 4, scene 1.
19. Bath Record Office, B091.5.
20. *The Examiner*, 16 June 1816.
21. Campbell, 2.357.
22. Ibid., p.358.
23. Roberts, p.110.
24. Campbell, 2.365.
25. Parsons, p.274.
26. Ffrench, p.241.
27. Ibid., p.245.
28. Ibid., p.246.

Epilogue
1. Campbell, 2.378.
2. Kemble, 2.64.
3. Lawrence, p.189.
4. Ibid., p.209.

5. Ibid.
6. Kemble, p.45.
7. Manvell, p.311.
8. Lawrence, pp.222–3.
9. Campbell, 2.376.
10. Shaughnessy, p.11.
11. Fitzgerald, 2.384.
12. Campbell, 2.378.
13. *The Morning Post and Daily Advertiser*, 16 December 1782.
14. Hazlitt, William, 'Mrs Siddons' in *The Examiner*, 15 June 1816.

Index

Abington, Frances, x, xiv, 102, 185
Amelia, Princess, 91
Ancaster, Duchess, of, 17
As You Like It, 22, 25, 52, 91, 109, 111
Augusta, Princess, 89

Baillie, Joanna, 70, 128
Ballantyne, James, 101, 114, 126
Barry, Elizabeth, 22
Bate, the Reverend Henry, x-xi, 19, 22–4, 26, 185
Bath, 6, 11, 29–39, 41, 43, 65, 71, 85–7, 93, 101, 110, 114, 120, 129, 143, 149, 156, 163–6, 187, 189–91
   Abbey, 32
   Axford's Buildings, 32, 47
   Cotillion Balls, 30
   Milsom Street, 33
   Old Orchard Street Theatre (aka Theatre Royal), 29–31, 33, 35, 39, 143, 166, 187, 189
   Royal Crescent, 33
   Southgate, Street, 32
Belfast, 63, 118, 150
Bell, Professor George Joseph, 48, 172
benefit nights, 1, 12–14, 29, 31, 36, 42, 61–3, 69, 105, 118, 121, 150, 176
Bere, John de la, 25
Bickerstaff, Isaac, 20
Bird, Sally, 131–4, 142–5, 185
Birmingham, xiv, 6, 26, 28, 119, 135–6, 15
   New Street Theatre, xiv
The Blackamoor Wash'd White, xi
Boaden, James, xii, 10–12, 41, 53, 64, 80, 87–8, 94, 98, 102, 109–10, 121, 123, 126, 162, 178, 185
The Boy and the Frogs, 7
Boyle, Henrietta (O'Neill), 21, 24, 33, 55, 60, 185

Brecon 12–15
   Church of St Mary, 3
   The Shoulder of Mutton Inn, 1
Brereton, William, 43, 48, 55–6, 61–6, 102, 105, 185, 187
Briggs, Henry Perronet, 86
Brighton, 96, 135
Bristol, 6, 31, 33, 36–8, 79, 120, 134, 149, 191
Broadstairs, 166, 172
Bruce, Lord, 21
Buckingham House, 91
Burke, Edmund, 48, 98
Burney, Fanny, 33, 43, 46, 90, 92–3, 185
Byron, George Gordon, Lord, 47, 51, 74, 168, 171, 173, 185

Calais, 71, 100, 129
Cambridge, 172
Camp, Maria Theresa de, 106–7, 109, 173, 179, 186
Campbell, Thomas, xiii, 7, 12–13, 16–17, 21, 32, 43, 48, 59, 63–4, 70, 82–4, 94, 114, 117, 130, 162, 165–6, 168, 171–2, 174–5, 179, 185
Centilivre, Susanna, xiii
Chamberlain and Crump's Barnstormers, 20–1, 24
Charles the First, 10–11
Charlotte, Princess, 52, 89, 174
Charlotte, Queen, 69, 71, 88–96, 101, 119, 171–4, 186, 198
Charterhouse School, 69, 91
Cheltenham, 21–2, 38–9, 135, 147, 151, 185
   Birch Farm, 147
Cherry, Andrew, 172
Cibber, Colley, and Vanburgh, John, 92, 95, 119

Cirencester, 3
Clarence, William, Duke of, 53, 80, 93, 170, 182, 188
Cleone, 60
Clifton, 134–8, 141, 145, 191
  St Andrew's Church, 138
Coffey, Charles and Mottley, John, 36
Colman, George, 53, 108
Combe, George, 181
Congreve, William, 52, 110, 199
Coriolanus, 6, 94, 167, 17
The Country Girl, 53
Cork, 57–8, 62–3, 146, 150–1
Covent Garden Theatre, xiii, 22–5, 31, 43, 70, 81, 96, 101, 104, 107–10, 116, 125–8, 142, 144, 153, 157, 162, 167–8, 171, 173–6, 178–80, 188
Coventry, 7, 11, 14
  Holy Trinity Church, 19
Cowley, Hannah, xii
Crawford, Ann, 28, 42–3, 57, 186, 195
Cumberland, Ernest Augustus, Duke of, 90
Cumberland, Richard, 20

Daly, Richard, 55–8, 61–2, 186
Damer, Anne, 76, 171, 186
Delaroche, Frances, 149
The Devil to Pay, 36
Devizes, 86, 129
Devonshire, Georgiana, Duchess of, 33, 112
Digges, West, 58, 62–6, 186
The Distrest Mother, 35
Doctor Barrow's Academy, Soho Square, 69
Dodsley, Robert, 6, 60
Douai, 6, 26–7, 109
Douglas, 52, 58–9, 175, 197
Drury Lane Theatre, viii–x, xii–xvi, 6, 8, 17, 20, 22–6, 30–1, 33, 38–43, 45–7, 52, 55–6, 58, 63, 71, 81, 83, 86–91, 93, 95, 98–102, 104–11, 114–18, 120–6, 138, 153, 167–9, 171, 173, 180, 184, 187–92, 198
Dublin, 55–61, 64, 77, 101, 105, 146, 148–51, 153, 158, 186
  Crow Street Theatre, 57, 186

Dublin City Marshalsea Debtors' Prison, 57, 62
  Smock Alley Theatre, 55–8, 61, 186
Durham, 69, 108

The Earl of Warwick, 117, 167
Edinburgh, 59, 70, 112, 114, 118, 120, 149, 166–7, 173
  Theatre Royal, 58, 70, 108, 190
Edwy and Elgiva, 93
Epicoene, or The Silent Woman, xi
Erskine, Tom, 45
Evans, Mr of Pennant, 12, 186
Exeter, 11

The Fair Penitent, 44, 85, 193
Farington, Joseph, 80, 104, 128, 167, 169–70, 186
Farren, Elizabeth, 80, 95, 122, 124, 186
The Fatal Marriage, see *Isabella or The Fatal Marriage*
Fitzgerald, Edward, Lord, 60
Fitzgerald, Percy, 118
Fitzherbert, Maria, 92
Fitzhugh, Charlotte, 70, 75–6, 120, 128, 146, 150, 159, 164, 170, 175, 181, 186
Flaxman, John, 82
Ford, James, xiv, 53
Ford, Richard, 53, 93
Fox, Charles James, 48, 98
France, 26–7, 68, 72, 97, 99–101, 103, 125, 130, 145, 181
Franklin, Dr, 117, 167
Furnival, Fanny, 2

Gainsborough, Thomas, 83–5, 111, 183, 186
Galindo, Catherine, 148–58, 162, 164, 170, 176, 182–3, 186, 189, 191
Galindo, Philomen, 148–58, 161–4, 170, 176, 182–3, 187, 189, 191
The Gamester, 52, 64, 90, 135, 168, 170, 173, 197
Garrick, David, viii–xvi, 17, 20–7, 35, 38–40, 42, 44, 48, 57, 59, 71, 80, 84, 89-90, 101–2, 104, 175, 181, 183, 185, 187, 189, 191–2, 197
Genest, the Reverend John, 17

George III, 71, 88–91, 93–7, 99, 119, 131, 164, 186–7, 198
George IV, (aka George, Prince of Wales, The Prince Regent), 72, 88–90, 92, 95–6, 127, 164, 176, 187
Gibbon, Edward, 48
Gillray, James, 65
Glasgow, 58, 79, 118, 120
Gloucester, viii, 22, 24–5, 71, 135
  St Mary's Church, 25
The Grecian Daughter, 7, 28, 39, 42–3, 48, 57, 80, 85–6, 89, 99, 168, 186, 195
Godfrey, Mary, 19
Graham, Dr James, 111–12
Gray, Thomas, 172
Greatheed, Ann, 71, 76, 145, 187
Greatheed, Bertie, 15–16, 71, 76, 87, 145, 187
Greatheed, Lady Mary, (née Bertie), 13, 15–18, 187
Greatheed, Peregrine, 15–16
Guy's Cliffe, Warwickshire, 13, 15–19, 71, 76, 87, 107, 183, 187

Hamilton, William, 47, 85, 187
Hamlet, 1, 32, 148–50
Hampstead, 73, 76
Harcourt, Elizabeth, 68, 73, 92, 95, 100, 166, 187
Harcourt, George, 68, 73, 92, 119, 187
Harlow, George Henry, 86
Harries, Mrs, 8
Harris, Thomas, 110, 126, 153, 187
Harrogate, 75, 121
Hastings, Warren, 98
Hatton, William, 112–10
Havard, William, 10
Haydon, Benjamin, 74, 97, 173, 176
Haymarket Theatres, 45, 95, 108, 121, 127
Hazlitt, William, 47, 52, 98, 174, 184, 187
Henderson, John, 29–30, 43, 187
Henry VIII, 32, 52, 78, 94, 101, 106, 117, 168
Hereford, 2, 135
Hoadley, Benjamin, xii
Holcroft, Thomas, 5
Holland, Henry, 121
Holyhead, 55, 146

Home, John, 52, 59, 175, 197
Hopkins, William, xiv, 105, 188
Hopkins, Patty (Pop), (aka Priscilla Brereton, aka Pop Kemble), 55–6, 105–7, 125, 128, 141, 144, 175, 185, 187
Hotham, Sir Charles, 66, 74, 80, 106, 188
Hull, 119–20
Hume, Robert, 57

Inchbald, Elizabeth, 27–9, 56–7, 70, 105, 125, 127, 153, 160, 163, 181–2, 185, 188
Inchbald, Joseph, 27, 29, 105
Inchiquin, Lord, 55
India, 72, 151, 161, 173, 180, 190
Ireland, 43, 47, 55–60, 66, 69–70, 72, 102, 105, 109, 111, 114, 118, 126, 147–9, 151, 154, 157, 161–2, 182–3, 185–7, 192
Ireland, William Henry, 122–3
Irving, Sir Henry, 180
Irving, Washington, 171
Isabella or The Fatal Marriage, xv, 39, 42, 45, 57, 79, 83, 85, 89, 99, 126, 168, 195

Jane Shore, 17, 43, 79, 110, 111, 138, 196
Jeckyll, Joseph, 176
Jersey, Lady, 96
Johnson, Dr Samuel, 45, 48, 78, 188–9
Jones, Frederick, 153
Jonson, Ben, xi
Jordan, Dora, 53–4, 56, 79–80, 93, 95, 123–4, 170, 182, 188
The Jubilee, x

Kelly, Hugh, 38
Kemble, Anne, (aka Julia Anne, aka 'Ann of Swansea') 4, 10, 111–15, 162, 181, 188
Kemble, Captain, 2
Kemble, Catherine, 4, 10
Kemble, Charles, 4, 104, 108–10, 115, 126, 131, 147, 154, 173–5, 178, 180–1, 186, 188
Kemble, Elizabeth (aka Elizabeth Satchell), 108
Kemble, Elizabeth, (Sarah's sister), 4, 10, 18, 110–11, 113–15, 188

Kemble, Fanny (aka Fanny Twiss), 3, 10, 18, 55, 87, 110–11, 113–15, 142, 165, 168, 191
Kemble, Fanny (Sarah's niece), 86, 110, 131, 175, 177–80, 188
Kemble, Father John, 2
Kemble, Jane, 4, 14, 114
Kemble, John Philip, 3–4, 6, 9–10, 26–9, 45, 48, 55–8, 62–4, 69–70, 84, 94, 96, 98, 102, 104–3, 114–15, 117, 120–8, 141, 147, 153–4, 163, 167–71, 174–5, 180, 185–8
Kemble, Roger, 1–16, 18–20, 26, 40–1, 108, 147, 159, 162, 188
Kemble, Sally, 1–4, 6–16, 18–20, 109, 113, 129, 147, 159, 162, 188
Kemble, Stephen, 3–4, 69, 104, 107–8, 115, 189
King, Mary, 25
King, Tom, 22, 39, 63, 65, 106, 189
King John, 32, 52, 61, 90, 94, 117, 125, 167–8, 194, 199
King Lear, 32, 52
Kings Theatre, Haymarket, *see* Haymarket Theatres
Kington, Herefordshire, 3
Kotzebue, August von, 124–5, 194, 198

Lausanne, 107, 171
Lawrence, Lucy, 130, 134, 136, 144
Lawrence, Sir Thomas, 6, 71, 84–5, 104, 128–45, 147, 161, 163–4, 167, 169, 173, 177–9, 181, 183, 188–91
Leeds, 73, 118–20
Leinster, Dowager Duchess of, 60
Leominster, 1, 18
Leopold, Prince, 174
Licensing Act, 3
Limerick, 62, 150
Linley, Thomas, xiv, 33, 42
Little Haymarket Theatre, *see* Haymarket Theatres
Liverpool, 6, 26–9, 55, 101, 118–19
Llandrindod Wells, 1
Love in a Village, 7, 11
Love's Metamorphoses, xii

Macbeth, 16, 59, 97, 100, 109, 122, 127, 167–8, 174
Macaulay, Catherine, 84, 98

Macready, William, 90, 109, 156, 170
Macready, William Charles, 170, 173, 180, 189
Manchester, 26–7, 79, 118, 156–8, 170, 189
Margate, 69, 172
Massinger, Philip, 105
Master Betty, 126
Marie Antoinette, 101, 126
Measure for Measure, 52, 142, 167–8
Melpomene, 53, 65, 85
The Merchant of Venice, viii–ix, xi, 110, 172
The Miller of Mansfield, 6
Milton, John, 7, 17, 167, 172, 175–6
Mr Kemble's Company of Comedians, 5, 10, 13, 20
Modern Breakfast; or All Asleep at Noon, 108
Monckton, Mary, 45, 92, 189
Moore, Charles, 147, 189
Moore, Edward, 52, 64, 135, 170, 173, 197
More, Hannah, 33
The Mourning Bride, 52, 58, 86, 110–11, 199
Murphy, Arthur, 7, 28, 39, 42, 57, 186, 195
Murray, Harriet, 70, 126, 128, 145, 173, 181, 189

Newcastle, 114, 120, 170
A New Way to Pay Old Debts, 105
Northumberland, Duke of, 126
Nuneham Courtenay, 73, 92, 187
  Rectory Cottage, 68, 71, 73, 92, 187

Old Price Riots, 127–8
O'Neill, Elizabeth, 171
Opera House, Haymarket, 106, 121, 126
Othello, 32
Otway, Thomas, 21, 193
Oxford, 147, 172

Paddington, 73
Paddington Green, St Mary's Church, 180–1
The Padlock, 20
Palmer, John, 29–32, 34, 37–8, 110, 187, 189
Paradise Lost, 7, 172
Paris, 171, 174

Index

Pennington, Penelope, 33–4, 68, 75, 110, 134–41, 145, 189, 191
Pepys, Sir Lucas, 74–5
Philips, Anna Maria, 56, 58
Phillips, Ambrose, 35
Piozzi, Hester, 33, 43, 46, 48, 50, 68–9, 71–2, 75–6, 78–9, 93, 96, 107–8, 122, 124, 131, 133, 138, 145, 151, 155, 159–66, 168, 172–3, 175, 181, 183, 188–90
Pitt, William the Younger, 98
Pizarro, 125, 168, 194
Place, Dorothy, 145–7
Plymouth, 119
Pratt, Samuel, 33, 41, 87
Prescott, 3
Pritchard, Hannah, 48, 50–1, 116, 190
The Provoked Husband, 92, 95, 119

The Regent, 87
Reynolds, Sir Joshua, 33, 47–8, 57, 79, 81–5, 99, 130–1, 172, 177–8, 181, 183, 189
Richard III, xii
Robinson, Henry Crabb, 167
Robinson, Perdita, 118
Rogers, Samuel, 82, 110, 122, 169, 175
Romeo and Juliet, 32
Romney, Sir George, 79, 85, 189
The Runaway, xii
Rowe, Nicholas, 17, 43–4, 110, 124, 193, 196
Royal Academy, 47, 81–2, 84, 99, 131, 164, 176–7, 189
Rutland, Duke of, 61

Sadlers Wells, 67, 109, 147, 159
Satchell, Elizabeth, *see* Kemble, Elizabeth
The School for Wives, 38
Scotland, 47, 58–9, 78, 108, 134, 197
Scott, Sir Walter, 70, 128, 167
Sedgley Park, Wolverhampton, 6
Seward, Anna, 'The Swan of Lichfield', 33, 43–4, 52, 190
Shakespeare, William, xii, 1, 17, 22, 32, 52, 61, 78, 90–1, 94, 104, 117, 122–3, 127, 167–8, 171–2, 174–6, 178, 181, 187, 194, 196, 199
Shanes Castle, County Antrim, 21, 60

Sharp, 'Conversation', 17
Sheffield, 109, 119–20
Sheridan, Richard Brinsley, xiv, 30, 33–8, 40, 42, 51, 65, 94–5, 98, 102, 106–7, 116, 120–6, 153, 160, 167, 169, 190, 194, 198
Sheridan, Thomas, 33, 38–9
Shrewsbury, 109, 146
Siddons, Cecilia, 68–9, 72–3, 75, 101, 107, 122, 135, 145, 147, 162, 164–5, 171–2, 174–5, 179, 181, 190
Siddons, Elizabeth Anne, 36, 38, 71, 190
Siddons, Frances Emelia, 32
Siddons, Henry, viii, 21, 32, 36, 38–40, 45, 69–70, 85, 91, 100, 108, 126, 145, 161, 165–6, 173, 180–1, 189–90
Siddons, George, 47, 71–2, 86, 92, 95, 118, 151, 161, 165, 173, 180–1, 190
Siddons, Maria, 32–3, 36, 38, 68, 71–3, 75, 86, 96, 100, 109, 120, 125, 129–42, 145, 147, 161–2, 179, 185, 189–91
Siddons, Mary, 10
Siddons, Sally, viii, 14, 25, 32–3, 36, 38, 68, 71–3, 75, 80, 86, 100, 108–9, 120, 129–48, 151, 154, 158, 161–3, 183, 185, 189–91
Siddons, Sarah:
  early life, 1–19, 183
  earnings, 25, 29, 31, 36–8, 42, 57–9, 61–3, 65–6, 79, 108, 118–26, 128, 132, 135, 146–7, 151–2, 156–7, 159, 161, 164–5, 167–8, 170, 172, 176, 183, 190
  family, viii, xiii–xv, 8–9, 14, 16, 20–1, 25, 29, 31–2, 34, 36, 55, 66–7, 69–76, 86, 88, 95–6, 100–1, 107–115, 122, 125, 127–31, 133–8, 140–8, 151–4, 158–62, 165–7, 175–7, 182–3, 190–1
  health, xv, 15, 25, 40, 61–2, 64, 66, 68–9, 74–6, 95, 120, 123, 126, 128, 146, 148, 150–1, 154, 160–4, 166–7, 170–1, 176, 179–80, 182–3, 191
  homes, 32, 38, 41, 47, 60, 63, 72–3, 92, 109, 122, 132, 142, 144–7, 154–6, 160, 164, 166, 168, 170–1, 173, 175, 179–80, 187
  portraits, xv–xvi, 27, 79, 81–6, 121, 129–31, 140, 144, 159, 164, 172, 177–9, 181–3, 186–7, 189

roles:
  Ariel in *The Tempest*, 7
  Beatrice in *Much Ado About Nothing*, 30
  Belvidera in *Venice Preserved*, 21, 58–60, 62, 89, 99, 119, 168, 193
  Calista in *The Fair Penitent*, 44, 58, 85, 89, 193
  Charlotte Rusport in *The West Indian*, 20
  Cleone in *Cleone*, 60
  Constance in *King John*, 52, 61, 90, 94, 117, 167–8, 194
  Cordelia in *King Lear*, 52
  Desdemona in *Othello*, 32, 117
  Elgiva in *Edwy and Elgiva*, 93
  Elvira in *Pizarro*, 125, 168, 194
  Emily in *The Runaway*, xii
  Epicoene in *Epicoene or The Silent Woman*, xi
  Euphrasia in *The Grecian Daughter*, 7, 28, 39, 42, 58, 80, 85–6, 89, 99, 168, 195
  Gertrude in *Hamlet*, 30
  Hamlet in *Hamlet*, 26, 28–9, 32, 148–50, 172, 187
  Hermione in *The Distrest Mother*, 35
  Hermione in *The Winter's Tale*, 52, 94, 101, 117, 168
  Isabella in *Isabella or The Fatal Marriage*, xv–xvi, 15, 39–42, 46–7, 57, 83, 85, 89, 99, 119, 126, 168, 195
  Isabella in *Measure for Measure*, 52, 142, 167–8
  Jane in *Jane Shore*, 43, 58, 83, 89, 110, 138, 196
  Juliet in *Romeo and Juliet*, 32
  Katharine in *Henry VIII*, 52, 94, 99, 101, 106, 117, 168, 199
  Lady Anne in *Richard III*, xii–xiii
  Lady Macbeth in *Macbeth*, 32, 47–54, 59, 71, 81, 84–5, 90, 97–8, 100–1, 103, 109, 114, 116, 118–19, 122, 126–7, 167–9, 173–4, 191
  Lady Randolph in *Douglas*, 52, 58–9, 61, 175, 197
  Lady Townley in *The Provok'd Husband*, 95, 119
  Leonora in *The Padlock*, 20
  Macbeth in *Macbeth*, 172
  Maria in *Love's Metamorphoses*, xii
  Margaret of Anjou in *The Earl of Warwick*, 117, 167
  Mrs Belville in *The School for Wives*, 38
  Mrs Beverley in *The Gamester*, 52, 64, 90, 135, 168, 170, 197
  Mrs Haller in *The Stranger*, 80, 124–5, 168, 198
  Mrs Strickland in *The Suspicious Husband*, xii
  Nell in *The Devil to Pay*, 36
  Portia in *The Merchant of Venice*, viii–xi, 8, 30, 39, 172
  Rosalind in *As You Like It*, 22–3, 52–3
  Rosetta in *Love in a Village*, 7
  The Tragic Muse in *The Jubilee*, 71
  Venus in *The Jubilee*, x
  Volumnia in *Coriolanus*, 6, 94, 167
  The Young Princess Elizabeth in *Charles the First*, 10
  Zara in *The Mourning Bride*, 52, 58, 86, 110, 199
Siddons, William, 31, 40–1, 55, 71–2, 74, 79, 95, 100, 102, 114, 131–2, 134, 137–8, 140, 143, 145–6, 159–60
  acting career, ix, xiii–xiv, 10–14, 20–1, 23–5, 28, 188, 191
  early relationship with Sarah, viii, xiii, 10–14, 17–19, 29, 32, 38, 92, 183
  health, 68, 76, 120–1, 156, 160, 162–4, 166, 186, 191
  manager, xiv, 23–5, 32, 35, 38, 57, 62–7, 120–1, 123, 125, 135, 151, 153, 156, 161, 164, 170
  problems in the marriage, 31, 67–8, 75, 80, 133, 135, 140–2, 145–7, 151–2, 154–6, 159, 161–4, 182–3, 190–1
  later life 73, 165–7, 176
Smart, Sir George, 176
Smith, Gentleman, 48, 191
Southerne, Thomas, xv, 39, 195
St Kitts, 16
Society of Artists, 81
Southampton, 76
Stanhope, Charles Spencer, 170

Steevens, George, 114
Stourbridge, 7
The Stranger, 80, 124, 168, 198
Stratford-upon-Avon, 1, 17
Stuart, Gilbert, 82
The Suspicious Husband, xii
Swansea, 113

Tamerlane, 124
Taylor, John, 67
The Tempest, 7
Thompson, Benjamin, 124
Thorneloe School, 8
Thrale, Hester, *see* Piozzi, Hester
Truro, 119
Twiss, Fanny, *see* Kemble, Fanny
Twiss, Francis, 114, 142, 165, 191
Twiss, Horace, 114, 157, 168–70, 173, 180, 191

Vaughan, Thomas, xii
Venice Preserved, 21, 58, 60, 62, 79, 89, 99, 109, 168, 193
Vortigern, 122

Wakefield, 119–20
Walsall, 10, 14
Ward, John, 1–3, 5, 8
Ward, Sarah, 1–2, 5
Warwickshire Company of Comedians, 1–2

Wednesbury, the church of St Bartholomew, 14
Wellington, Duke of, 174
Westminster Abbey, 112, 121, 180
Weston, Sophia, *see* Pennington, Penelope
Weymouth, 38, 95, 119
The West Indian, 20
Whalley, the Reverend Thomas Sedgwick, 33–4, 41, 56, 66–7, 71–3, 87, 92, 120, 151, 157, 173, 181, 191
Whitlock, Charles Edward, 114
Wilkinson, Patty, 72–3, 134, 142, 145–50, 154–7, 171–2, 174, 181, 191
Wilkinson, Tate, 28–9, 119, 134, 172, 191–2
Windsor Castle, 88, 91–2, 94, 171
The Winter's Tale, 52, 94, 101, 117, 168
Wolcot, John, 91
Wolverhampton, 11, 20, 26
The Wonder, xiii
Woodfall, William, 28
Worcester, 7–8, 10–11, 18, 20, 27, 135
Wroughton, Richard, 123
Wycherley, William, 53
Wynne, Bridget, 100

Yates, Mary-Ann, x, 43, 82–3, 86, 117, 192
York, 28–9, 79, 119–20, 134, 192
  Blake Street Theatre (aka Theatre Royal), 28, 119, 192
Younge, Elizabeth, x, xii, 58, 192